# THE LOST AND FOUND OF GREEN TREE

# THE LOST AND FOUND OF GREEN TREE

A NOVEL BY

BOBBIE CANDAS

*For*
*ElDora Criswell and Arlis Linder*
*Sisters in adventure and inspiration*

# CONTENTS

# WELCOME TO WONDERLAND: A DRAMEDY

An excerpt

by Bobbie Candas

# PROLOGUE

*M*y latest issue of Silver Screen is calling this decade a time of amazing progress for the modern woman and they're calling it, 'The Roaring Twenties.' Well, I can assure you, the only roaring going on in Green Tree, Iowa, is the occasional motorized tractor chugging down Main Street.

The name of Green Tree probably has you conjuring up images of a lovely hamlet, with winding hilly streets, surrounded by a thick forest of evergreens, populated by lots of interesting people.

No. There's just the one tree. A big, unshapely elm, growing off to the side of the brick county court house which is the center of a grid of straight, flat streets servicing the surrounding farming community, populated by, well…mostly farmers.

Of course, there's a few of us town-folk too, running the integral businesses supporting the area. But there's no movie theater, or community stage. No elegant restaurants, and only the one clothing store. There's a popular hardware store—for my needs, useless. And I'd have to say the same for the Farm and Implement Store. Although, I should add that we do have a coffee shop which sells cherry-flavored soda-pop, a personal favorite, a pool hall selling ice cream, and the drug store which just added a modern pay phone to the wall.

Also, I'd be remiss not to mention a fabric store run by my grim auntie who is assisted, under forced labor, by me, Nanette Jorgenson.

Amongst all this, I can absolutely assure you that in Green Tree I saw no possible future employment for dynamically inspired women, such as myself. By my teen years I already knew I was meant for bigger things.

# CHAPTER 1
# NANETTE JORGENSON

*I* stood confidently on the makeshift plywood stage in front of the courthouse, lined up next to nine other hopeful girls, each of us praying to hear our name called. It was August, a warm late afternoon. My face muscles were beginning to ache after showing off my glistening smile for at least forty-five minutes. The Green Tree judges of the 1927 Harvest Celebration were about to decide the winning candidates for the Corn Queen's Court. Whoever was selected as queen would be the envy of every girl in town and had the honor of presiding over the Harvest Celebration parade, the corn-eating contest, the fall fruit-pie competition, and the Harvest Celebration dance.

We were judged on poise, beauty, ability to communicate, posture, and popularity; all attributes many friends have told me I excel at.

Our Green Tree mayor, dressed in a dark plaid suit, bow tie and straw boater, was droning on about all the upcoming festivities which were essentially the same ones we had every year. Just get on with it...announce my name. I was born for this. If my name wasn't announced as queen, I might not accept the role of princess or duchess. I didn't like playing second fiddle and certainly hated third.

With a crowd of next year's potential voters in front of him, the mayor couldn't simply get to the point, feeling compelled to remind us of all the good things the funds generated by the festival would do for the village. While he talked, I looked about, nodding to a few friends standing in the crowd. I saw my best friend, Catherine Anderson, and her cute younger brother, Sam, with that girlfriend of his, Mariah. What did he see in her? I then waved at Melinda Perkins. She wasn't really a friend, but was strong competition and I was happy she'd decided not to run for queen this year, so I was being nicer to her.

Then finally... "Alright. So now folks, here's what we all came to see. Our beautiful line-up of Corn Harvest Court hopefuls. Gosh, I wish we had room for all of them in the parade. Have you ever seen such a lovely group of young women?"

The mayor's pandering was followed by a light smattering of applause and a few whistles. The sun was about to set, the mayor was losing his audience, and my feet were beginning to hurt standing tall in Auntie's borrowed high heels with my hands on my hips, continuing to flash my broadest smile.

The mayor raised his hands as if he was stopping a tidal wave of applause. "OK... Alright. Let's quiet down. The judges have given me their decisions. Ladies, if I call your name, just step over here next to me. So—without further ado —for our Corn Harvest Duchess, we have... Miss Amy Shulwater."

Amy Shulwater? With the chipped tooth and frizzy hair? I guess there were perks when your father owned the implement dealership. Light applause rose from the crowd, as a young boy rushed over from the side of the makeshift stage with a dozen ears of corn tied together with a green ribbon, handing them to the new duchess. Some towns offered rose bouquets, but in Green Tree, you got corn.

The mayor jumped in with a handshake and then read from his card, "Congratulations Amy! Next, for the title of Princess, we have another town-beauty... Miss Miranda Plum." Miranda stepped forward, gushing, accepting her gift of corn.

This was it; my big moment, or utter defeat.

"And now... good people of Green Tree, the recipient of our tiara, the satin banner, and *two* dozen ears of corn goes to our 1927 Queen of Corn... the lovely Miss Nanette Jorgenson."

Was it my imagination, or had the crowd erupted in massive applause? Forget the produce, just put that crown on my head and pin the banner across my chest. I stepped over to receive my handshake and congratulatory hug. Queen Nanette was crowned!

That week was magical for me and transformative. I cut my long blonde hair into a permed and crimped bob, almost giving Auntie a heart attack when she saw my thick eight-inch braid cut off and sitting on my vanity. I led the parade while waving from the back of a decorated, spanking-new red truck, borrowed from a dealership in Clear Lake. Auntie provided me with a silver sparkling fabric which I sewed into a draping drop-waist dress, hemming it rakishly short, exposing my knees. I felt special; little girls pointed at me when I walked down Main Street, while friends from school would stop and congratulate me. Topping that, I danced with every young man in town at the festival celebration. But most importantly, at the dance I met James Iverson.

He was from neighboring East Point. Four years older, and the most handsome man I'd ever seen; a tall, strapping guy with a manicured dark mustache, whose father happened to own a bank. I'd given him a wink on the dance floor and he'd eventually made his way over to me. When he asked me to dance, that was it. I'd found my man.

AT THE HOT CUP, sitting next to a table of grizzled farmers, I was gossiping with my friend, Catherine Anderson. We both took long sips of our colas, gearing up for our weekly gab exchange. "So, how are all your brothers doing, Catherine? I still think young Sam is the cutest."

"Forget it Nanette, you're too old for him. Besides, he's crazy about Mariah. They've been dating over a year now."

"Don't be silly. He's cute but not my type. I'm ready for someone more mature in the business field. Speaking of which, at the dance, did you notice a tall handsome gentleman? Mustache, suspenders? We danced together at least five times."

"Gosh, yes… I think every girl at the dance was ogling him."

I lowered my voice, saying, "Name is James Iverson. Son of a banker, great dancer, and even better *kisser*."

"You've kissed him already! Nanette, be careful."

"Oh, don't be such a bluenose. It was only a little kiss. He drove me home from the dance, and guess what?" I pounded my hand lightly on the café table. "We have a date for next weekend. I'm over the moon! *Never* felt this way about a guy before."

"Nanette, you're so lucky. Why can't I ever meet someone like him?"

"You will, Catherine. Just get your brothers to introduce you to their friends. You're bound to meet a great guy."

She nodded, playing with the straw in her drink. "I suppose, but all their friends are farmers too."

I glanced around, making sure nobody was eavesdropping.

"True. James seems different, not like all these boys we grew up with. A college man…. and a banker."

"Yes, you mentioned that."

I checked my watch; I was running late as usual. "Darn. Auntie is watching the clock; I'm supposed to be getting the groceries. I'll let you know how the date goes."

"OK. Please keep me posted, Nanette. I'm dying to hear how it goes." As I walked out, two more girls from school walked into the Hot Cup, waving at Catherine. I knew she'd spread the gossip about my date with James.

James Iverson. I couldn't get his face out of my mind. When I told Auntie about him, she approved of my Saturday night date. Although, at eighteen, I was officially an adult. No permission should have been necessary. But when I was twelve, my dad passed away, and his Aunt Edwina had been clucking over me like her prized hen ever since.

I checked my *Silver Screen* and *Photoplay* magazines religiously and had cut out photos of several styles of dresses I wanted to copy and sew for myself. Auntie owned a small fabric and yarn store in Green Tree, so I'd always had access to my own creations. That week, I made a light green cotton dress with white piping, with the green fabric perfectly matching my eyes, and I accessorized it with a long string of pearls. Fake ones, but who could really tell?

Now that I had the crimped hair, the dress, and the right makeup, I found it hard to tell the difference between myself and motion picture star, Marion Davies. I wanted to stun James Iverson. I stared at my reflection and then back again at the magazine photos of Marion. The comparison was pretty darn close. If Marion could attract the attention of publishing tycoon William Randolph Hearst, I could certainly hold the eye of James Iverson from No-Where, Iowa.

Peeking out the window, I watched James drive up in his shiny dark-blue Chrysler Roadster. So stylish, I had to pinch myself. I took a minute to ask him into our small home and introduce him to Auntie. She'd made me promise to do this and immediately began grilling him. "So, James, Nanette tells me you're an East Point resident. Have a cousin still living there. Would you know Bonnie and Steven Billows?"

"Why, yes ma'am. The Billows... a fine family. I believe they've held accounts with our family for years. Miss Jorgenson, if it's alright with you, I'd like to take Nanette to see a new film in Clear Lake. It starts at eight-thirty, so we'll need to head out."

"Certainly, of course. You two enjoy this lovely evening." I could tell Auntie approved. She wasn't giving him her usual squint-eye.

He'd decided that we should see *Phantom of the Opera*, starring Lon Chaney. Clear Lake was a thirty-minute drive from Green Tree, allowing us a little time to get to know each other better. When we sat down near the back of the dark theater, he immediately put his arm around me, and the movie became so scary I had to hide my eyes against his jacket a few times. Before the film was over, we'd kissed twice and my heart was almost jumping outside my chest. Leaving the theater, James placed his hand around mine and I felt like we melted together.

He suggested we take a drive by the lake. "It's beautiful this time of year, Nanette. Only us, the water, stars, and the moon. You'll love it."

"Sure, sounds magical. Just as long as I'm home around midnight." Auntie was a stickler on the curfew, but perhaps tonight she'd allow me a little leniency with James being such a promising beau.

We drove past some cottages built along the water and cruised a bit further, parking in a grove of overhanging willows near the lake's edge. It was dark, with a background sound of frogs croaking melodically. We drove across freshly cropped grass which invaded my senses, a salute to summer's final hurrah. And as promised, a big bright moon danced across ripples on the black lake. I felt like I was on a film set. He pulled a silver flask from his inside jacket pocket, took a long swig and handed it to me.

"Maybe I'll try a sip. I really don't drink." It was strong whiskey, too bitter for me. I handed it back quickly. "It's gorgeous here, let's walk a bit."

"In a little while." He stretched out his arms above his head. "I'm feeling really comfortable, but it's even better in the back seat. Let me show you." Always the gentleman, he got out, opened my door and let me slide across the spacious, padded back seat. It was lovely. He leaned over and kissed me, but this time he inserted his tongue. It was one of those French kisses the girls at school were always giggling about.

He looked down at me. "You're so beautiful, but you know that, don't you?" His hands moved slowly lower to my breasts, gently rubbing them, as he groaned in anticipation. I pushed his hands away, surprised he'd try such liberties already.

Nervously, I asked, "Maybe we should get out and walk? It's so nice by the lake."

"It's nicer here." He pushed me back, pressing my head down on the arm rest. "You're going to love this. Pretend you're my very own little movie star."

Before I could sit up, his weight was on top of me and his hand was pushing up my dress and snaking into my panties. I wedged my elbow out on the open side and tried to stop him, but his right hand knocked my arm away and then jerked more aggressively on my panties, ripping one side as he yanked them down. "Come on Nanette, you want this as much as I do." I heard his belt unbuckle and the sound of his zipper.

"No, I'm not ready. It's too soon. Not like this." I struggled to keep my legs together, grasping the skirt of my dress tightly.

But he roughly batted my hand away again, then thrust his fist between my thighs, pushing my legs apart. He began pushing hard, but nothing was happening. James asked me hoarsely, "Your first time?"

I nodded, repeating myself, "James, no! Get off. I'm not ready." This was all going terribly wrong.

He ignored my pleas, continuing to ram his penis into me, eventually sliding inside, as he grunted on top in jerking motions for what seemed agonizingly long. He finally stopped, got off, went out to his trunk, and handed me a small white towel. "Here, you might need this," and then he walked over to the lake's edge, turning his back to the car.

I quickly removed the remains of my panties, putting them in my handbag and then wiped the blood and wet stickiness from the seat and between my legs. I was in shock as I watched James outside the car. I was so afraid he'd come back and want to do it again. As the shock began to wear off and the reality of what had just happened hit me, I began to cry. I felt dirty and disgusted with myself.

James was now leaning against the hood of the car, puffing on a lit cigar and continuing to take leisurely swigs from his flask. He eventually came back, opened the door, then looked at his watch. "Well, it's getting late. Probably don't have time for that walk. Guess I better get you back home."

"I'm staying back here," I said in a defiant voice.

"Suit yourself."

There was no discussion of what had just happened.

I no longer cared about James Iverson. I hated James Iverson. I sat next to the window and stared out at the dark farm roads, and rode home in silence. Could I have kicked him, bucked him off, screamed? Nothing about what had happened was how I'd dreamed it would be; it was dirty, painful and felt all wrong. How did he go from fairytale prince to, to… that? Arriving at my house, I opened the car door myself, slamming it abruptly on James and never heard from him again. That, at least, was a relief.

Although my fears and nightmares often trailed back to that terrible night, I put on a show to others, pretending my life was absolutely normal. All that continued until October, when I realized I'd missed my period--twice. How could that be possible? Some of the girls at school who'd whispered about 'doing it,' said you never got pregnant on your first time. I couldn't tell anybody. Like I'd tried to tell James, I wasn't ready for any of this. This could not be how my life was supposed to play out. I became sick to my stomach. Often.

Then, I quickly developed a plan.

## CHAPTER 2
## MARIAH ANDERSON

*I*'d never forget that day back in September 1924. Gosh, that seems so long ago. I'd been at Green Tree High School for only a few days, coming from a country school with a total of twelve students, grades first through eighth. Now at Green Tree High, there were thirty-two students in just my freshman class. One of my first assignments was an oral presentation on Germany for world geography class.

The night before, upstairs in our small crowded bedroom, I practiced my report out loud so many times that my two sisters, Arlene and Janeen, were throwing their shoes at me to make me stop.

"Mariah, if we have to hear about that darn Danube River one more time, Arlene and I will beat you with these shoes instead of just throwing them. We have studies of our own. Shut up, please!"

"Sorry, I'm so nervous. Imagine, standing in front of over thirty students. I want everything perfect."

In preparation for the task, I'd done three days of library research and created a poster from butcher paper. The morning of my big report, I'd borrowed my older sister's new light-pink lipstick and curled my shoulder-length dark hair. I wore a knitted pull-over sweater over a starched white collared blouse, and a pleated skirt Mother had recently sewn for me. All of this preparation, just to give a five-minute report.

Standing in front of the class, most kids looked back at me with bored expressions. I cleared my throat, nervously pulling on my sweater, and began, attempting to exude a sense of confidence.

At lunch, I joined a table of girls I'd recently met at band practice. While unwrapping my cheese sandwich, I watched a handsome blonde boy, dressed in overalls and plaid shirt, walk over to our table. Sitting down next to me, he introduced himself and offered me his hand to shake, as my new girl-friends giggled and rolled their eyes. I grasped his rough calloused hand and shook it while he announced, "Mariah, I'm Samuel Anderson. Don't know if you've noticed me, but I'm in your geography class. Four rows over, two chairs back. Just wanted to stop by and say I liked your report. Seems like you really did your homework."

I was suspect that any boy from Green Tree would really be interested in a report on Germany. I nervously strung a few random sentences together. "Uh... thanks? I enjoy reading about new places. I plan on traveling a lot someday."

"Why?" He blinked, looking suddenly surprised.

"Why not? There's certainly something more interesting in this life besides cows and corn. That's about all I ever see around here." I took a few bites of my sandwich, and watched all the girls at my table turning their curious heads toward us.

"Nothing wrong with cows and corn. Kept my family fed for years. And I tell you, Mariah, farming's changing."

"Maybe... Send me a letter all about it when I'm up in New York working in a skyscraper office."

"And of all places, why would you want to go there?"

"Because it's not here." Our banter had the girls' heads switching back and forth, not wanting to miss whatever was about to happen.

"Just so you know… there are so many new planting techniques coming out. I been reading up on it. Farming's exciting." Sam slapped his hand on the lunch table, signifying he'd won the discussion.

I shook my head and laughed. "Challenging maybe, but I don't know about exciting. My parents have farmed for years." I shrugged my shoulders, looking around the table. "I just know I want more. Someplace where I'm not always side-stepping cow-pies, or worrying about rain and drought. But I like your passion about farming, Sam." I started wrapping up the remainder of my lunch. "I guess we all need to be inspired by something."

Sally Neilson, sitting on my other side, nudged my elbow. "Seems like farming isn't the only thing Sam's excited about."

Ignoring her comment, he lowered his voice and said, "Mariah, I'd like to buy you a slice of cake at the Hot Cup this Saturday. Let's talk more about this."

"This may sound strange but I really don't like cake." I picked up my books for class and stood up. "But I do love pie."

"They got that too."

"All right, farmer Sam. I'll meet you for pie, but don't plan on changing my mind about farming."

INITIALLY, I was a little leery of this over-confident, tall, fair-haired boy. He seemed too sure of himself, to the point of being cocky. But honestly, I was flattered that Sam seemed to like me, a little nobody farm-girl with straight brown hair and hand-made clothes. But eventually his steady persistence and laughing blue eyes won me over and we began seeing each other regularly outside of school a few times a week.

I told my two sisters that I'd never met a boy my age who already knew what he wanted and was hell-bent on getting it. Those plans included having his own farm, marriage, and a family. In his mind, everything was all laid out. But I knew there was plenty of time for things to change; we were young, with years ahead of us, and that first love was so intoxicating.

At fourteen, with Sam in my life, the simplest of things felt fresh and new; the thrill of holding hands walking down Main Street, or sitting on a blanket together at outdoor movies on the courthouse lawn. We'd share a bag of popcorn, and watch the silent movies of my favorite actress, Mary Pickford, while Sam loved laughing through the Buster Keaton and Chaplin films.

There was one early date I'd never forget. A company passing through town set up a temporary roller-rink in our village park, and all our gang from school decided to give it a try. Sam sprung for the forty cents on our rentals as we both clamped the metal skates onto our shoes and had them keyed tightly to the soles. I'd only tried skating once before and Sam was a total novice, so we gingerly clung to the rails spaced around the rink which was set up on a platform. A large amplified Victrola played all the popular songs from the radio. When they put on my favorite, *Five-Foot-Two, Eyes-of-Blue*, I forced myself to push off from the sides and courageously skate to the tune of the music. As I gained more confidence, I pulled Sam along and soon we found ourselves skating hand in hand. We went round and round the platform, gaining in speed. It was exhilarating. When the song ended, everyone else dashed to the sides, waiting for the next record. But Sam pulled me to him and in the middle of the rink, wrapped his arms around me, and gave me a long kiss. I knew people were watching, but I had to kiss him back. If I'd been alone, I would have kissed him all night. I adored feeling Sam's strength wrapping around me and his hot breath in my ear, whispering, "You're the one."

I felt a deep shudder go through me as we broke apart, and then began skating to the next tune. That first passionate kiss resonated, making me realize Sam might be more than a passing romance.

## CHAPTER 3
## NANETTE

*I*'d always wanted to get out of Green Tree, move to a larger town, and find an exciting job. With a possible pregnancy, there was now more urgency for my move. Nobody I knew could find out about this. I looked at a map and chose Mankato, Minnesota, about eighty miles north of Green Tree; not too far, but large enough to allow me some anonymity for a while. I wasn't sure what I was going to do *if* I was pregnant, but at least I could figure it out privately, on my own.

Aunt Edwina had one part-time assistant at the fabric store and me, but she could easily run it without my help. Besides, she'd never paid me for working there, but instead, gave me a meager weekly allowance. After dinner, I announced we needed to have an important conversation.

I started by serving tea and her favorite dessert, pineapple-upside-down cake. I'd actually paid a neighbor down the street to bake it. Sitting across from her at our dining table, I moved aside the bowl of waxed fruit and picked nervously at our lacy white table cloth.

"I've been contemplating this for a while now, Auntie. You

know I've always wanted to get out on my own eventually." She raised her eyebrows and stared at me, saying nothing. "Well, I think it's time. Ever since graduation I've been thinking about it….time for me to fly my wings and try new things." *Exceptionally good title for a future movie; I should write that down later.* I took a deep breath, and just told her. "I've decided I'm applying for jobs in Mankato."

"Mankato? That's Minnesota!" She said it as if I'd just announced I was moving to the North Pole. She shook her head, looking resolute. "No, Nanette. And besides, what if that nice gentleman, Mr. Iverson, comes round again."

"I told you already, he wasn't the man I thought he was. I have *no* interest in dating him… ever."

"You were always too picky. He was a good catch."

I rolled my eyes and ignored her comment and put a large slice of cake in front of her. "Take a bite, you'll love it. Besides, Auntie, a girl needs to see a few places before she settles down. I have skills. I type, excellent at selling, and I sew. I'm certain I'll find a good job there. There's just the issue of some seed money to find myself a little place to get settled. Will you help me, Auntie? Please?"

She took a big fork full of cake with sweet pineapple, laced with brown sugar crumbles. She savored it, took a sip of tea, and licked her lips. "I don't think so. Here's an idea. What if I start paying you at the store? I hate the idea of you being out there in the world all alone. There's too many unscrupulous people out and about these days. It's wild in the cities and Mankato's just too far."

Her comment immediately had me thinking of the predatory James Iverson. "Auntie, danger can lurk anywhere, but we can't let it consume us. And I've already checked. Mankato's only a two-hour train ride." It was actually closer to three hours, but who was counting? "And I could come back to visit some weekends." Auntie took another bite, listening and nodding. "This is actually a perfect time to apply. Most businesses are going gangbusters right now. If I hate it there, I can always come back, run your store and let you retire."

"Retire? Me? I don't know what I'd do with myself if I wasn't working. I don't need to retire!"

"How's the cake? I know it's your favorite."

"Delicious; your best yet, Nanette."

"You think so? Thanks. So then… if you're fine without me at the store, and based on your advice and business savvy, how much money do you think I'll need to find an apartment and maybe get a proper working wardrobe?"

"Hmm. Let me think on that. Oh, speaking of work clothes, we received the most adorable patterns for suits today. You'll need a smart suit, perhaps in a tweed."

"I agree. Let's discuss the money later. First, we'll need to pull a new wardrobe together. I appreciate your advice and style tips, Auntie, and I'll make you proud. There're so many details we need to consider." I jumped up, leaned over, and gave her a big hug. "Thanks so much. You're the berries! Got to go; I'm meeting Catherine."

As I walked out the door, she suddenly got up and yelled after me, "I didn't say yes. You're not going anywhere. There's more to talk about… Nanette?"

I squeezed an official 'yes' out of her within two days. Phase one of my evolving plan was coming together.

During my final week in Green Tree, my morning sickness began in earnest, confirming my pregnancy fears. I wasn't showing at all but I was having trouble hiding my nausea, making quick runs to the outhouse throughout the day.

By early November, I was on a train to Mankato with three suitcases of clothing, shoes, and hats. Auntie had given me enough cash to cover a few nights in a hotel and two months' funds for food and rent for a small apartment. If I didn't find a job during that time, I had promised to return home. In addition, she'd given me strict instructions to write her one letter every week, or she threatened to come there herself and drag me home.

The train trip to Mankato was a nightmare, with the rocking car motion making my vomiting bouts even more intense. I arrived green and exhausted; my face covered in a sheen of nervous sweat. Standing on the depot platform in my new travel suit with three large suitcases, I had no idea on how to get to the Front Street Hotel, where I'd reserved my first two-night's stay. The town looked larger and busier than I'd imagined, but apparently not large enough to have taxis.

In front of me, I watched a workman unloading wooden crates of produce from a freight car onto his dray wagon. Perhaps he could help. Dragging my three suitcases over one at a time, I walked up to the tired looking man. "Hello sir, any chance I could get directions for the Front Street Hotel? Would it be far?"

He stacked another wooden crate of cabbage in the wagon, while glancing up at me. "Nope, not too far. A little less than a mile west." He jerked his thumb in the hotel's direction.

"I see." I looked to my left, sighed, and stood there staring despondently, considering my options.

"Is all them cases yours?"

"All mine."

He stepped over, put them in the back with the cabbage crates and said, "OK, then. We best go now. I've got a delivery to make. You can get up front." He settled on the springy front bench and grabbed my hand, helping me step up.

"Why, thank you. My goodness, is everyone in Mankato as nice as you?"

"Nope, I just have a weakness for pretty girls with lots of suitcases."

"Well, you're very sweet. I'm Nanette Jorgenson and you're the first person I've met in Mankato."

The man nodded, touching the bill of his ragged cap. "Pleasure to meet you, Miss Jorgenson. I'm Obidiah Dawson, lived here all my life, and know lots of people. So, Front Street Hotel?" He snapped the reins on his two broad-backed black horses, turning them around. "What brings you to town?"

"Work. Just moved here from Green Tree, Iowa and decided to branch out a bit." The breeze picked up as I held on to my cloche hat with my hand. "Actually, I'm looking for a job and an apartment."

"A lady on a mission. I like that. This here is Front Street, main business street of Mankato. Not a bad spot to start your job search." Obidiah pointed out local landmarks as we made our way down to my hotel. Along with horses and wagons, there were numerous cars zipping up and down the asphalt road and several two, three, and four-level red-brick buildings on both sides of the street. It was impressive. We passed all of the larger buildings and eventually arrived at a dreary looking two-story wooden establishment with peeling paint and a sagging front porch. A creaking sign swung from the top level, *Front Street Hotel*. The place looked run-down and far from exclusive.

Noticing my unenthusiastic expression, Obidiah said, "Yeah, not exactly what you kids would call the bees' knees. You sure this is where you're staying?"

I took a deep breath and smiled. "I'm sure it'll be just fine. Wish me luck, Mr. Dawson." I climbed down, thanked him, shook his hand, and yanked my bags out of the back. "Do you suppose they'll come out to get my bags?"

He laughed at me as he began moving his horses. "No, Miss Nanette. I doubt any bellhops will come scampering out here. Good luck to you."

Here I was, arriving at a flea-bag hotel in a horse-drawn cabbage wagon. Not an auspicious beginning to my new life and definitely *not* movie star material.

# CHAPTER 4
# MARIAH

*B*y the middle of my junior year in high school, Sam was still the only boy I'd ever dated. Everyone knew we were a couple. Forgoing all his extra-curricular activities, including basketball and track, Sam began attending only a half-day of school. Instead, he focused his efforts on farming a new piece of land his father had rented from a retiring farmer, Lars Stevenson.

One late afternoon, after band practice, I walked out the school's side door and was surprised to see Sam sitting on the hood of his dad's old Model A.

He opened the door for me and we both got in. "Thought I'd give you a ride home today, but I've got a few things I need to get off my chest." He turned away from me and stared out the front window. "Been thinking about it a lot. There's something I need to say. Something important."

"You seem nervous. What's wrong?"

Clearing his throat and still looking straight ahead, he said, "Mariah, I love you more than I can express. You told me a long time ago you wanted to move to a big city, experience the world, travel to far-flung places. But I can't give you that. I'm committing full-out on this new land Dad's rented. I promised my father I'd give it everything I had. It's a chance to be on my own and try out all the new methods I been researching. Dad believes I'm ready."

I nodded and smiled. "I know. You told me already. And you're lucky to get the opportunity, especially at your age. He must really believe in you."

"He does. But I can't do it alone. I don't want to do it alone. It has to be with you. That's the only way I can see it. The two of us together, Mariah. A partnership. Maybe down the line, some years from now, I'll take you to Paris or that Germany you know so much about." He turned to look at me and took both of my hands. "What I'm trying to say is...will you marry me, Mariah? I love you so much and I'll do my darndest to make you happy."

I sat quiet for a moment, thinking, then looked down at the school books on my lap. I did want more from life than living out on an isolated Iowa farm. What about a career of my own in New York or Chicago, or taking a trip to Europe? But, if I was honest with myself, could I imagine a life without Sam? My days began and ended with me thinking about him, imagining his grinning face, entwining our arms around each other, passionately kissing him. If I left Green Tree, wherever I traveled or worked, I'd be thinking about him, longing to be with Sam. So, what was the point of moving elsewhere? As much as I hated to admit it, he'd changed my mind about being part of a farming family. If Sam was with me, I was on board.

I looked up, smiled, and threw my arms around his neck and kissed him hard, not caring who noticed. "Yes....yes! I'll definitely marry you. I love you so much. But not until I graduate. I must graduate high school."

"Whatever you want. I'll wait. But I've decided this is my last year. Work on the property is nonstop. I can't spend any more time doing class work. Several of the guys are dropping out after this year."

"I hate to hear that, but I understand. My Dad never went beyond eighth grade and did fine."

"You're going to love the house, Mariah. In the evenings, I'm going to work on fixing it up, just for you. It's old and needs updates, but I'll make us a good home. Can you see it…a place of our own?"

"Yes. It may be rented but we'll make it ours, a special place."

That afternoon, the drive back to my house was a turning point. I'd committed to a new life, separate from my parents, older brothers, and sisters. It was scary but also thrilling to think about. As long as I had Sam, I knew I'd be fine. He made me feel safe, beautiful, and desired; important requirements for a sixteen-year-old girl. I convinced myself I was ready to make this journey with him as Mrs. Mariah Anderson, while my dreams of travel and a life off the farm became a wistful memory.

# CHAPTER 5
# NANETTE

*D*ragging my first two bags to the hotel's porch, I critically eyed the worn and cracked leather armchairs spaced across the front, under a torn awning. I retrieved my third bag from the street, and held one of the large double doors open with my foot, while grabbing my other two bags and dumping everything inside. Checking out the interior, a damp musty smell mixed with the scent of tobacco greeted me and then gnawed at the yellow bile bubbling up again in my stomach.

I was nervous, having never stayed in a hotel, and unsure of the protocol. Auntie had insisted I stay at an all-women's place, but actually this was the only hotel the phone operator could locate for me when I called to make an inquiry. And anyway, what difference did it make? In the small lobby, there were two men in suits and bowler hats, both reading newspapers. As I walked in, feeling queasy, one of them glanced up, folded his paper, and left it on the arm of the lobby chair.

Walking out the door, he smiled at me. "Good day, miss. You look a little lost, may I help?"

I took out my embroidered handkerchief and wiped my brow. "Thank you. Just a little overheated. Uh, registration?"

He pointed to a small counter in the corner. "You have a lovely day."

While walking to the registration counter, I grabbed his abandoned newspaper, and stepped up to the counter. A balding man with glasses looked up from his desk.

"Yes, madam?"

"Hello, you're holding a room for *N. Jorgenson* for two nights."

He paged through a ledger. "Hmm, I see that, but is the room for you?"

"Yes."

"Well, if that's the case, it's quite impossible."

I was nauseous and agitated. I needed a room immediately. "Impossible? Why, for heaven's sake?"

"Because you're a woman. A lovely woman, no doubt. But... we do not allow unescorted women here. It's simply not proper."

I was surprised and confused, but tried my best to remain calm. "So... you do take women, just not unescorted women?"

"We take *married* women who are traveling with their husbands or families."

"Oh, I see. Yes, of course. Understandable. My husband, uh... Nathan Jorgenson, will be along. He's coming from Chicago and meeting me here. We have business in Mankato-- real estate. I'll need to check in now though, freshen up and meet him at the station later. Let me get the room prepared for him. He likes things just so; you know how husbands can be. What room are we in?"

The clerk looked uncertain. "Well... if you're sure he'll be here later, I suppose you can register for the two of you; sign here, names and address please." He handed me a large metal key. "Room 2 F, upstairs, to the left. Bathroom's at the end of the hall."

"And I'll need someone to bring my bags to the room please." Ridiculous… needing to have a man tag along merely to rent a dive hotel room. I was fuming, although I kept my face calm and my smile glued. "Thank you, and what's your name, sir."

"Harold White, hotel manager."

"Well, Mr. White, I appreciate your understanding." It looked like Nathan Jorgenson's train would be running very late today or might not arrive at all.

I quickly walked upstairs, then dashed to the communal bathroom, as a bout of morning sickness erupted. I dry heaved into the toilet. By now, there was little left to throw up except a disgusting yellow liquid. I wet my handkerchief in the sink, located my room, and fell across the squeaking narrow bed, placing the wet cloth over my forehead. I suddenly missed the comfort of my own familiar room, the stocked kitchen, the path leading up to our flower-laden front porch, even Auntie's nosey and concerned questions seemed endearing at the moment.

I closed my eyes, dying for a nap, but was interrupted by a voice and rapping on the door. "Your bags, Mrs. Jorgenson."

I jumped off the bed and opened the door. "Oh, thank you, Mr. White. Very kind of you."

Placing the three cases on the printed linoleum floor, he smiled and stood there, waiting.

"I guess I better get to unpacking a few things."

"Yes, lots to unpack. Would you like me to open the window?"

"Certainly, thanks."

"Will that be it, madam?"

"Yes, thanks again."

What was he waiting for? Money, a tip? I'd never tipped

before. What was appropriate? I fumbled for my pocketbook. "Here you go." I handed him a quarter, which he looked at with disdain. I anxiously searched through my coin purse, handing him another coin, plastering on my best smile. "Mr. White, your service is simply impeccable. Good day."

Back on the bed, I leaned against the rickety headboard, put my damp handkerchief across my forehead, sighed and decided to open the newspaper I'd swiped downstairs. Hmm, where to look for a job? Flipping through the pages, I was distracted as my eye spotted an ad for a movie playing downtown: *The Gold Rush*, starring Charles Chaplin. Well, why not? For an aspiring actress needing to study acting skills, a movie theater might be the ideal place to apply for work; something to tide me over until I was discovered. Job-search completed, it was time for my nap.

# CHAPTER 6
# MARIAH

$\mathcal{U}$nlike his brothers, Sam's love of farming was more than a job; it was all he ever wanted to do. From an early age, he'd always been curious about crop rotations, more effective seed hybrids, and unique plowing techniques. He'd told me about experimenting on his dad's farm, and tinkering with machinery was his child's play. In this regard, he and his father, Alfred Anderson, shared a common passion.

With three-hundred and twenty acres, my future father-in-law owned one of the largest farms in the county, managing it with the help of Sam's three older brothers, all still living at home with their mother, Gerta, and sister, Catherine. Although he was the youngest, Sam was eager to be independent and strike out on his own. With the aid of his father, they convinced a retiring farmer to lease his farm to Sam. Once settling into it, he had managed two successful harvests, and now he only needed his recently graduated wife to join him. Together, we convinced ourselves we'd make a formidable team.

It was late May, 1928. Our wedding was a small, modest affair. For something old, I wore an antique gold locket my mother gave me. For something new, I purchased an impractical but beautiful pair of white satin pumps. For the borrowed, I wore my older sister's wedding dress; the price was right and I loved the simple bias-cut style. And for something blue, I selected a simple blue ribbon to wear around my neck adorned with the gold locket. I thought the bride's good-luck mantra was silly but I wasn't willing to test my luck on this marriage.

I walked down the aisle beaming, staring ahead to Samuel who stood confidently at the altar. I was proud of him looking so handsome in his new and only suit. As I stepped across from him, Sam, in silence, mouthed, "I love you." At that point, any nerves or doubts I was holding on to flew out the church doors. I knew I was making the right choice.

My family attended a country church surrounded by rich green fields of knee-hi corn stalks and the gravestones of family and friends who had passed. We were blessed with a dazzling, crisp, blue-skied day with a slight breeze. Between my family, the Anderson crew, a few of our closest school friends, and essential relatives, our wedding guests filled most of the pews in our Lutheran church.

After the service, everyone filled their stomachs with plates of food contributed by many of those attending, while my uncle took a few photographs of Sam and me, and our families. These formal family photos were rare, and weddings often provided the few times everybody could gather together in front of someone who owned a camera. Sam's parents, Alfred and Gerta, seemed a bit in shock after the ceremony, keeping to themselves. Their youngest and seemingly favorite son was flying from their tightly woven nest.

His mother, Gerta, gathered her brood. "Sam, get your brothers. Alfred, gather round. You too, Catherine. Let's get a family photo." She pulled her husband, crew of four sons and daughter together, but seemed to purposely exclude the new bride, while I stood off to the side waiting.

After my uncle shot the picture, his parents began walking

away, as Sam spoke up. "Ma, Dad...we didn't get one including Mariah. Come on, let's do one more." Sam pulled me close; we were front and center. His mother, to our left, remained rigid and curt. Later, Sam quietly said, "Sorry. Mother is kinda like our general; thinks she's the commanding officer. But, thank God, I've gone AWOL."

Luckily, the Anderson farm was eight miles away from our place, so I wouldn't have to look at her disappointed face daily.

As a wedding gift, Sam's parents gave us their old Model A, an exchange which seemed to miff his older brothers. My parents gave us a few dairy cows, not terribly exciting or romantic, but my dad was always the practical one. For our honeymoon, we drove the Ford thirty-five miles to the larger Minnesota town of Albert Lea where we checked into a downtown hotel for two days.

It was a weekend I'd never forget. It was the first time either of us had stayed at a hotel. It was just a simple room, with a springy double bed, a desk and chair, and a bathroom down the hall. But it was our room and our bed. We had made love before, a few rushed and secretive times in the backseat of the car, but it always felt off, like something special was missing. Now we had the luxury of lying in a comfortable double bed in private, exploring each other's bodies for hours.

As the sun came up through our hotel window, I looked over at Sam who was awake and smiling, his head propped up above two pillows. I asked, "So, after almost four years of waiting, was it worth it?"

He grabbed and kissed my hand, "So worth it. You're perfect. All I ever wanted."

From my calendar calculations, our family was started that day, and the twins came tumbling out nine months later.

# CHAPTER 7
# NANETTE

*T*he sound of traffic woke me with a start. A breeze blew through the short dingy curtains hanging at my hotel window. I stretched, feeling exhausted, not wanting to move. Pushing myself out of bed, I stared through the window looking out onto Front Street. The commotion seemed to be caused by cars honking at an ice-delivery wagon blocking their way. I checked my watch; it was already three o'clock and my stomach was shooting out hunger pains.

I passed a tiny round mirror hung above the dresser, and my reflection caught me by surprise. Disaster; my hair and face looked terrible. Makeup smudged, with more lipstick on my pillow than lips, and my waved bob in disarray. I opened one of my bags, pulling out a hairbrush, lipstick, powder and rouge. I needed to impress for my first possible job interview. Having slept in it, my suit was wrinkled, but it would have to do.

Walking quickly down the stairs in my new heels, I saw Mr. White checking in another guest, and hoped to exit before he noticed me. As I grabbed the front door, I heard his annoying voice. "Mrs. Jorgenson, just *now* leaving to meet your husband?

"Yes, I fell asleep. He's going to be upset; need to hurry. Will we see you this evening?"

"No, I get off at five. Good day to you." That was convenient, no elaborate lie needed for Mr. White until tomorrow.

The honking cars were now slowly going around the large ice wagon, and I saw a young delivery man walking back carrying empty ice tongs. I scurried up the sidewalk to ask him directions. It had worked for me this morning, maybe I'd get lucky again.

"Sir... sir? Any chance you know how to get to the Mankato Movie House?"

Ignoring me, he climbed onto the bench of the wagon, then pulled off a kerchief tied around his neck and wiped his tanned face. I stepped directly across from him, and asked again more loudly. "Mankato Movie House? Do you know how far?"

He stared at my face, smiled and leaned over, reaching for my hand. In a strong accent, he said, "I take." Was that an Italian accent? Whatever it was, I liked the sound.

"Well, thank you. Is it close?"

He nodded, clicked his team of four horses forward and we continued down Front Street. One block down, he stopped in front of a restaurant. Smiling again, he said, "Ice."

He went to the back of the wagon and pulled out a massive block, carrying it through the back door of the restaurant. Then he climbed up again. This continued with three more stops as the ice-man made his deliveries. He said only "ice" as he got down, but then smiled at me each time he came back. I kept sneaking side glances at him as he managed the team of horses. Strong chiseled chin, long nose, with dark curling hair showing below his hat, and biceps that bulged under a rough and soiled cotton shirt. But at the rate of his deliveries, I figured I'd be better off walking to the theater than hitching a ride with my handsome ice-man. The view was good but the conversation was limited.

After his third delivery, I explained, "I'll walk to the theater. In a bit of a hurry." As I turned to step down from the bench, he reached for my arm and said, "I take." Attractive as he was, trying to explain my needs to someone with a vocabulary of 'ice' and 'I take' was frustrating. He continued, making two more stops. Finally we arrived at a building with a marque and he said, "Movie" and then pointed at me saying, "Movie star," grinning with a broad smile, as if he'd made a joke. Well, maybe there was more to this delivery man than just big biceps. His vocabulary was expanding.

I looked bashful, casting my eyes down, then pointed to myself. "Me? No, not a movie star. But maybe someday. Thanks for the ride."

As I jumped off the step, I heard, "Tomorrow, I take?"

"Maybe?" I shrugged my shoulders demurely and said, "I'm Nanette. What's your name?"

He pointed to his chest. "Romero."

Romero… it did sound Italian. We didn't have any of those in Green Tree. Dark, mysterious, strong. Very Rudolf-Valentino-like, my favorite exotic movie star.

I waved goodbye and turned toward the glass cubicle in front of the theater. An older gentleman in a burgundy uniform with gold braid was sitting inside selling tickets. I leaned into the opening. "Hello sir. I'm Nanette Jorgenson and I'd like to speak with the manager, please."

"He's inside; but I can't let you inside unless you buy a ticket."

"But I'm here on business. I want to inquire about a position."

"Far as I know, there ain't no jobs here. If you wanna to go inside, you need to buy a ticket."

I was so hungry and I'd already wasted fifty-cents on my tip to Mr. White. I certainly didn't want to pay to see a man about the mere possibility of a job.

"What's the ticket cost?"

"Twenty-five cents, miss."

"So, if I pay twenty-five cents, will the manager see me?"

"Don't know. He might be busy."

"Oh, for heaven's sake. You're running quite a racket here, sir." I dug in my purse and gave him a quarter, and walked through the lobby. Seeing an usher, I used my most authoritative tone and said, "Sir, I need to speak with the manager. It's quite urgent."

"Sure, miss." He pointed to a hallway beyond the concession stand. "Name's Mr. Grant. Just knock on the door. He should be in there."

I took a deep breath, knocked with exuberance, and heard a high-pitched nasal voice say, "What is it now, Daniel?" I opened the door a few inches, poking my head through.

"Hello, Mr. Grant, it's not Daniel. I'm Nanette Jorgenson. Do you have a couple minutes?"

He looked at his watch as if there was a massive line of people demanding his time. "I suppose. What can I do for you?"

I sat down on a small wooden chair in front of his desk. The office was tiny, not much more than a closet, with a few movie posters tacked on the walls. Grant was a small man with pale skin and reddish thinning hair. Someone who looked like he'd stayed in a dark theater too long.

I punched up my enthusiasm level and began. "My goodness, how lucky you are to work in this fine theater surrounded by all these movie memories."

He was now flipping through the newspaper. "Uh-huh… well, let's get to it. I've got a lot on my plate today."

"It's just that the movies…they're all I dream about, really. And that's why I'm here today, Mr. Grant. I wanted to inquire about a job. I'm new to the city and this was the first place I wanted to apply. Now, some of my best skills include handling money and giving change; I'm also trustworthy, prompt, and *excellent* with customers."

"Well, you're certainly not shy; I'll give you that. Unfortunately, I have no openings. All my staff have been here a while now."

"I see." I sat for a second gathering my thoughts. "But, Mr. Grant, are they *good* at their job? Really good?"

He closed his paper, and ran his hand through his thinning hair. "I believe so, my dear."

"Does your ticket seller get customers excited about the movies you're presenting? The man selling tickets today certainly didn't seem to do that. Does the person at your concession counter always sell a drink *with* your popcorn? Does your usher keep your lobby and theater sparkling clean? If you hire me, Mr. Grant, I promise I will increase your ticket and concession sales. I'm assuming your salary is based on overall business performance?"

"That's certainly none of your business. Anyway, it's *not possible* to hire you. All of our uniforms are designed for men."

I laughed at the minor obstacle. "That's no problem. I can easily make a skirt to go with your jackets. I suggest you try me out at least part-time; you'll be impressed. If you don't see improvements and increases on the days I work, I'll turn in my uniform."

He pulled a clipboard off the wall and studied it. "I do spread myself pretty thin during some of my employees' days off, and then again, people get sick, have emergencies."

"I'm your girl, Mr. Grant; you obviously need some help here with your spotty schedule. What does the position pay?"

He looked around his desk flustered, seemingly confused at the turn the conversation was taking. "Well, I don't rightly know. Let's see… the men make forty-five-cents an hour, so, as a part-time woman, I suppose thirty-five cents?"

"I'll take the job for forty-five cents an hour and not a penny less. Remember, Mr. Grant, that will still be a bargain because I'm going to make *you* more money. Now, let's discuss my schedule."

I left fifteen minutes later, with a burgundy and gold jacket tossed over my shoulder and a job paying a fiercely negotiated forty-cents an hour, which included all the movies I cared to watch and free popcorn. I'd allowed Mr. Grant to bargain me down a nickel just to let him keep his pride. The job started in two days.

Now, time to find some inexpensive food. I was so hungry, and pie sounded especially good if my unsettled stomach would allow me to hold it down. I noticed a small café across the street. Traffic was clear at the moment. I walked quickly across with my eyes on the prize—the café showcased three different pies on a stacked pedestal. With my hungry eyes glued to the window, I accidently stepped into a massive warm pile of horse shit. The nasty scent bloomed around me as I pulled my sticky brown foot and new shoe out of the mess. Continuing across the street, I tried to scrape the excrement off my shoe onto the curb before entering, but the smell grew only stronger. I attempted to step inside, but customers at the front tables turned suddenly towards me, wrinkling their noses, looking disgusted. Backing out, I decided to return to my hotel, clean my shoe and foot, and then try a restaurant closer to where I was staying.

By the time I arrived, it was well past five o'clock so I had no fear of Mr. White being there. The smell of the shoe wasn't as bad as it had been earlier but the scent still lingered. On the front porch, I wrapped the shoe in my handkerchief and hobbled in, walking up-stairs, ignoring the registration desk. A minute after I locked my door, there was loud knocking outside.

"Mrs. Jorgenson?"

Now what? I opened the door a crack. "Yes?"

A young man in white shirt sleeves stood there, clearing his throat, looking nervous. "Mrs. Jorgenson, Mr. White wanted to make sure I checked on you."

"I'm perfectly fine. Thank you for checking." I closed the door, but the knocking resumed. "What is it?" I asked through the closed door.

"Has Mr. Jorgenson arrived?" I opened the door again.

Putting on a sad face, I said, "He's been delayed, unfortunately. Long delays along the line from Chicago, apparently. Hopefully tomorrow. Thanks for asking, though." As I began to close the door, his foot crossed the threshold.

"Well, madam, in that case, I'm going to have to ask you to leave. Mr. White was quite explicit with me that you could only stay here *with* your husband."

*Maybe tears? They were usually effective.* "I can't believe this. It's just that I'm so exhausted, waiting at that train station for over two hours, and now you're throwing me out?" I collapsed on the bed starting to wail. "Sir, surely you can see this is not my fault and you're tossing me to the street?"

"Sorry ma'am. Rules is rules. Mr. White's the boss."

"This is absurd." I wiped my tears with my jacket sleeve. He wasn't budging, leaning against the door with his arms crossed. "Alright, it's a tacky little room anyway. Excuse me while I visit the powder room; I expect a full refund and I'll need my bags carried downstairs."

I hobbled to the bathroom taking my shitty shoe with me. Where to now? I'd suddenly hit an impasse.

# CHAPTER 8
# MARIAH

*T*hey arrived, almost together, in our small drafty farm house.

Jo's wail broke through the tension, quiet, and cold as I envisioned Sam downstairs nervously stubbing out a cigarette, with a long stem of ash clinging to it in the bowl. He only smoked when he was nervous and I could smell the smoke snaking up the stairs. I'm sure he was glancing up the narrow wooden staircase, pensive, waiting for confirmation. Then my baby's wails were replaced by my own as I screamed out in agony once again. The waiting had been going on for hours. Samuel had chores to finish and a barn to close up, but I knew he wouldn't leave while I was upstairs in our bedroom going through this agony.

Then the room turned silent, no shrieking from me for at least a few minutes. I heard his heavy boots climbing the steep stairway to the two bedrooms at the top. He softly rapped on the door and asked, "For God's sake, how are things going in there? I'm at my wit's end waiting."

His sister, Catherine, called out, "All Good. Very busy here. Go tend to your darn cows, why don't you? It may be a while."

After hitting the door in frustration, I heard him sigh and then trudge downstairs. As I counted breaths between the next contractions, I pictured him in the mud room, putting on his heavy belted coat, wool cap, and thick work gloves. Our cows would be ornery tonight. They didn't like to be kept waiting.

Lying back against the black iron bed, I smiled for a few brief seconds of relief, but that was broken by several waves of excruciating pain. It was hard to focus. I was hot and sticky but the bedroom air was so cold I could see Catherine's and my mother's breath coming out in small puffs. I tried panting away the sharp pains of labor, as my mom instructed. My mother, Renalda, held her new granddaughter, Jo, in a corner wooden chair, while Catherine held my hand and whispered encouragement for one more hard push.

"You can do this, Mariah. You're almost there. Remember, the pain is temporary."

It may have been temporary, but so was life. "I don't know if I can do it again. I've pushed all I can. It's more than I can bear." In anguish I called out, "My God, Ma, how could you ever do this time and again? I never realized…." Then I grabbed a damp cloth on the nightstand, putting it in my mouth as I gritted my teeth. Holding fast to Catherine's hand, I pressed down with one final, excruciating shriek as my second baby, Sarah, made her delayed entrance into the world, joining her eager twin. Even in those first few minutes, Sarah was always a few steps behind Jo.

I shuddered in relief after hours of struggle. We were truly a family now, with two daughters, both perfect to my eye. Jo, towheaded with a light sprinkling of down-like hair, and Sarah, with a thick dark shock of hair. As my mother cut and tied Sarah's cord and then bundled her up, she said, "You rest now, Mariah. You'll soon have double the work, but twice as much to love."

At that moment, an overwhelming sense of maternal duty overruled the fear that had dogged me these last few months. I'd doubted I was up for this herculean task of nurturing and raising a family, but now I felt content, amazed, fatigued, but excited by the challenge. Mother laid the twins on my chest for a moment of exhausted bliss before their weak crying commenced.

Only after cows were milked, pigs fed, and tools put away, did Sam return to the house. After removing rubber boots and washing in a pan of cold water in the kitchen sink, he walked into the small front parlor. I was lying on the short sofa, covered in a quilt, while my mother and Catherine talked softly, sitting in chairs across from the bright burning embers in the fireplace, each holding one of our beautiful daughters.

Seeing me on the sofa, Sam came directly over and knelt down. "What are you doing down here? Should you be moving so soon?"

"Shhh, you'll wake the babies. I'm fine. Catherine and Ma practically carried me down. It's just too cold upstairs. I was afraid for the babies."

"I'll bring our mattress downstairs."

"So go look!" I whispered. "Go see what we created. They're amazing."

My mother had suspected and suggested twins, but the actual confirmation was still remarkable to Sam.

He grinned widely, "So, two for the price of one! You were right, Renalda. And who do we have here?" Samuel peeked into the blanketed bundle she was holding and scooped up Sarah.

Catherine whispered, "That little dark beauty is Sarah, and I have Jo. Quiet now, Sam. They just went to sleep."

He gingerly picked up Jo as well, holding them both, and grinned down at their tiny sleeping faces. He softly spoke to us, saying, "I'm one lucky man with three beautiful girls to take care of now." It was a lot of responsibility for a young man of nineteen, but Samuel seemed to have been planning for this his entire life.

## CHAPTER 9
## MARIAH

*I*n late-summer, with the stove heated up, the hot still air in the small kitchen made me yearn for cold winter days. I twisted my long dark hair up in a bun, pulling it off my neck, while sweat dripped down my back. Then I scoffed, knowing in the winter we had to layer up four garments thick just to keep warm inside. Now here I was, wishing for bone-chilling winds to come blowing through. I reminded myself, count your blessings and enjoy the moment.

I checked the clock. It was 2:30, which allowed me about an hour for dinner preparation before my napping twins would wake for their feeding. Because I was still nursing, all tasks needed checking off before Jo and Sarah woke with hungry cries. I quickly rolled out a mound of lefse dough; the potato flatbread helped fill Sam's stomach that was never quite satisfied. Samuel worked so physically hard that he burned through calories like a work-horse. Between meal preparation for him, breastfeeding two demanding babies, and keeping up with my large vegetable garden, I had to squeeze in chores of laundry, dish washing, collecting eggs, and keeping an ever-growing sounder of pigs satisfied. As a fine dust blew through my screens, sweeping often ended up last on my endless to-do list.

I slid my circle of flattened lefse onto a pan on the stove top, and glanced around at my simple life. As tough and demanding as some days were, I knew we were lucky. We had a solid non-leaking roof over our heads, a round pine table with four sturdy chairs surrounding it, and a linoleum floor in a pretty floral pattern which Sam had installed as an early wedding gift. As a young married couple, we understood there was time down the road to accumulate better furniture, maybe a heating system, and in time, hire some household help. Perhaps it wasn't the life I'd dreamed of, but I was with a man I loved fiercely. We had two thriving daughters, and a rented home we thought of as ours.

As the lefse baked, Samuel surprised me, poking his head in the window, as beads of sweat streaked through a layer of dust across his face. "Hey there, how you doing, beautiful?"

I smiled back, pushing strands of hair out of my face. "Not feeling very beautiful; just rushing to get some dinner started."

"Good, and set a few extra places. David and Billy-Boy, from the Thomas farm, are helping me with the pump. OK if I invited them?"

"Don't know what I have to feed the three of you, but I'll find something."

Then, from upstairs, the crying commenced.

THAT EVENING AROUND SEVEN, our neighbors had left and the twins' final feeding was done. Samuel was in his usual spot, sitting in the brown upholstered chair reading his newspaper from the light of an overhead oil lamp. I was bone-tired, sitting in my rocker, and leaned over to set Sarah down on a blanket.

"Well, that's done for the night. These two are wearing me out, Sam."

He looked at me, peeking over his paper. "Well, I hope you're eating enough. I honestly don't know how you do it."

I shrugged at his concern. "I'll be fine, but just look at these two. I sat back and watched, amazed at their eight-month growth. After a few minutes I announced, "Well, I'm putting these little ladies to bed. Want to say good night with me?" I glanced at Sam but his head was already beginning to nod, dozing off after his tiring day. "Never mind," I whispered to the girls, as I climbed up the steep stairway. "Your Daddy worked hard today. I'll say good night for both of us."

I would have to supplement their feeding soon. Like Sam said, I needed to keep up my strength to hold the house together. We were a two-person company, committed to keeping our fragile and fickle business functioning and profitable. Our farm was one-hundred-and-sixty acres of rich blue-black Iowa soil. Lars rented both the acreage and house to us. We planted and harvested the crops, with fifty percent of the profits going back to Lars. Any improvements we added to outlying buildings and livestock were our responsibility, but we also got to keep those profits. The few dollars our egg and dairy money earned each week was precious and used as credit toward other needed staples. The occasional slaughtered swine or cow was also a big boost to our monthly earnings, and kept us fed with a steady supply of smoked meat.

I assumed, one day, we'd buy the farm, but for now we scrimped by. Married for less than two years, Sam and I had already worked through several challenges. After learning how to balance our books, I'd learned so much about the perils and success of a farmer's tenuous budget.

Although we both had extended family throughout the county, there were some days I felt so alone, as if it were Sam and I against the world and all it could throw at us. With no phone and miles between family members, it could feel isolating. I still thought about what it might be like living in a bigger city, working independently, but I knew those thoughts were now only silly dreams. I was a fully committed wife and mother and there was no going back.

After putting the girls down for the night, I came downstairs and saw Sam awake again, checking the sports page. "They went right to sleep, thank goodness. Let's see if I can find some music."

Sam nodded. "Sounds good."

Like most farms in the area, we had no electricity, but Sam had recently purchased a large battery-operated radio for fifty-five dollars on credit. I admonished him for his reckless spending but reveled in this connection to the world. Both he and I would dial through the static most evenings, eventually tuning into programs broadcast primarily from Des Moines or Minneapolis. Our new prized possession was placed on a square table between my wooden rocker and the armchair. Samuel often dialed into baseball games and I loved listening to the comedy shows like *Fibber Magee and Molly*. In the evening, as the darkness of the surrounding acreage closed in around us, we'd put tasks to the side briefly, as we tuned in, imagining the faces of entertainers we listened to each night.

After an hour, Samuel stood up and stretched, picked up a lantern and said, "Well, that bathroom isn't going to build itself. I'll get a little more framing done before I go to bed." The indoor bathroom, a rarity among farms, was going to be another of his generous gifts for me. We were building it as an extension off the mud room in the back. I got up reluctantly and sighed. "I'll help. It'll be so worth it in the end." We joined in together for one more hour of labor.

~

By October, the last of the preserves had been squirreled away in the cellar, our corn harvest had been excellent, and my garden was sputtering out the last of the fall produce. Our newest joy was our completed bathroom, with water piped in from our windmill tank. The simple room, with tub and toilet, was glorious and the envy of most of our neighbors, still using outhouses. Sam had purchased the needed tools, lumber and supplies from his uncle's hardware store and was paying him back in small monthly installments. I allowed myself a weekly guilty pleasure, luxuriating in a hot Friday evening bath, as Samuel looked after the girls.

Tuesday evening, while I was shutting windows in the front room, Sam said, "Special news, Mariah. Best listen for a minute." A news report was interrupting the *Amos 'n Andy* show. Static crackled through the room, followed by beeps, then the deep and serious voice of a newscaster came through clearly.

"*We interrupt this program to report today's dramatic market sell-off on Wall Street in New York, with stock prices tumbling to record lows after several years of unprecedented highs with frenzied trading. Thousands of Americans, from wealthy tycoons to poor widows, have lost their savings, and today, eleven high-flying financiers committed suicide, reacting to the downward spiral of the market.*" The announcer went on for several more minutes relaying the shocking news, calling it, 'Black Tuesday.'

"Oh my God, Sam. That's devastating. I had no idea the stock markets were so unstable. And those poor men…jumping out of windows. Can you imagine feeling so desperate? And to think, I used to dream about moving to Manhattan."

He shook his head, remaining silent for a few seconds. "Sounds terrible. Shocking news. But keep in mind, Mariah, we're in farming. It's necessary, steady work. Be thankful we'll be safe from all that big-city banking business."

I naively nodded my head in agreement.

## CHAPTER 10
## NANETTE

*D*azed, sitting on the front porch of the hotel surrounded by my suitcases, I looked out despondently on the street, enveloped by the night's chill and darkness. A few hotel guests walked past, coming and going, but nobody offered to help. I put the Mankato Movie House jacket over my suit, clashing terribly, but it was thick and warm. I had no idea moving to a new town would be so challenging. Here I was, on my first night, thrown out with no place to go. Not to mention, probably pregnant, incredibly tired, and beyond hungry. If Auntie knew about all this, she would be furious with me.

Eventually, the annoying hotel clerk came out to the front porch. "I'm sorry madam; you can't stay here. Best move along now."

"Horsefeathers!" I was trying to decide what to do, but nothing was jumping out at me. "What's your name?"

"Finn McDonald."

"Now Finn…"

"Don't 'now Finn' me, Mrs. Jorgenson, You're a lone

woman all bundled up here, just sitting amongst your bags. It don't look right, ma'am."

"Finn, you can call me Nanette. I'm simply taking some time to contemplate my options. Here's an idea. You hold my bags for me while I look around for a place to stay. Will you at least do that for me?"

"Nanette…No ma'am, can't be libel for them. Can't clutter up the lobby."

"Finn, you're a weak man. Just following rules for the sake of rules. I'm disappointed in you."

"Sorry to hear that. I'll be inside calling the police now"

He was a tough nut to crack. As he turned to go inside, I started crying again, making loud outbursts. "Go ahead. Call the coppers. I'll take my chances. Hopefully, they'll be more charitable than you."

Within ten minutes, a black and white vehicle pulled up and a tall uniformed policeman got out and ambled up the walkway. Close up, he had a sympathetic looking face, as he stood in front of me with his hands on his hips, listening to me sniffle.

"Madam, are we having a problem this evening?"

I increased my tears. "I've been flung out of this hotel! Only because my husband has been delayed. Could you help me please?"

"First of all, let's calm down. How about this; are you willing to stay at the Young Women's Christian Association for the evening?"

I turned off the tears and asked, "The what?"

"You would have to share the room with others, but it's clean. Only God-fearing, respectable women are allowed to stay there."

"Well, certainly. I believe I fit the criteria and it can't be worse than this place. But could I impose on you to take me there? I have all these bags and no idea where it's located. As a matter of fact, Officer, I would love to buy you a slice of pie if we could go to a restaurant first. Are you hungry?"

I dried my sniffles and broadened my smile. As I stood up, I pulled off my silly looking uniform jacket.

"I can certainly drive you over there, but I'll have to say 'no' to the pie invitation. Let's hurry along and get you situated."

"I can't thank you enough, Officer…?"

"It's Officer Olsen."

I grabbed one bag and he took two as we walked toward the police car. Sitting down inside, I said, "Officer Olsen, I believe Mankato has some of the nicest people. With the exception of the crew at the hotel… They're horrid. But honestly, everyone else I've met here has been wonderful."

"Good to hear. Now about the Young Women's Christian Association, they have chapters in many cities now, and they're offering women safe and inexpensive places to stay."

This was all news to me. Green Tree had no such thing, not even a small hotel. We pulled up to what looked to be a large converted brick home, with the lights on throughout.

"Mrs. Jorgenson, I took the liberty of checking from the station to see if they had a vacancy. They're holding a bed for you."

As we walked up the sidewalk with my bags, I felt I had to come clean with the pleasant Officer Olsen. "Since we may see each other again one day, I feel compelled to be honest with you, officer. I'm not married. There was no husband coming from Chicago. The hotel manager insisted I had to be married to stay there, which is, of course, ridiculous. So, he forced me into a difficult and precarious position with the truth. I came to Mankato to look for a job and an apartment. I wanted you to know my real story."

"Well, Miss Jorgenson, I'd pretty much figured all that out since there were no train delays at the station today and we only get one train a day from Chicago. And then there's your movie theater uniform. Now, you either stole that jacket or you're working there."

"Yes, I actually got a job there today. I'm excited." I shook his hand at the door. "I must tell you; the city is wasting their money on you being a mere policeman. You should be a detective! Maybe I'll see you at the movies?"

He lifted his hat, gave me a slight grin, and set my bags on the covered front porch. "Perhaps. Stay out of trouble now, Miss Jorgenson."

# CHAPTER 11
# MARIAH

*A*lthough not immediate, Samuel's prediction of being safe from the 1929 crash proved incorrect. As time passed, a rolling tide of tightening credit in banks across the country was drowning customers in unpayable debt. This included the small rural banks supporting the farming communities. Because so many people living in cities had lost factory jobs and shuttered small businesses, most Americans were buying less food, clothing, and manufactured goods.

Everybody was tightening their belts. Problem was, we had bumper crops of corn that year. Our herd of dairy cows had grown, but prices on food and dairy were in free-fall because there was so much surplus and less demand. Prices on corn reached a pitiful eleven cents a bushel and eggs were as low as eight cents a dozen. Some of the smaller farmers were resorting to burning their corn in the winter for fuel, not being able to afford coal.

Many farmers, deep in credit for purchases on machinery or livestock, couldn't pay their monthly loan payments and eventually banks were calling in notes on past due accounts and auctioning off farms. Within a few months, even in our seemingly safe Iowa county, several neighbors had been forced off their farms by banks, involuntarily leaving the area in search of work in bigger cities, hoping for better.

It was a sobering thought for Sam and me, and we felt fortunate we hadn't taken on more credit to buy the gas-fueled tractor Samuel had his eye on earlier. Always more cautious of making big purchases, I'd encouraged Sam to wait another season or two and continue to plow our fields the old-fashioned way, with Buck and Shorty, our team of reliable horses. For a young farmer eager to take on more land, a bigger tractor was a necessity, but now that farm commodity prices were falling, the idea of taking on additional acreage and livestock didn't feel like a smart move. But at least we had our basic housing and food needs met, which was more than many had.

We held tight to each other and gathered strength from our young marriage and kids. I'd discovered we each had qualities that made the other stronger. At night, in bed, Samuel would cradle me in his arms, imagining his next big project, filling me in on all his dreams and plans.

"By next year, Mariah, things should turn around. If they do, I'm looking to take on another forty acres and plant soybeans. Wave of the future, mark my words."

And I'd prudently reply, "I believe you Sam, but let's wait and see."

CHURCH ATTENDANCE WAS AN ALMOST mandatory weekly event. Sam's family was a member of the Lutheran church in town, while I had grown up attending the country church, where we had married. As a new family, we decided we'd attend both, taking turns each Sunday, allowing us to build a bond of friends and acquaintances throughout the community.

At our country church, after the Norwegian service, my

oldest sister, Janeen, came up to me in tears. "Jim's leaving tomorrow. Taking the car to Chicago. Who knows when I'll see him again."

"What are you talking about? What happened?" I asked, pulling out a handkerchief for her from my handbag.

Between sobs, she explained, "The dairy is cutting back, probably closing. The owner released all management this week. It's just a skeleton staff now."

I hugged my sister hard. "I'm so sorry, Janeen. We've been hearing rumors. How are the kids handling it? Why Chicago?"

"The dairy owner has a contact there, someone who might have a job for Jim, but it's so far away. If things work out, the kids and I may eventually have to move."

"Chicago? All of you? I'm sure it's only temporary; things will turn around."

Janeen looked away and wiped her nose. "Lord willing, I hope so. I can't imagine moving. Especially to Chicago! But it seems like problems are snowballing, not getting better. After next month, we can't make rent on the house. I talked to Ma yesterday. The boys and I are moving back home while Jim's away."

Janeen was the first of my siblings to marry and move into Green Tree. I had envied her life in town, with access to most needs within walking distance. She had electric power, a good school close by for her four sons, and a husband working in a secure management job with a steady paycheck. But now that stable world had turned upside down. It was frightening how life could turn on a dime. Janeen and her boys would be moving into my parent's already crowded household. Mom and Dad's place would be housing themselves, my two older brothers, a younger sister, a hired man and his wife, who slept in a small room off the back porch, and now Janeen and her four sons.

"What did Ma say?"

"You know Ma. She nodded her head and said it'll all work out. She started clearing the basement right after we talked. The kids will bunk down there and I'll room with Arlene. Little sis is not too happy about it, but we're family."

"Absolutely. I'm so sorry, Janeen."

My mother and one of her neighbors were on babysitting duty in the church basement. Joining her there, Ma took Janeen's hands and looked into her eyes saying, "We're all ready for you and your brood, excited to have you back. Feeling better today?"

Janeen tucked her light blonde hair back behind her ears. "Better, yes… but worried. I know things could be worse, but I hate giving up our home and losing Jim." Hugging our mother, she said, "Thanks for putting us up, Ma. I don't know what else we can do right now with him leaving."

She patted Janeen's shoulder. "It'll all work out. Who knows? A new adventure in a big city might be exciting for you and Jim."

I added, "Yes, Chicago might be great for your whole family."

Janeene's eyes teared up again. "I don't even want to think about that!"

I began bundling up Sarah and Jo in boots, coats, hats and mittens; a task that always seemed to take forever. But I enjoyed the lingering… chatting with girlfriends and neighbors who were also collecting their kids. Although times were leaner, there was always a strong sense of friendship and food to be shared within our church community.

As we came outside to return home, a cluster of men stood in the churchyard, circling Jim, discussing the dairy's turn of events and offering advice. I saw Sam give Jim a firm hand-shake and an encouraging pat on the back. None of us were sure how long it would be before we saw Jim again. As the four of us piled into the car, I couldn't shake the sense of unease which was weighing me down.

# CHAPTER 12
# NANETTE

*W*alking into the YWCA's cheery home-style lobby, I was put at ease. There were a few sofa and chair groupings centered on either side of a large fireplace, with some younger women clustered together talking, while another read by herself under lamplight. I checked in at a small desk where a stern looking woman was folding towels.

"Hello ma'am, I'm Nanette Jorgenson. I was told you were holding a room for me."

She was older, wearing a dark suit, round spectacles, with her graying hair pulled back in a tight bun. "Ah yes… and you're lucky you arrived on time. We don't receive guests after eight PM."

Checking my watch, I saw it was five minutes before eight. "Goodness. I had no idea. I *am* lucky. Can you tell me where I might go to get a bite to eat?"

"There's a café about two blocks to the west. The Good Egg, but everything around here closes by eight, and besides, the rules don't allow you to leave here in the evening after eight. Now, sign in and I'll give you the rest of the rules." She pulled out her registry book and a numbered sheet, reading it to me. "There are no gentleman callers allowed beyond the lobby and they may only come during visiting hours, which are from five until eight PM. Understood?"

"Alright."

"Rooms are fifty cents a night and you will share a room with three other women and must keep your area tidy and neat." She eyed me suspiciously with the last comment. "All lights out by ten PM. You will be expected to be available for a prayer meeting every morning from six to six-thirty. This is mandatory. We do serve a continental breakfast from six-thirty-five until seven-fifteen."

"Well, I certainly won't be missing that," I said with a smile.

Ignoring my comment, she continued. "There is no cooking allowed on the premises and you must keep the bath-room area clean. You will be issued one towel and one wash cloth which you will turn in for laundering every Saturday. And any time you are in the lobby, you must be dressed appropriate-ly." She set down her list, eying me skeptically and asked, "Any questions?"

"No, everything understood." This place made Auntie's rules seem down-right liberating. "I'm sure it will be just fine. Thank you."

"Perfect. Then we'll both stay on good terms with each other. You'll be in room three, bed two."

I sensed the police officer may have mentioned to her that I had a bit of a rebellious streak in me, which, of course, was not true. But it didn't matter anyway because tomorrow I would definitely begin my search for an apartment. I didn't come all this way to live in a house of silly confining rules. But right now, all I wanted to do, besides eat, was wash up and go to bed.

I lugged each suitcase up the stairs, one at a time, with absolutely no help from those giggling girls in the lobby. My room already had one woman asleep, snoring in the far corner. Thankfully, bed two was on the opposite side. I slid two of my suitcases under the bed and pulled out a sleeping gown and toiletry case from my smaller bag, and went to the restroom. Three girls were already standing in line in the long hallway waiting their turn. I joined the line and leaned against the wall, feeling I could easily fall asleep standing up before my turn arrived. Had it really only been early this morning that I'd left Green Tree? It felt like a week ago.

Later, someone was shaking my shoulder rather aggressively as I lay in bed. I turned, squinted, and looked up at her in the semi-dark room. "Sorry, doll. Wanted to warn you; you got five minutes before prayer meeting. You don't want to be late for that."

I stared at her face for a second before I realized where I was. "Morning all ready?" I sat up, looking around, and realized I'd slept so soundly I hadn't heard a peep as my three other roommates had gotten up and dressed, with the other two already downstairs.

"Best be quick, doll. No praying... no breakfast."

That got me motivated. I raced to the bathroom, urinating and then vomiting. I would not miss another meal. I yanked the first dress I found from one of my suitcases and threw it over my head, as I slipped my feet into heels, and rather scandalously, didn't bother with stockings. I finger combed my permed bob, folded yesterday's newspaper into my pocket, then raced downstairs. I hustled into the large dining area that held two long tables of twelve chairs each. There was one chair left to be filled. It appeared I was the last to arrive.

The priss and prim house mistress and reader of rules, was standing at the far end of the room and stared at me as I plopped into my chair.

"Now that we are *all* here, let us bow our heads and pray." I closed my eyes, pressed my hands together, and got busy. I prayed to find an apartment…very soon. I prayed not to be pregnant. I prayed to find another job, in addition to my part-time position, and then remembered to pray that I be discovered by a Hollywood agent that might be passing through Mankato, hoping he would whisk me away to California and all my problems would disappear. Were these prayers, dreams, or wishful thinking? Did it matter?

After five minutes of personal prayer, another holy-roller joined Miss Priss at the front and gave us our morning bible reading, as I slowly pulled out the newspaper, put it in my lap, bowed my head in prayer and attempted to read the rooms-for-rent section of the paper.

After Holy-Roller finally finished sermonizing, praise be to God, breakfast was served. As I waited patiently for the passing of coffee, hard rolls, butter, marmalade, and a scoop of oatmeal, I felt the firm hand and bad breath of Miss Priss on my shoulder. I looked up with a gentle smile.

"Good morning, ma'am."

"Miss Jorgenson, we do not read newspapers during prayer services. All attention should be given to the Lord."

"But it was, ma'am. I prayed fervently hard the entire time. The newspaper is for reading later, in the lobby. And I must tell you, I thanked God this morning that you took me in last night and gave me a place to lay my head. I slept so well and your breakfast this morning looks top-notch."

At that moment, the platter of rolls was being handed to me. I was not losing this opportunity. As I grabbed two, I passed the platter on, telling my table-mate, "Bless you, sister." Miss Priss moved on.

After breakfast, I scurried upstairs before she could condemn me for my indecent un-stockinged legs. I made up my bed, pulled out a pen and began circling possible addresses. I found five possibilities, and checked with my roommates about locations. They concluded I'd have to cover two to three miles. Putting on my makeup, most comfortable shoes, coat, and dashingly fashionable cloche hat, I left, on the hunt for my first apartment.

I stepped out into a blue-sky morning with a brisk wind; perfect walking weather. Amazing how a good night's sleep and a filling breakfast could give you a fresh perspective. Last evening, I was ready to give up and move back in with Auntie, but this morning I could only think about the positives. I already had a part-time job… in a movie theater! I'd met three friendly gentlemen: Produce-hauler, Obidiah Dawson, Romero, of the ice-delivery profession, and Officer Olsen, a helpful and handsome policeman. A girl could do worse finding new friends in a single day.

Walking two blocks of residential streets, I turned left looking for Elm Heights Road and noticed The Good Egg restaurant Miss Priss had recommended last night. Passing it, I recognized Romero's ice wagon and team of four horses on the side street which got me thinking that maybe I should linger here a little longer.

Perhaps my fervent morning prayers were paying off.

# CHAPTER 13
# MARIAH

*I* envied my daughters' easy contentment. If only all problems could be solved by cookies and paper dolls. Glancing at my twins' guilty smiles, I knew Sarah and Jo had snatched the last two oatmeal cookies from the church kitchen when they thought I wasn't looking. An extra cookie was a valuable commodity for a kid at age four. After an hour-long sermon and another thirty minutes spent collecting gossip from our far-flung neighbors, Sam drove us home over the rutted snowy roads.

Samuel and I were in the front seat talking about the possible dairy closing in Green Tree, resulting in Jim's job loss. Poor Jim. I'm sure he felt overwhelmed right now, with my sister and their four young sons depending on him. There was also talk of yet another farm foreclosure in our county. We kept our voices low not wanting to concern Sarah and Jo, as they sang together in the back seat.

Sam put his arm around my shoulder, pulling me closer as he drove. "Mariah, we're gonna make it through this. I gotta say, '32's been a tough one; next year's bound to be better. We're young, got our health, and lots of good family around."

"Hope so, but this financial stuff… it's all getting too close."

"Don't forget that new seed. Next summer's corn crop is gonna be our best yet. Don't let yourself get down about all this."

I kissed his cheek and sighed, as the twins watched and giggled. "Guess I'm just ready for some good news."

With one arm on the wheel, he gave me a quick, reassuring return kiss and hug, then turned his head to the back seat, laughing with the girls. "Hey, can't a guy kiss his beautiful wife without you two hooting about it?" Sam was always one to see the glass half full, even if it was cracked and leaking. And he had a way of setting my head straight when I needed it.

At home, the overcast December sky went quickly dark in the late afternoon. I tried to shake off my sense of unease as I cleaned the kitchen after serving a warm stew dinner. Lately, I'd been making it heavier on potatoes and carrots, lighter on the meat, but it was still warm, seasoned, and filling. As I washed dishes, Samuel bundled up and trudged through the light snow, carrying a kerosine lantern to do his milking. Now that our cows were up to a dozen, it took him about two hours, twice a day, to complete the chore. If the herd continued to grow, Sam would need to hire a part-time farm-hand, but for now it was manageable.

After finishing with their paper dolls, I directed the girls into the bathroom, getting them ready for bed. I stood back and watched them as they put on their thick flannel night-gowns, and double pair of socks, despite the extra time it took. They were learning to dress themselves, although I had to laugh at their young contortionist attempts.

Before leading them upstairs, I rubbed a circle in the steamed-up window, glancing at the barn. It had been over two hours since Sam had left. Leaning close, I noticed a flickering bright flame shining from the side window near the back of the barn. I looked again, wiping the circle wider with my sleeve, and let out a little gasp.

Grabbing Sarah and Jo's hands, I led them quickly to the parlor. In a firm, rushed voice I said, "You two sit right here. Do *not* get up. Do you understand?" With wide eyes, they nodded and stared as I ran out the back door, grabbing only a sweater off the wall hook, oblivious to the freezing temperature.

My heart was beating so loud I thought my eardrums would burst. Why hadn't Sam run into the house for help? As I ran to the watering trough, skidding on frozen ground, I hit my chin against the rough wood. Ignoring the cut, I pulled myself up with shaking hands and grabbed the small rubber hose that connected our water tank to the trough. If pulled tight, I knew the hose went about halfway through the barn's length.

The barn door was still closed. With the chance of a fire, the first thing Sam would do is open the doors and get the live-stock out. I flung open the large, heavy wooden doors, as anxious bellowing cows cried out, and a thick curtain of black smoke hit my eyes and invaded my nostrils. It was impossible to see a foot ahead. Stumbling into the barn, I released the stan-chions, which held the cows in place for milking. As each cow rushed out the door, I counted eight. Then, I heard the terri-fied neighing screams of our two plow horses, Buck and Shorty, still in their stalls. As the acrid smoke rushed out through the doors, the flames grew larger, eating up and swal-lowing fresh oxygen flowing back inside. I doused myself with the icy-cold water from the hose and ran to the stabled horses to free them, hoping they'd survive the poisonous smoke. They both galloped out frantically, nearly trampling me, as I released their gates and pressed my back against their stalls.

I continued calling out Samuel's name in a series of shrieks. Panicked thoughts pushed me forward, telling me he has to be here; he has to be alright. Edging to the back, near the end of the milking area, I was conflicted. Would the fire spread to other buildings? Should I stop searching and get help? What about the twins, left alone in the house? I was tormented with opposing thoughts.

I tugged desperately on the hose, stretching out its entire length as the flames competed against my weak tube of water. The flames were winning, growing higher, hungry to lick the stored hay in the loft above. As I tried to clear a path, I tripped. Feeling the floor around me, I realized I'd stumbled over Sam's body. My hands grabbed his limp long legs. It was too dark to see his features but I could tell he'd fallen backwards with his head leaning to the side. I felt a patch of slickness on his face. He seemed unconscious, unable to move or speak, but I continued talking to him.

"Sam, I'm here. We'll get out of this. I love you so much. You're going to be OK."

Fear of the smoke kicked my adrenalin to its highest level. As I continued pleading with him to wake up, I reached under each of Sam's arms awkwardly and walking backwards, I began dragging his body out of the barn, and coughing up smoke while blinding tears ran down my face.

"I've got you, Sam. Keep breathing. We're almost out." I tugged and pulled, going too slowly, wasting precious time.

Outside, I took in hungry gulps of the dark, frigid air, pounding on Samuel's chest, then caressing him. In a pleading tone, with tears dripping on his face, I whispered, "Wake up Samuel. Come back. You are my life." I gently laid him out on the snow-dusted yard, then ran to the garden shed, grabbed the wheel barrow, put him in it haphazardly. and pushed it back to the house. Dragging him inside, I placed him on the scuffed planked floor in the mud room.

I closed the door between the front room and kitchen, and lit a lantern. Holding it up to his face, I came to the sickening revelation that he was never coming back to me. The left side of his skull was crushed, probably from a fatal cow kick. Laying my head close to his chest I listened for a heartbeat, feeling for a pulse that was now gone. My stomach lurched as my hand grazed his head injury. I sat back on my knees, stunned, and began wailing while my entire world broke apart. Sam was everything to me and now that world was crashing in around me. Everything we had built together was in shambles.

The twins walked timidly into the room, ignoring my earlier directions.

"Daddy sleeping?" Sarah asked.

Then Jo handed me her blanket saying, "Don't cry Mama, don't cry."

I walked them quickly away and grabbed their coats off the hooks. "Daddy's hurt. His head is very bad. There's been an accident. I need you to be really strong for me and Daddy. Can you do that?"

They nodded their heads as I bundled them in boots, hats and put coats over their nightgowns. I grabbed a big quilt out of a cabinet and ran them out to the car parked in the machine shed. After covering them in the back seat, I said, "Try to sleep, girls. Do *not* get out of the car. Mommy has to go to the barn."

Sarah whined, "It smells bad Mommy."

"I'm going to try and make the smoke go away. Stay here." They held hands and whimpered together, fearful of me leaving them again. If the fire was spreading, I wanted to be able to make a quick get-away, with the girls already in the car.

As I hurried back, I saw several cows wandering back to the warmth and familiarity of the barn. I clapped my hands, yelled, and ran at the meandering livestock to keep them from returning.

All the roofs of our five farm buildings were covered with a thin frosting of snow which I prayed would keep the flying embers of the fire from spreading. With a lantern now lighting my way, I went back trying to slow the fire's progression. Flames were beginning to shoot up through the loft's floorboards. The loose hay was feeding the fire; all those weeks of labor, cutting and drying the hay, loading and storing, all that work was nourishing this greedy, life-sucking fire.

The outside air was now also thick with smoke. I hoped the Thomas family, our closest neighbors, would smell it soon and come to help. I grabbed a second hose to attach to the one I'd already dragged through half of the barn. After connecting the two, I had forty more feet, but the water pressure was low. I wrapped my head scarf around my nose and mouth and gingerly climbed steps to the loft trying to saturate the remaining piles of hay to keep the rafters from cratering.

A desperate sense of preservation was the only thing keeping me from dwelling on Sam's bloody body lying on the mudroom floor. If I kept moving and fighting the fire, maybe I could alter events. Maybe I could bring Sam back?

As I began to make progress dampening the hay, headlights from a vehicle swung in front of the barn. Finally, someone was here to help. I saw three silhouettes in front of the headlights standing with pails in each hand, calling out for Samuel. They had to be our neighbors, Mr. Thomas, his son, David, and their hired-hand, Billy-boy. I climbed down, sprinting cautiously across the barn floor and ran into old-man Thomas, throwing my arms around his neck, sobbing uncontrollably, suddenly releasing all the pent-up emotion raging in my head.

"Sam's dead! He's dead... I don't know what to do!"

He shook my shoulders, trying to control my hysteria. "Mrs. Anderson... Mariah, we're so sorry. Billy, take over the hose. David, round up the livestock and tie 'em up in the shed. Your girls, Mariah...Where are the twins?"

I stood staring back at him in shock, with tears running through the soot blackening my face.

"Mariah! The twins? Are they safe?"

I nodded. "Yes, yes… in the car, bundled up."

"Drive to our house. Eleanor is up. She'll put them in a warm bed for the night. And Sam, where's his body? You're sure he's gone?"

Coughing and sobbing into his shoulder, I said, "Yes, in the mud room. It's horrible." I looked back up at him. "I'll take the girls. Bless you. I'm grateful you came."

In the back seat, the girls looked to be asleep. I grabbed the steering wheel with all my strength, trying to keep my hands from shaking uncontrollably. I drove the half mile to the Thomas home and carried my sleeping twins inside with Eleanor's help. After tucking them in together on a small bed, I thanked my neighbor, hugging her tight, whispering, "Eleanor… what am I going to do? Sam's dead."

"We're here to help. Whatever you need, child."

"I have to go."

I ran to our car, backing out of the gravel driveway. I longed to keep driving, past the fields, farms, and back roads I knew so well. Head west and just keep going. Drive all the way to a roaring ocean that I'd only read about. Just go. I imagined myself wading into cool rolling waters. Just go.

Then the worried eyes of my beautiful twins floated in front of me, anxiously calling for me as they woke up in a strange place. And I saw the disappointed look in Samuel's face as I considered abandoning all we'd worked for.

I turned the wheel, sobbing, and headed back to the smell of smoke and fear.

## CHAPTER 14
## NANETTE

*I* waited, leaning against the ice wagon, relieved to see Romero walking from the back of the Good Egg toward the horses. Recognizing me, his face broke into a wide welcoming smile, then he pointed at me, saying in his romantic Italian accent, "Movie star!" Laughing again at his knee-slapping joke, he said, "I take? I take to movies?"

"No, not today. Not movies, but houses. I look for houses," I slowly explained.

He had a perplexed look on his face but quickly climbed up on the wagon bench, extending his strong, large hand. "I take," he said. Once upon the bench, I pulled out my dog-eared newspaper and pointed to the circled addresses.

"I need to go here. Then here. Then here. Looking-for-houses." I pointed to a home across the street. "Houses. I go here, here, here."

"Ah… houses, la case. Si, la case. Y qui, y qui, y qui," he said pointing to the paper. The guy was catching on. He pointed to the back and said his favorite word, "Ice y case."

"Yes, first ice, then house," I said. I could work with that arrangement. "And Romero, I'm Nanette."

"Si, Nanette. Movie star!" He slapped the back of the horses and we were off.

With five rental houses to check and multiple ice deliveries, it would be a long day. But the alternative of hanging around the lobby with Miss Priss hovering nearby made me happy to be sitting downwind of four massive horses and next to a handsomely musky ice-delivery man.

Romero patiently waited as I made inquiries at the apartments, then I waited during his ice stops. The first two places I saw were totally unacceptable. The first reminded me of the downtrodden appearance of the Front Street Hotel, offering a room and an outdoor privy with numerous boarders in one large old house. At the second, I would have to share all common spaces with the homeowner, a leering middle-aged man. Totally inappropriate for someone of my tender years. At the third rental, my hopes were high. It was a cute, small two-story bungalow that looked well-tended. I knocked on the door and waited. Eventually, a haggard looking woman holding a wailing baby opened the door... barely.

"Yes?"

"Hello madam. I'm Nanette, and you are...?"

"The lady of the house. What do ya' want?"

In order to be heard over the crying, I raised my voice. "I'm new in town, looking for an apartment. Could I see the space that's for rent?"

"And who's that?" Her eyes darted out to the street, as she pointed to the ice wagon.

"Him? Only a friend who's helping me out today."

"No, sorry. I never rent to single women. You could up and marry him, then disappear... and you probably don't even have a job. Too risky."

As she popped a rubber pacifier in the baby's mouth, two more young children, a boy and a girl, poked their heads out through the door and pushed it open. "We want to play outside," the boy demanded. The two of them rushed out as their mother loosened her grip on the door.

She yelled after them, "Stay out of the street," without bothering to look in their direction.

With the door wide open, I took a minute to point out the error of her opinions. "Ma'am, I'm so pleased to tell you I *do* have a job. The Mankato Movie House. I was recently hired as the assistant manager. I can provide excellent references from Green Tree, Iowa, and can also assure you, I have absolutely no intention of running off and marrying, of all people, an ice-delivery man."

"I don't know. With that face of yours, I don't see you staying single long. Last renters were here five years; family of four. I'm gonna miss them. I'll tell you what. I'll show you the space and if no one else more promising comes by, I'll consider you."

It wasn't much of an offer but I followed her toward the back of the house, then took the outside white wooden stairs up to a separate backdoor. Inside, the space was bright and airy with a lovely bay window looking out onto the street. It was sparsely furnished with the basics, had a tiny separate bedroom, a Murphy bed in the front room, no kitchen except a hot plate and a small ice box, but there was a small indoor bathroom with a shower, which I'd only read about and had never seen before. Amazingly modern! I had to have this space.

"Ma'am, your notice stated that rent is forty dollars a month. Is that correct?"

"Yes."

"Well, I have an excellent offer for you. I will pay you thirty-five a month…but would love to offer you child-care services one day a week and would be more than pleased to go to the market for you at least twice a week. It'll free up your time and allow you occasional visits outside the home."

The lady, still holding the squirming baby, considered for a second. "Interesting offer. My husband is on the road three weeks out of every month, so I make the decisions on the rental unit. The idea of a few hours to myself sounds good. But here's the big question… what's going to happen when *your* baby comes?"

"My what?" I was shocked she could see it. My figure was still perfect.

"Your baby; the one in your womb that you keep touching protectively, each time you speak."

"Madam, I have no idea what you're talking about."

She stared down directly at my stomach. "I've been through it three times, so I *do* know what I'm speaking about." At this point she let her fidgeting baby down on the floor to crawl, while she leaned over, looking out the window to check on her two other children. "Hell's bells, I don't see 'em. I've got to go. Look, Nanette, you seem like a pleasant enough person…" She grabbed the baby who was already crawling toward the stairs, as I pulled out my handkerchief and began dabbing my tearing eyes. "OK, stop with the waterworks; I can't believe I'm saying this. The place is yours for forty-bucks a month *with* the babysitting *and* the market shopping. We got a deal?"

"We do." I said with a smile, "And what's your name?"

"Your landlady," she yelled, as she ran down the stairs in search of her wandering children.

I continued to stand there, staring at the details of my very own first, fabulous apartment, then quickly figured how much money I would make working three days a week, at forty cents an hour. Not near enough! And then I considered, how does one become a full-time assistant manager at a movie theater?

From the apartment, I elected to walk back to the YWCA, letting Romero get on with his day. He'd been such a good sport to help me out. The weather continued to be a lovely cool temperature and I was in the best mood, already putting thoughts together for my first letter home to Aunt Edwina, which I immediately wrote once back in my room.

*Dear Auntie,*

*I miss you and our lovely home so much, but I think you'll be pleased with what I have achieved in so little time. First, I have already made three good friends, one of whom is a Mankato policeman, so rest assured, I'll be well protected. Secondly, I've been hired full-time as the assistant manager of the Mankato Movie House. Isn't that exciting! Now, I told the manager that I'd been assistant manager of Superior Fabrics in Green Tree and I'd provide a reference. I realize that was a little white lie, but I did work there occasionally when you were gone, so I believe I didn't stray too far from the truth. Could you kindly write and mail an excellent reference for me?*

*I just located a wonderful little apartment. And my landlady and I have become fast friends already. It's furnished but needs several additions to make it look the way that you would approve of. Do you suppose it would be possible for you to ship me, via train, my sewing machine and several yards of blue and yellow fabric for curtains, pillows, table cloths, etc. I have some wonderful decorating ideas!*

*Auntie, I may also need a little more money than we planned because rents here are more expensive than in Green Tree. Perhaps one-hundred dollars or so, just to tide me over until I get settled. I'll include my new address so that you can mail me the funds. I think things are going swimmingly and it will all work out fine!*

*Your loving niece,*

*Nanette*

*P.S.—If you happen to see Catherine Anderson around town, let her know my news. She must come and visit me in a few months. I even have a Murphy bed and my own shower. Isn't that the cat's pajamas!*

# CHAPTER 15
# MARIAH

*I* arrived numb, angry, and almost in denial that Sam was actually gone. But he had to be. There were over seventy people surrounding me, telling me how sorry they were. Sarah and Jo spent most of the afternoon staring up at everybody's tearful sad faces, or hiding behind my skirt. The funeral service was held at Sam's family church in town which was filled to capacity. Both of our extended families and Sam's old school friends had all come to say their goodbyes. His death seemed to be a big blow to the community, one more recent tragedy in a list of bad things that seemed to be raining down on Green Tree.

My heart went out to Jo and Sarah. It had to be difficult for a four-year-old to understand. Their tall smiling dad, who'd always found time to swing them around at the end of his exhausting day, would no longer be at home for dinner. I'd tried to explain everything in the best way I could. They were sad and confused, while I was devastated, felt cheated, and somehow guilty. I couldn't bring myself to speak, but instead, I simply nodded to people, going through the motions of being polite. Everybody approached us, giving me long hugs, words of condolences, and covered plates of food.

At the burial, the sun finally came out, punching out thin golden shafts of light through the December afternoon clouds. It felt disingenuous that on this saddest of days, the sun had finally decided to show itself after days of gray.

Samuel's parents, Gerta and Alfred, were also beside themselves with grief. At the funeral, Sam's sister, Catherine, took me aside to a quiet corner of the church, explaining that in her parents' eyes, Samuel, their youngest, had always held the most promise in carrying on the success and legacy of their hard work.

"You know he was the best and the brightest, and mature in so many ways for his age. And Mariah, the sad truth is, Mom and Dad only recently adjusted to how committed Sam was to you and the girls, branching out on his own, and now, shockingly, his life has been snuffed out in a freak accident. They're having trouble coping."

Catherine began crying, while she tried to explain her parents' cold reaction to me. I simply nodded, wanting to wallow in my own misery. Nobody could take this heart-break away from me. I only wanted to shroud myself in the darkness of our house. Sam was the reason I had stayed in Green Tree; the twins and our farm were everything to us.

And now to add further misery to our lives, my father-in-law, Alfred, was blaming me for his loss. After the service, I passed by a circle of older men and overheard him, as he tearfully murmured to his friends over coffee. "The boy never had an accident in his life until now, never got sick, never a broken bone. And now, the light of my life has gone out. I don't know, maybe *she* rushed him into all this. Working him too hard, trying to build *her* fancy bathrooms, working day and night for *her*."

As he mumbled to friends, I had to walk out. It was all too

much. As the mourners left the churchyard, my mother helped me gather up the covered dishes brought by friends. While putting them in our car, Ma gently asked me about my plans. During those first tumultuous days after the fire, everyone had been too polite to broach the subject and I had no desire to think about it.

"Mariah, have you thought about the farm? Will you be moving? What does Lars say?"

In a voice lacking emotion, I responded, "My landlord has nothing to do with my life. We'll make do. We'll keep going."

"But you can't stay out there alone. There's too much to do."

I felt exhausted and had no real answers for her, as I put the twins in the back seat. "I don't know, Ma. I can't think about it now. The farm is all I have left of Samuel. My life is there. We can't leave and we have nowhere else to go." I slammed the car door, leaving her standing in the gravel parking lot.

Driving home at dusk, we scurried back to our private lives. Over the past week our farm had become a sad, quiet place. I sensed the girls saw the change in me, but it was difficult for them to understand. Jo was a pleaser, always trying to nudge a smile out of me, trying to make me laugh again. Sarah was my loyal follower, offering hugs when I gave her the time. When I allowed myself to look in the mirror, my eyes looked dead, and my nose was red, perpetually running from a deep cold and cough I couldn't seem to shake. I spoke as little as possible, walking about the house like a ghost, basically ignoring everything for days.

During those dark days after Sam's death, I rarely got out of bed. If the girls were hungry, I had them eat food off the covered plates neighbors had given us, or I'd hear them fending for themselves, bumping down the stairs on their bottoms, eating from jars of preserves. We wore the same clothes day after day because I couldn't be bothered to do laundry. Old food clung to dishes which teetered on the kitchen counter; the dirty floor was still flecked with ashes from the fire, with mud and Sam's blood spread across the back room.

Sleeping through much of the day, I ignored most of my endless chores. In the afternoons, I got up to throw ears of corn and old vegetables into the pig trough and sprinkled a bit of feed in the hen house. For a meal, I'd heat up oatmeal for Sarah and Jo, plunking thick globs into their bowls. They would both look up to me for a hint of a smile, but I couldn't even pretend to give one. It was impossible to force myself to feel better. I told them to eat and then trudged back to bed, locked in my dark sadness.

THE DAY AFTER THE FIRE, neighbors David and Billy-boy returned, and with the help of our horses, hauled the charred remains of four burned cows out of our barn. They dug a large hole near the pasture, buried the dead livestock and took our eight remaining cows and two horses to their barn for feed and care. In addition, David Thomas brought us over three bottles of milk daily. The Thomas family were neighbors I would never forget for their kindness during this dark time.

One saving grace of the horrible fire was that it had not spread to our other buildings. In that regard, we were spared. But for now, because of damage done to the barn, the structure was probably unsafe. The roof's gaping hole let in too much cold and snow to keep the livestock inside.

About a week after the funeral, I heard a vehicle drive up to the back door while I was lying in bed. Peeking through the curtain from my upstairs window, I saw Sam's mother and sister coming to visit. Always a stickler for a clean, organized household, I knew Gerta would be shocked at the condition of our house and the grime accumulating on her two grand-daughters. As I reluctantly pulled myself off the bed, I heard Greta's shrill voice echoing up the stairs.

"What are you girls doing? You could fall off those chairs. Get down now!"

Jo answered, "We need cups. Cups for milk."

"Catherine, find Mariah. Girls, I'll get your milk glasses. You two sit down at the table. What's going on here? This house is a mess."

As I dragged myself down the stairs, I overheard Jo saying, "Mommy sleeping. She's sick."

Then Sarah added, "She's crying a lot too."

Catherine met me at the bottom of the stairs with a strong hug, as I shook my head. "I know... I look terrible." As we walked into the kitchen, Gerta told the girls, "Grandma and Grandpa are sad too. We all miss your daddy. Finish your milk, girls, and let me wash you up. You two need a good scrubbing, and where's your hairbrush?"

I leaned against the kitchen wall with arms crossed, just watching. Gerta stared at me for a few seconds, with her narrow lips twitching on her long thin face, and then led the twins into the bathroom. I was wearing the same cotton-print house dress and old black cardigan sweater that I'd worn day and night since the fire. For the funeral I'd changed into my Sunday dress, but put the old dress back on as soon as I returned home. The sweater still had rusty brown stains on the sleeves, blood from Sam's head wound. The blood and smokey scent, now woven into the sweaters' fibers, were all I had left of Sam and I wasn't ready to let it go.

Following behind the twins to the bathroom, I watched as Gerta brushed Jo's fly-away blond locks and neatly pulled back Sarah's thick dark hair with clips. A wheezing, cracked voice emerged from my chest, "Hello, Gerta. Girls, please tell your grandmother thank you."

She turned and looked at me with disapproval. "Mariah, what is all over your sweater? You need to wash that. And this house is a disaster." She walked over to me, taking hold of my cold chapped hands. "We really need to talk privately. Catherine, dear, will you take the twins upstairs and show them the new books you made for them?"

Excited about a new diversion, the girls eagerly followed their favorite aunt upstairs as if she were the pied piper. I'm sure they were glad to see someone with a happy face for a change. My mother-in-law began wiping down the kitchen table. Then, with the practiced hand of an experienced cook, she quickly filled the wood stove with kindling, lit the fire, and had the tea kettle boiling in minutes. I stood there and stared, unable to move or talk, watching overly-efficient Gerta resurrect my kitchen. I felt useless and knew I looked my worst with my hair flat and unwashed, and my face pale and gaunt. I continued to simply watch, as I wiped my dripping red nose on the sleeve of my dirty sweater.

She set a cup of hot tea on the table in front of me. "Alright, let's sit down, Mariah. Alfred and I understand you are feeling hopeless right now, but life must go on, dear. These girls have to be looked after, livestock must be fed, and there's spring planting around the corner. You must know in your heart a farm is way too much work for one person to handle and almost impossible for a mother with young children to look after."

"Gerta, I've been so tired, but I'm getting better. I promise. I've been thinking…Maybe I could have the girls sleep with me and hire a farmhand to move in and help with the spring planting. There are so many men looking for work now."

"Well, that wouldn't be proper, would it? Besides, you know with corn prices so low and the cost of seed going up, you could never make a go of things; not after paying a farmhand

*and* sending Lars his portion of the profits. There would be nothing left."

Not liking the direction this conversation was heading, I began tensing up, offering alternative plans. "But perhaps I could find someone that would work for only room and board with reduced wages, paid at harvest."

"Actually, Lars and Alfred have already talked. It's been decided, Mariah. Lars does not think it practical for you to remain here with your limited knowledge of farming."

Anxiously, I responded, "But I grew up on a farm. My parents are farmers. I know enough. Maybe not everything Samuel knew, but he shared a lot with me. I could always go to my dad with questions." I now realized Sam's parents would not be allies I could count on.

"I'm sorry. There's no more discussion about it. Henry will take over this farm. Lars wants to guarantee a good crop with an experienced farmer." Henry was Samuel's oldest brother, who I knew was engaged to be married soon.

"Mariah, Lars wanted you to know he won't charge you for the barn damage as long as you agree to give him the remainder of your cows in exchange for repair payments. And Henry will pay you later in installments for your pigs and hens. Of course, prices on these are low right now, but that money might help you out a little."

Panicking, I said, "But this is *our* home...We've worked so hard on it. It's all we have."

"But you're renting, Mariah. Be realistic. You and the girls can't stay here. It's just not possible. Lars depends on his portion of the harvest for income. You could never manage. And we will be giving the car to Henry while he's living here."

"The car? The Model A? That car was for me and Samuel. Your wedding gift to us!"

"No, Mariah. That Ford was our old car. The title is still held by Samuel's father. He loaned it to Sam when he took over this farm, but now we'll need to pass it on to Henry, once he moves here."

All this talk of sudden change made me feel light-headed and dizzy. I wasn't ready to uproot; move, and leave everything Sam and I had improved upon over the last five years. Whenever I walked in our bathroom, I'd see his face smiling up at me as he hammered away on floorboards. At the kitchen table, I imagined him eagerly wolfing down his dinner, enjoying every bite and talking at the same time. His well-used leather work boots were still sitting in the mud room. I couldn't leave this house behind with our lives so intensely visible in every corner.

Listening to Gerta announce decisions made by Alfred and Lars set off a ringing in my ears. I couldn't hear anymore and felt a hot flash envelop my body. My mother-in-law's mouth was moving, but I couldn't understand what she was saying. The ringing got louder as I stood up from the table. I leaned forward, gripping the table's edge, and then crumpled into a heap on the floor.

Lying there, I first heard mumbling and then distinct words hovering over my ears.

"My goodness gracious. Here, Mariah, drink some water, dear. Lost you for a minute. And you're skin and bones. Are you eating enough?"

Gerta was on the floor, cradling me in a sitting position. "Here, drink some more. You're probably dehydrated. You must take better care of yourself. I know these are troubling times."

I coughed on the water, then took a second sip, regaining more of my senses, as I sat up leaning away from her. In a raspy voice I spat out, "Troubling times?... Troubling times! The love of my life, the father of my two daughters has died and now you're telling me to get out of our home and leave behind all that we've worked for! These are not *troubling* times, Mother Gerta. This is the depth of despair."

I pulled myself back onto the chair at the table as Gerta tried to remain calm at my outburst. "I know this is painful, Mariah. We are mourning Sam's loss too. You have no idea how it breaks our hearts. I've suffered losses greater than you know. Years ago, my oldest daughter died after her first year. Putting that tiny, innocent body in the ground almost killed me. But you'll get stronger, Mariah. It takes time. You're young; you will survive this. The information about the farm comes from Lars and my husband. I'm only the messenger."

I cleared my throat, trying to appear strong. "The planting season doesn't start until March. Lars signed an annual agreement with us. I have about two months. Let me explore *my* options and I will be keeping *my* car until then. I will let Lars know what I plan on doing. I see now where your loyalties are."

Shocked at my reply and bold rebuke, Gerta said, "My loyalties are with my family; *all* of my family and my grandchildren. Speaking of which, you, my dear, are not doing a good job with. Your girls looked dirty and hungry." Saying this, Gerta walked to the mudroom and grabbed my broom and dustpan. "Not to worry, things will work out. Alfred and I will do our best to find a place for you; perhaps you could stay on here for a while as an extra hand for Henry's new bride. I must say, she appears like someone that'll need help. Now let's get this kitchen cleaned up."

I stood up and grabbed my broom from her hands. "I don't need your help. It seems your family is all too eager to sweep us out of here without regard for our needs. And you *dare* suggest I become a hired hand in my own home! I think it's best if you leave right now. I can take care of this by myself." I began briskly sweeping the dirt and ashes toward her boots.

Her voice became nervous and shrill. "I only came in charity, thinking of what's best for you and my granddaughters, and to convey Lar's message." She walked to the stairway and called for Catherine and the twins to come down and say goodbye.

Jo came down holding up her new book. "Look Mommy, Aunt Catherine made this. So pretty."

Anger made my voice shake. "They sure are. Thank you, Catherine."

My sister-in-law and I exchanged looks, both of us understanding her father's message to vacate had been delivered. Catherine was a good friend. Two years older than her brother, they had been close, and being the only daughter in a family of men, she enjoyed sharing a sense of sisterhood with me. I hoped my breach with her parents wouldn't break our bond.

"Girls, tell your grandmother and aunt goodbye. They have to leave now."

They each hugged a thigh of their grandma, scratching their chapped cheeks on her rough tweed skirt. Gerta patted the tops of their heads, then smoothed down her gray bun. She peeled the twins off of her, saying "Thank you, little ones. Aunt Catherine and I need to go now." The girls looked sad, realizing their play with Catherine was cut short. They took their new books over to the fireplace to look again at the hand-drawn pictures.

After Gerta and Catherine left, I locked the door behind them, wanting to shut out the world and stay safe in our own little corner.

I took off my damaged black cardigan and held it close to my nose, deeply inhaling, trying to resurrect memories. I lit kindling in the fireplace and sat down in Sam's brown upholstered chair, and looked into the mesmerizing flames beginning to take hold. I suddenly shook my head, thinking, wake up Mariah; he's gone. Memories of Sam would always linger; he'd be right with me, pushing me on. But the girls and I couldn't survive on memories.

## CHAPTER 16
## NANETTE

*A* month in, I'd quickly settled into my apartment. Once Auntie shipped my machine and fabric, I was busy sewing up a storm. The blue and white checked curtains I'd hung made a huge difference in brightening up the place. I was currently working on decorative pillows when my landlady, Clarice, knocked and then poked her head inside. She was holding baby Jonathon, who was usually glued to her hip. I continued sewing as she walked in.

"Hi there; there's hot water in the kettle. Help yourself to a cup of tea."

Clarice headed over to my hot plate and kettle. "I was curious what you were up to with all the racket you're making up here."

"Curtains. Don't you love them? It only took me a day or two to whip them up. But don't they jazz up the room? And today it's pillows. I simply love an accessorized room."

"You're right." Clarice looked around appreciatively. "I don't know why I never thought to hang them in here. Hey, do you have any sugar?"

"Next to the cups. You know, Clarice, if you like the idea of new curtains, pillows, bed covers...I can make anything for you in exchange for a month of free rent. What do you think? It'll give your place a whole new look, like straight out of the *Ladies Home Journal*. Do you think your husband would approve?"

"Theodore? Bet he'd never even notice. But I could probably use a little update; some new color would be nice. Hey, how do you have the time for all this? Shouldn't you be at work?"

"Oh, Mr. Grant gave me another day off, and I wanted to get all this decorating business done." My landlady was still under the impression I was the assistant manager but I had yet to convince Mr. Grant to promote me or give me full-time, although I hadn't stopped asking.

"Well, it looks lovely. So, Nanette, how are you feeling, with... you know?"

"With, I know... what?"

"The baby," she said pointing to my stomach. "Look, you might be able to fool other people, but after another month, it's clear to me you're pregnant. Maybe it's none of my business, but if you're ready to talk, I'm here to listen. Mind if I set Johnnie down." She laid him on the sofa and sat down next to him.

"He's looking sleepy. Must have just eaten. Where are the other two?"

"Locked in their bedroom playing cowboys and Indians. I had to take a break."

"I don't blame you, but they're sweet kids."

"Some days...but we were talking about you."

"Oh, Clarice." I took a deep breath, and looked up from my sewing. "All right...You guessed it. I suppose I'm about three-and-a-half months along. You're the only person I've admitted it to."

"I told you I had a sense about these things."

"It's one of the reasons I moved here. I had to get away.

My aunt would have a conniption if she knew. Babies… they're so cute, but seem like *so* much work. It's hard enough just getting by on my own. I kept hoping I was wrong about the pregnancy. Honestly, I'm scared."

"That's what I was afraid of. How old are you?"

"Just turned nineteen. Old enough to know better."

"What about the father?"

"Ugh, don't even mention him. A terrible mistake and a scoundrel to boot. It sounds crazy, but I hoped the problem would simply disappear."

"Trust me. You'll start hearing some comments. Give it another four or five weeks."

I looked down at my frivolous yellow pillows and shook my head. "A baby would derail all my plans for the future—the perfect husband, a great job, my possible movie career. Everything would be ruined."

"I don't know about ruining your life, but it certainly changes things. Nanette, if you don't think you can go through with it, I might have a suggestion. But think about it long and hard before you decide."

Clarice's comment shook me up. When she said, *think long and hard*, I simply shrugged my shoulders and began babbling about the new movie at the theater. But later that evening, after meeting Romero for a sunset walk, I began considering my options. I calmed myself in my shower, turned off my lamp, got into bed, and forced myself to think about the reality of my situation. It wouldn't be too long before I'd feel the quickening; the movement of my very own child within me. Much later than that, it would be difficult to change my mind. What would life be like with a baby? I loved children; I'd always seen myself having a few. They were so fun, but only amusing for an hour or two. After that, kids became a serious business, often loud, tedious, and time consuming. And this baby was a product of a rape. I had never admitted that to myself until this moment.

I was currently surviving on Auntie's money. With the extra hundred she'd sent, I was fine for now, but I'd never be able to support myself *and* a child with the pittance I made at the theater. I had to find another job, or get promoted. But working two positions, how would I care for a child? This was all so daunting. And what suiter would want an unwed woman with a baby? I thought about Clarice…barely thirty with three children, and she looked positively ancient.

This baby did not fit into my life right now. Certainly later, with the right husband a child would be wonderful… but right now, not a good idea. I should have thought this through before? Time was ticking.

# CHAPTER 17
# MARIAH

*I* was extremely angry with Gerta and Alfred, but I did credit her visit for snapping me out of my gray cloud of despondency, forcing me to take action for the twins and myself. Although still mourning Samuel, I had to fight for what was ours. I couldn't let him down.

I glanced over at Sarah and Jo playing and asked, "I bet you two are hungry; when was the last time we sat down together and had a real meal?"

"Long time, Mommy," said Jo. "I want pancakes!"

"I think that's a grand idea. But you can have them only if I have some help. Who's first?"

Jo answered for them, "We both help. Me first, Mommy."

I quickly heated up the griddle on the stove and then went to work mixing the batter, explaining each ingredient to the girls.

I asked, "Jo, you pour the first one."

Jo dragged over the step stool leaning against the kitchen wall.

"We'll take turns. Jo, dip the ladle in the bowl, fill, and pour in the pan. Excellent. Now Sarah, step up."

They each took turns, pouring the mixture on the griddle, watching it with excitement as it bubbled up, turning golden brown, studying the exact time to flip. Sarah called out with excitement. "I turned it Mommie. All by myself."

The scent of warm pancakes cooking in butter filled the house and it was glorious. As a treat, I fried up some smoked bacon. We smeared our pancakes in butter and plum jam and drank big glasses of fresh cold milk. I remember that dinner as one of my favorites; it was the afternoon I returned to my girls. I attempted to smile; desperately pushing encouraging, kind words out of my mouth. I reminded myself that my twins were suffering from their father's death, probably as much as I was. They needed me and I'd been neglectful.

As we ate, Jo said, "We happy you here, Mommy."

"Jo, I've been here every day. I'm not going anywhere."

And wise Sarah said, "No Mommy, you was gone; looking for Daddy."

As the girls napped, I spent the afternoon sweeping and mopping floors, dusting furniture, bleaching the bathroom and washing dishes, getting our house back in order. There was still laundry to wash and hang in the cellar, but that could wait for another day. We ended the evening with me plopping Jo and Sarah into a warm bath. As they splashed around, I pulled my wooden rocker up close to the tub, and asked them to sing their favorite songs to me. Jo led off with *Twinkle, Twinkle Little Star* as Sarah followed along.

It would be a long while before the pain of their father's death left us, and months before I wouldn't look for him walking in from the barn, think about what food to prepare for Sam, or long for his strong arms to encircle me each night. But that night, as I tucked the twins into bed, I knew at least they were comforted again and hoped their sleep was sweet.

The next morning, still in night gowns and socks, with the sun already up, Sarah and Jo bumped down the stairs on their bottoms, their favorite way to traverse the steep stairway. I'd been up for two hours and had our farm's ledger book and papers scattered across the table. Hearing their thumping, I cleared my paperwork into a pile. They seemed happy to see me up, with breakfast ready.

"Scrambled eggs and biscuits for my twin angels. How are you feeling?"

"Hungry," said Sarah.

Although the kitchen was warmed by the stove, it was cold throughout the rest of the house. "It's too cold, Mommy," Jo said.

"I know. Looks like it's going to be a really frigid one today. Fill up on hot food and we'll bundle up in sweaters and coats for our chores. When we finish, if you're very helpful, Mommy will let you look through her favorite picture books."

After making our rounds to the hen house and pig barn, the twins sat at the table turning pages, looking at drawings in cherished books from my childhood collection. As they poured over the pictures in detail, I rechecked the ledger book, adding up numbers that didn't seem to make sense. Hearing a truck drive up to the back door, I glanced through the window seeing our neighbor, David Thomas, dropping off our milk.

He was a shy, quiet man, in his early thirties, with dark hair and pale green eyes, with a larger build than Sam had. David seemed content living with his parents and working with his father. At church, Samuel and I had often tried to coax words out of him to strike up a conversation. Being the only son on an isolated farm, we thought he might be lonely, although he and Billy-boy seemed to be good friends.

David attempted to leave our milk bottles at the back door,

but I quickly jumped up, opened the door, and invited him in. "David, I wanted to thank you and your family for helping us with our cows, and bringing over the milk…exceptionally kind of you. Sorry, I didn't thank you earlier. I've been ill."

He looked down at the ground as he spoke to me. "No problem, Mrs. Anderson. Happy to do it."

"Please, call me Mariah. Come in for a few minutes. I have fresh biscuits and coffee."

"Sorry, I'll have to pass. Work to get to. Thank you though."

"Actually, if you could spare just a little time, I have a few livestock questions to ask you. I'd really appreciate it. Unfortunately, I've let things go these last few weeks and need some advice."

With eyes averted and speaking in a low quiet voice, he said, "Well, livestock's my area of interest. I could try to help." Probably relieved he wouldn't have to make idle small-talk with me, he agreed to come in. As long as I kept the conversation focused on cows, I'd probably get some answers.

I sent Sarah and Jo to the parlor with my old books, as I plied David with questions at the kitchen table. Over the years, I'd often helped Sam with the accounts, keeping current with incoming funds and outgoing expenses, but the last six months he'd taken over the books.

"David, I see that a year ago we sold two cows, based on weight, for $104.00 and $120.00 each, but a month ago, Samuel sold one for just under $60.00. Is that right? How could that be?"

"Mrs. Anderson, sorry… Mariah. The price of cattle, actually all livestock, is in free-fall right now. If it drops much further their price will hardly be worth the cost of feed, care, and pasture maintenance. As you know, it's a tough time. My father is starting to dig into savings just to keep Billy-boy on the payroll; 'course, he's like family to us. We can't let him go."

"I knew it was bad, but didn't realize how much livestock prices have dropped, and so quickly too. I think when Samuel took over the accounts, he was probably trying to protect me from the downturn. He was always such an optimistic person. Wanting me to think everything was OK."

David coughed and looked out the window. Maybe this talk was getting too personal. I steered the conversation back to livestock. "Do you mind if I ask a few questions about our farm? I have some important decisions to make and I need an expert."

Sitting in his faded overalls and torn winter jacket, he looked down at his hands, "I'm no expert, but I'll give you my opinion."

"Our landlord, Lars, wants me to move off the farm and let Samuel's oldest brother, Henry, take over. He's marrying soon; I guess it makes sense, wanting an experienced farmer to take over. Do you think there's any way I could run this farm with the help of a hired-man? I truly understand a lot about planting, harvesting, budgeting."

David nodded his head, looked out the window again and cleared his throat. "Mariah, if times were different, maybe. Doubtful, but maybe....but right now, with the direction prices are going, I don't think you could make a living at it. Between paying a field hand and paying your landlord, there'd be nothing left to live on except egg money, and even that's pitiful right now."

"I was afraid you'd say that." I grasped a piece of paper I'd been adding figures on and crumpled it in a ball.

"You got a nice little home here. As neighbors, we'd hate to see you leave, but I'd say chances right now are slim to none for much success, and that's even if we had perfect weather and good rain, which you can never count on."

I leaned in towards David, tapping my pencil on the table. "I sort of came to the same conclusion earlier this morning after checking the books, but I wanted to hear it from someone I trusted. OK, and what about this? With the cows, pigs and chickens I have left, do you think I'd be better off selling them now, or hanging on to them and eventually selling them to Sam's older brother, Henry?"

"I'm in this business for the long haul, so I'll hang on to what is feasible, but for you… I'd say sell it *all* now. Prices are dropping each month. Who knows how low they'll go before things turn around? And the price of milk isn't any better. The government might intervene eventually with milk and crop subsidies… but who knows? It'll be a while before your brother-in-law could start paying you back. If you sell everything right now, you'd be able to put together a little nest egg to stick in the bank.

Pinching the bridge of my nose, I felt a headache coming on. "I appreciate your honesty. I think you're right, David. One more favor? Could you go out to the barn with me and give me an estimate on what repairs might cost? Lars is expecting me to trade all my remaining cows to cover the barn repair.

He checked an old gold pocket-watch he pulled from the top of his overalls. "Dad and I were wondering about the barn. Sure, I'll take a look. It was so smoky and dark that night, I couldn't tell how bad the damage was. Smart of you to pull out that extra hose and start drenching your hay. That's probably what saved the place from collapsing."

I called for the twins to bundle up. "Girls, we're going back into the barn to explore. Let's bring some milk to the orange mama cat."

None of us had been in the barn since Sam's accident. It was a good-size barn, painted white. Inside, there were four horse stalls and space for twenty-five cows to be housed during the winter. The hay loft covered the width of the barn and was built about two-thirds of the way from the front. The fire had started near the back, under the loft area.

Even with the doors flung open and the large gaping hole in the roof, the empty barn felt dark and gloomy, still smelling of burnt wood, smoke, and damp mildewing hay. It definitely needed a good cleaning which would take a full day or more to muck out. Surprised at our disruption, our large orange barn cat scampered away, followed by her three nursing kittens, while Sarah and Jo made a dash to catch and cuddle the tiny fur balls. As David and I walked farther to the back, the rapid fluttering of wings startled me as two barn owls flew through the hole in the roof.

I held a lantern close to the wood as David began examining weak spots. He grabbed a hammer, paint brush, and can of white paint from Sam's workstation, and began hammering the planks, testing the durability of the weakened areas. He took his time, carefully examining the walls, loft rafters, floor boards, and roof structure. I followed behind, and began checking as well. David hammered as I marked an $X$ with the paint, indicating the damaged boards.

"Actually, it's not as bad as I thought," David said. "The roof area will be the most expensive to replace, but it's only the back third of the barn that needs the most work. The structure's still strong. Surprisingly, I don't think it will be a huge job." After walking back through counting the boards I'd marked, David began calculating. "Let's see, lumber is running about thirty-cents a board. With lumber and materials, I think seventy-five dollars should cover it."

"But the labor of good carpenters will be expensive, won't it?"

David nodded but added, "Billy-boy is the best carpenter I know. He fixes everything at our place. Let's say you pay him his full monthly salary of thirty-five-dollars, then my dad won't have to dip into savings to pay him. I'll wager it'll take him less than a month to fix the barn, so I think he could still find time to do some of his regular chores too."

"Lars wanted my eight remaining cows to cover the barn repair." I did the quick math in my head. "But you're estimating a little over one hundred dollars total for the barn repair, right? If I sell all my livestock, I should come out *way* ahead." With that realization, I came to the conclusion that Lars was attempting to take big advantage of me.

"Give or take, sounds about right. You should sell it all.

"Can you see if your father and Billy-boy will agree to the plan? I'll be happy to cover Billy's monthly wage, if I can get my cows and pigs sold quickly."

He nodded and said, "I'll let you know tomorrow."

I quickly shook David's hand eagerly, as he looked down at the ground, uncomfortable with my openness. "You've made me a happier person today, and it's been a while since I've felt that way. I need both sales to move quickly before Lars and the Andersons figure out a way to stop me and take my livestock. Thank goodness, our first two cows were a wedding gift from *my* mother and father. At the time I thought, how unromantic, but now I love them for it."

# CHAPTER 18
# NANETTE

*I* wrestled in my sheets most of the night wondering what Clarice would suggest regarding the pregnancy. But I had to go in for a long shift at the theater, so my answer for her would have to wait. As I walked to work, I tried to think of ways to get myself promoted. Moving up was always on my mind. I stopped at a corner grocery and bought a pint of milk hoping it would settle my stomach. As I finished the small container, I had an epiphany.

Entering the lobby, I stopped at Mr. Grant's office, where he was closeted away reading the newspaper comics.

"Good morning Mr. Grant. I had a great idea I wanted to discuss with you."

Not even bothering to look up, he asked, "Have you warmed up the popcorn machine yet? And make a new batch of lemonade. Time to get moving."

"Yes, sir. I'll get right on it. Speaking of popcorn, that idea I had—"

"An idea about popcorn? Nanette, popcorn is popcorn. I'm busy. Oh, also take inventory. The supply man will be in today. Cups, bags, napkins."

"Perhaps we can talk later then, Mr. Grant. It's a *really* good idea."

"Just close the door."

While thinking about tiny Mr. Grant and his small mind, I angrily ladled the cooking oil into the large silver pan in the popcorn machine, followed by a cup of seeds. Why bother wasting my breath? The man wouldn't know a good idea if it smacked him in the face and knocked him over. I poured water into the powdered drink mix, threw some old lemon slices into the batch for visual effect, and stirred. I was born for bigger things than simply making popcorn. I'd been a Green Tree Corn Queen, for goodness' sake! Pulling out the new stock of candy, I placed all the new pieces to the front of the display. If I was running this place, I'd set up a grand opening for a top movie every month. Mr. Grant simply had no imagination.

A few minutes later, I had my first customers, a man and woman who looked to be courting. I immediately tried to upsell. "Good day! You two are in for a treat. I've seen *The Merry Widow* twice already. You'll love it. So, what can I get you? Two popcorns, two soda-pops?"

The guy said, "Sure."

But, as usual, the lady said, "Oh Thomas, I couldn't possibly finish that whole bag. Let's just share." The guy shrugged his shoulders telling me, "Just one and the two drinks."

It happened all the time with couples. The women always wanted to share. That was what I wanted to speak with Mr. Grant about. Later in the day, I had my inventory counts ready for the supply representative, who swung by once a week. While he was leaning over the counter checking out my legs and slender ankles, I said, "You know, I had a question for you, Mr. Sturgis. Do you carry smaller bags, maybe half the size of the ones we currently sell popcorn in?"

"Yeah, we call it the mini, sell it for cosmetics, small produce, stuff like that. Got a bundle in the truck."

"Could you let me try out that size with a complimentary half-bundle? If we like it, we'll order a lot more. And how about a bigger cup? Can we get a sample sleeve of those as well?"

"Why not? No skin off my nose. Try 'em out and let me know if Mr. Grant wants more."

"Perfect." Since Mr. Grant was too busy reading the comics to listen to my ideas, I would have to run my own test study.

The next couple that came up to the counter became my first trial subjects. "Hi there; great afternoon, isn't it? Two popcorns, two colas?"

The lady predictably said, "I don't know, that's such a big bag. Let's share, Clyde."

Then I offered, "Oh ma'am, we have a new smaller size just for the ladies, only seven cents. The regular is ten."

"All right, I'll take the small and a lemonade please." Turning to the man, she asked, "What are you getting, darling?"

"Give me a regular and a soda-pop."

"And sir, if all that popcorn makes you thirsty, I'd suggest our new large drink. Most of the gentlemen prefer them. Oh, and we just received a new candy bar. The Baby Ruth. They're delicious; a great value for the size."

"OK, why not, kiddo?"

The sale would have originally been twenty cents, but I had increased their total to thirty-seven cents, almost double. And I had until ten o'clock tonight to further test my theory.

After our fourth and final movie showing, I counted out my cash drawer, swept the area, and wiped down the counter. Mr. Grant carried the till from the ticket kiosk over to my area, and asked for my total. I handed him the money, saying I'd done a total of thirty-five dollars.

"You better count that again, dolly. That total is almost the same as all our ticket sales. That can't be."

"No, I counted twice. It's correct." Then, quite proud of myself, I explained my new size strategy. But was shocked when he appeared angry.

"You just can't order new size products and create your own prices. You're barely part-time. Who do you think you are?"

"Somebody that nearly doubled your concession total tonight *and* increased profits. I'm trying to help and it didn't cost the theater a thing. Mr. Sturgis gave us sample sizes to try out. I only wanted to show you the possibilities we are ignoring. You're very clever, Mr. Grant, and I can be a valuable asset. Tell your bosses the size additions were all your idea. Meanwhile, I can train the other associates on my selling techniques. Give me more hours and I'll make you more money."

"But you can't do whatever the hell you want. It's not proper protocol."

"Well, you're right. It's certainly up to you. If you think it's a bad idea, I'll have Mr. Sturgis pick up the free supplies tomorrow."

"Now, hold on a minute. Give me a night to digest the information."

Excited about his hesitation, I pushed forward. "Mr. Grant, you'll see a difference within the week. And you're going to love the raise your bosses will give you. Now, I have lots of other ideas too, but I'm going to need you to give me full-time hours to implement them. What do you say?"

"I said I'm sleeping on it, Nanette. So, what other ideas do you have in mind?"

"I guess I'll need to sleep on those a little longer too." I was desperate to make more money, but Mr. Grant was too obstinate to see my talent.

Walking home in the dark, my mood was not as upbeat as

it had been earlier. Hopefully Clarice would have some better news for me in the morning.

## CHAPTER 19
## MARIAH

*B*efore repairs could begin on the barn, it needed a thorough mucking out. I put brooms in both Sara's and Jo's hands, while I took the large shovel from the garden shed and began scooping out charred straw, old manure, and burned wood. At their age, the girls' sweeping talents were minimal, but I only had them helping to keep us together. It was a big job, taking hours of steady work and my small assistants seemed to enjoy chasing kittens more than sweeping.

That evening, I tuned the radio to a musical program hosted by Jack Benny. Sam had loved that radio, but tonight was the first time since the funeral that I'd felt ready to listen to the light banter and lively music. I brought a kerosene lamp to the kitchen table, and began calculating how much cash I could generate before leaving the farm. I soon realized my little nest egg might be the single thing that would keep me off the soup lines now popping up in many towns.

The following morning, David Thomas knocked on our door, bringing us more milk. I eagerly let him in, welcoming the company.

"David, I don't know what I'd do without this. Thanks again."

"Sure. Just wanted to let you know—Billy and Dad think your offer is fair; paying Billy's monthly wage in exchange for the barn work. January and February are always slow, so he's eager to start."

"Oh, I'm so relieved to hear that. What about getting the cows to market?"

"If you can cover my gas money and a little extra, I'll haul your eight and a few of our calves to the stockyards in Albert Lea. I think we'll get the best price there. I'll go Monday and then next week I'll haul the swine."

"Perfect, and it'll wipe me out, but I have just enough in the bank for Billy to buy the lumber he needs for the repair. I turned to pour him a cup of coffee. "David, you have no idea how this eases my mind." Setting our milk bottles on the table, David nodded, tipped his old cap and quickly scurried away before the coffee was offered.

WITHIN A FEW DAYS, Billy-boy was up with the dawn, driving the Thomas' wagon, led by our two horses, Buck and Shorty, into our farmyard. The girls dressed quickly, curious to check out this new young man invading our territory. He unloaded the lumber and began repairs by pulling out the burned or weakened wood in sections.

I joined the girls as Billy got started. He was as out-going as David was quiet. And he appeared happy to put up with the numerous questions Sarah and Jo were loaded with, such as: what his name was, did he have any pets, and how old was he? Crucial questions for four-year-olds. For his sake, I eventually called the girls over to help me in the hen house. After a few hours, I asked Billy to come in for his second breakfast. We fed him eggs, sunny-side up, thick slices of bacon and homemade bread with preserves.

Hungry for company, we all sat at the table watching him eat, but my prying questions didn't seem to bother him a bit. "So, Billy, how long have you been with the Thomas family? Been a while, hasn't it?"

Between bites, Billy filled me in. "Well, let's see. 'Bout four years it seems. The day I wandered onto their farm asking for work was probably one of the best things that's happened to me in a long while."

"So, you like it there?"

"Miss Mariah, the Thomas family is the greatest. Put me to work, gave me a nice place to lay my head, paid me fairly, and made me feel like I had a home. I wandered around for a while after my parents passed with the cholera. Water went bad in our area of Mississippi. It took them so fast. I was out and on my own at fifteen, scrounging for food, and working any place I could find. Them was tough times, ma'am."

As Billy continued to eat and speak in unison, the girls appeared enamored, sitting and staring at his animated eyes and eager round face.

"Billy, I had no idea. I'm so glad you found a home here."

"You and me both. I started riding the rails to get out of Mississippi. Met a guy on the trains advising me to stay on until I hit Iowa. Said the winters were long, but the soil was rich, and the farm work plentiful. He was right. I don't plan on leaving any time soon, if I can help it." Billy pulled out the checked fabric napkin tucked into his shirt, and wiped his mouth. "Well, Mariah, I appreciate the breakfast. The scent of your bacon pulled me in like a rope. I 'spect you're wanting me to get back to work now."

Late that afternoon, Lars, my conniving landlord, drove into the yard. It didn't surprise me. Word got around quickly in Green Tree, especially in the winter when farmers congregated for morning coffee at the Hot Cup. I was certain Billy-boy's lumber purchase would have tongues wagging. Through the bathroom window, I watched Lars park his truck and wander directly into the barn to check on proceedings. The twins and I quickly put on coats and boots. I wanted to be the one answering the questions.

I called out, approaching him in the barn, trailed by Sarah and Jo. "Afternoon, Lars. Cold enough for you today?"

He shrugged. "I've seen worse. So, Mariah, what's going on here with my barn? I thought we had an agreement?"

"What agreement was that, Lars?" I asked, feigning confusion.

"That I'd take your eight cows in exchange for handling the barn repairs. I want someone capable fixing it."

"Oh… that was a kind offer but I decided to take on the cost of repairs myself. According to your rental agreement, care of the farm buildings is our responsibility."

"Well, I don't know about that. Everything needs to be done well and proper."

"David Thomas assures me their man, Billy, is an excellent, experienced carpenter and I plan on having things fixed quickly. The roof shingles will be done once the ice melts, but the planks in the walls, floorboards, loft and ceiling are being replaced now."

"Yes, but Alfred Anderson told me that you…"

I interrupted him, saying, "Let's check on the progress and see how Billy is doing. I think you'll find him knowledgeable." As I talked, Sarah hid her face in my work trousers, while Jo grinned broadly up at the old man's frowning face.

Lars, now silent, appeared confounded, and grudgingly walked up a few steps to the loft. Billy climbed down the ladder and greeted Lars with a smile, explaining his plans and timetable. "I picked up the best white oak I could find. Sturdy stuff. When I'm finished, you'll never know we had that hell of a fire here."

Lars fingered the new planks that had been replaced on the loft floor, grunting his approval, telling Billy, "This'll do. How you paying for all this?" It angered me that he asked Billy that question instead of me.

I jumped in saying, "I have it taken care of, Lars. I wanted everything in good shape for my move in March."

"March? I thought Henry Anderson was moving in right away."

"According to our agreement, I'll leave March first, time for Henry to begin the new planting season. That way, I'll have time to find a job and a place to stay."

He took off his denim cap, raking his fingers through his gray, combed-back hair, shaking his head a few times, knowing he was losing money in not getting my cows. "I'll need to look into all this."

"I have the rental agreement on our table if you want to read it."

"I'm busy right now. Good day, Mrs. Anderson."

"To you as well; give my best to your sweet wife."

He looked at me, nodded again, was going to say something, and then just walked to his car, slamming the door behind him.

Jo eagerly called out, "Bye-bye," to the unfriendly old man driving away. In a mischievous mood, I said. "Looks like your mother just outfoxed that old silver-haired fox." The girls looked confused but giggled along, happy to see me laughing.

## CHAPTER 20
## NANETTE

*A*t nine AM, I knocked on Clarice's door.

"Whatever you got, I ain't buying."

"Clarice, it's Nanette. Have time to talk?"

"Hold on." A minute later she swung open the door. Her apron was spotted with milky spit-up, as she dabbed at her stained dress and apron. "Jonathon isn't holding anything down this morning, feels like he has a fever."

"I'm so sorry. What can I do?" I walked into the mess that was her front parlor, filled with piles of laundry, and the baby's crib.

"Just hold him for a bit while I boil up a tonic. My mother showed me this. It should bring down his fever."

"Happy to help." I patted the warm baby on the back, holding him to my shoulder, while Clarice chopped up odd looking roots at her dining table. "Uh, Clarice, the other day you mentioned you might be able to help me, remember?"

"Yes, and I said to *really* think hard about it."

I looked at all the chaos around me and took a deep breath. "I'm pretty convinced I'm not ready for all this mothering business. Don't have the means or the mind to do it now. What did you have in mind?"

"Are you absolutely sure?"

"Yes."

"OK, keep all this to yourself. My mother's a midwife. Has helped women with pregnancies for years, but she also knows all about herbs and potions to make the monthly menses return. She compounds a mixture and sells it on the side—a mix of pennyroyal and rue, tastes like the devil, but usually gets you results in a day or two. But I have to tell you, Nanette, there are no guarantees and a few women had complications."

Just then, her other little boy and girl ran out of their bedroom and started jumping all over me, clamoring for attention. "Kids, leave Miss Jorgenson alone. We're talking. Go play outside."

Clarice lowered her voice and leaned over to my ear. "Between you and me, I used it about five months after Jonathon was born. Simply couldn't handle another child so quickly."

"I trust you, Clarice. It sounds like your mother has a lot of experience with this sort of thing. How can I get some? I can't put off this decision any longer."

"I agree. At three and a half months, we need to move quickly. As far as costs go, let's say you sew me some curtains and pillows and you got yourself a bottle of *little ladies' helper.* My mother lives a few miles out of town. I'll need three dollars for transportation. I know a guy who'll take me there and back."

"You got a deal."

After Clarice forced a foul-smelling mixture down the baby's throat, he seemed to calm down. I offered to babysit the three kids, while Clarice picked up the potion. Our relationship was becoming a growing dependency on each other; almost like having an older sister. Something I'd never experienced before, but I liked that feeling and trusted her.

A few hours later, she returned with the tonic. "Nanette, this is enough for two doses, in case you need it later on. Take this when you're scheduled off work for at least two days. You're going to feel some cramping, nausea, and of course, bleeding. You'll be *really* uncomfortable. I certainly was. Remember, only take half the bottle."

After yesterday's long shift, I was off for two days so I decided to take the potion that afternoon. I'd eaten a light breakfast, but decided to go without lunch or dinner in case there was vomiting. I thought again of the implications and could not see a real downside. Within a few hours the tonic began having its effect. It started with my stomach churning in agony, as I lay on my bed with a hot wet towel over my abdomen. The pain came in raging waves. As soon as I began to feel somewhat normal, the intense cramping would return. As the day wore on, I got extremely hot and feverish. I moved to the toilet, feeling faint. Then I recalled my eyes closing as I became unsteady, bent over on the commode. My apartment had gone dark when I felt someone shaking my shoulder.

"Nanette, wake up. Nanette! You're burning up." I was groggy and looked around, realizing I was on the bathroom floor. I'd never felt so terrible. Clarice tried to pull me up and walk me to bed, but my body felt like it was on fire, shooting out little arrows of flame to every part, and the cramping was still severe. Then I noticed blood all over my nightgown. I refused to move; the pain was too intense.

Checking the toilet, Clarice said, "There's a lot of blood in the toilet too. At least it's out. The worst is over; you should be feeling better soon." She pulled me up, helping me limp over to the bed and replace my soiled nightgown. Then she laid a towel underneath me. "I'll make a cool compress for your forehead and give you an aspirin powder for the pain." She handed me a packet of powder and a big glass of water. "Drink up, and keep drinking lots of water. You'll be feeling better soon. Get some rest."

"I never imagined it would be this bad." I placed my hand against my chest. "My heart is racing… I'm wringing wet."

"Nanette, give it a little more time. If you still feel bad in a few hours, bang on the floor. I'll come up. I'd stay longer but my husband came home this afternoon and I can't say *anything* about the tonic. He won't allow that stuff in the house. I'll tell him you have the flu."

I whispered to her, "The way I feel now, I'd welcome the flu." After Clarice left, I curled up in a tight ball, and whimpered helplessly to myself.

I had no idea how long I laid in bed, but the pain was so severe, sleep was impossible. Something had to be wrong. I had drenched both sheets with my sweat. I eventually grabbed a shoe by the bed and began flailing it against the floor.

Clarice came quickly up the stairs and turned on my bedroom lamp, asking, "What is it?" She reached over to touch my head. "God, Nanette, you're still on fire. Something's wrong. I've never seen anybody this sick or feverish. I think we should consider a doctor."

"What about your mother?" I asked breathlessly.

"I don't think her stuff would fix this. We need the real thing and we need to hurry. You may have an infection. We need to get you to the hospital." I stared blankly as Clarice paced back and forth, running her hands through her hair, genuinely concerned.

She stopped pacing, looked at her watch, and announced. "My neighbor has a car, but it's four in the morning. I don't think I can ask her. Besides, she hates me. The kids are always running through her garden."

I whispered, "Does she have a telephone?"

"I think so."

As she headed to the door, I called out, ""Wait—tell her it's an emergency. Call the police. Ask for Officer Olsen; I know him."

# CHAPTER 21
# MARIAH

*A* new year had slipped quietly in without fanfare. I hoped 1933 would deliver some happier times. With David Thomas' help, I'd nailed down some basic economic decisions, and I was now mentally ready to discuss future options with my parents. Prior to several days ago, my head and heart hadn't been in the right place to figure anything out. I'd been deep in denial and despair.

With the twins in tow, I drove the coughing Model A over the icy rural roads to my parent's farm. Although it was an unexpected visit, Saturday mornings usually found my family congregating around the kitchen table for breakfast, often going over weekly finances. Their small three-bedroom farm-house was now filled to capacity with soon to be thirteen people, anticipating the pregnancy announcement by Rose and Willis, their hired help.

Janeen's four boys were a rambunctious group, aged eight to two, looking like stair-steps in height. As we arrived, the three older boys were pulling each other around on an old sled over light snow that was just shy of allowing much glide action.

As I parked, they clamored around our car, happy for a new diversion.

The girls climbed backwards out of the car seat, while Jo announced, "We made cookies, sugar cookies!"

As my nephews started jumping around me at the mention of cookies, I held the coveted platter over my head and said forcefully, "Boys, two apiece and only if you behave." This quieted them down as they followed us through the back door and into the kitchen.

Cookies quickly depleted; I sent all the kids back outside. The boys offered to show the twins the secret fort they'd created in the tool shed. As the kitchen suddenly quieted down, I noticed my dad looking tired, as he put down his newspaper. Mother showed her perpetual smile, finishing up dishes while the rest of her family remained gathered around the kitchen table.

Dad looked over at me, studying my face. "How's my number-two daughter doing? Better today, Mariah?"

"A little better, yes… It's going to take time. Dad, how are *you* coping?"

With her two-year-old son on her lap, Janeen jumped in, "The boys are driving Pa crazy. He's not used to having so many kids around anymore. Sorry Dad; I know they're noisy."

He patted her arm, "We'll make due. But they need a firmer hand with their father gone. Your older boys need to do more studying and chores, and less playing. Town life has been too soft on them."

Ma interrupted the lecture that was about to be delivered. "They'll learn Walter. It's only been a little over two weeks. It won't be long before they learn their duties around here."

I asked, "Any news from Jim?"

"Yes, a letter a few days ago," Janeen said. "He got the position at the dairy there, thank God. It's a big operation, but he said housing costs are so much higher in Chicago. He won't have us moving up there anytime soon. He's staying at a boarding house, and supposed to send money home every few weeks."

I looked over at Arlene, now in her senior year of high school, "You're all dressed up. Where are you going?"

She smiled, smoothing down her hand-sewn suit jacket and matching skirt. "Ma didn't tell you? I got a part-time job at Magee's. Saturdays and Thursday evenings after school. They had one opening and over twenty-five women applied."

Magee's was the only women's clothing store in town, selling shoes, dresses, and a wide variety of hats. Although pay was minimal, the job had clout for Arlene, being a farm girl.

"Congratulations, Arlene! I'm so proud of you."

"Thanks. I saw a few of your girlfriends at the store last Saturday, Suzanne and Elma. They both offered their condolences and said to tell you hello."

At the sink, Mother called out, "Speaking of your job, Arlene... Your brother better drive you into town soon or you'll be late for work."

"Gosh, you're right. I hadn't noticed the time." From the mud room, she grabbed her hat and coat, and pulled galoshes over her dress shoes. As she and Clem left, she hugged me saying, "We'll talk soon."

With a smaller group in the kitchen, everyone got more comfortable over hot mugs from my mother's never-ending flow of coffee. It was a toasty farm kitchen, with delicious smells seemingly baked into the faded fruit-print-wallpaper covering the small room. It was a scent I never tired of coming home to. The well-worn planked pine table could seat eight and took up the majority of the floor space. Through the years, that kitchen had weathered so many family conferences, heated arguments, joyful meals, and tight budget planning, with numerous cuts and imprints on the table top to prove it.

With residual anger I'd been holding back, I relayed news

of my mother-in-law's recent visit. "Apparently Lars and Alfred decided I needed to vacate our farm *and* replace us with Sam's older brother, Henry, and his new bride. They just up and decided without consulting me! And topping that off, Gerta said I had to give our car back. They want Henry to have it now. Can you imagine! That was their wedding present to Sam and me. I think it is downright unthinkable. Who takes back wedding gifts after five years?"

My parents nodded, looking like none of this sounded out of the ordinary. My father had his hands folded and was looking down at the table. "We know this is quite difficult for you, Mariah, but moving is for the best. You and Samuel were making a go of it, but out there on your own, it would be almost impossible."

I was surprised my normally vocal father was taking this so complacently. "I may have to move out, but I won't let Lars and Alfred Anderson dictate the terms. Lars expected me to pay for the repair of the barn with all my remaining cows and Alfred wants me to just hand over my chicken and pig stock to Henry, and pay me back whenever he decides."

"Well Mariah, don't rock that boat," Dad said, taking off his glasses. "They probably know what's best."

"Yes, they know what's best for *them*, not for me. I've been talking to David Thomas…"

My brother, Wilbur, interrupted. "David Thomas? I'm surprised you got more than a mumbled good morning out of him. The man rarely speaks."

"You're right. He's quite shy, but he actually knows a lot about livestock. He's been helping organize the barn repair and he's going to help me sell my cows and pigs. I've decided *I'm* taking care of things on *my* terms. I have the Thomas' hired man, Billy-Boy, repairing my barn already. I'm selling off everything I can before prices go lower. At least the sale will give me a bit of money to put in the bank before I'm forced to leave."

My parents looked at each other with concern. But Janeen said, "Good for you, Mariah. Makes sense to me. Don't let Lars take advantage of you."

"That's what I thought. The Andersons were expecting me to just pack up and leave immediately, but I explained, by signed agreement, I wasn't obligated to move until March, so I have a little time. I need to find a job and someplace to live. Actually, that's why I'm here. I'm so isolated out there. Maybe you could put in a few good words for me if you know any families or friends looking for help."

My mother touched her wet eyes with a tea towel. "Mariah dear, we want you here, but we're up to twelve people now, and with Rose expecting… we're bumping into each other every which way. Walter doesn't have the stamina he used to. A small farm can only support so many people."

"Speak for yourself, Renalda," my father said irritably. "I have plenty of stamina, but I just don't know if we can take on two more crying toddlers in this household. You understand Mariah, don't you? But yes, we'll support your decisions and make inquiries for you. We may not tell you often enough, but we love you and our two beautiful granddaughters. And if push comes to shove, you know we'll take you in somehow for a while."

"Thanks, Pa. I appreciate you both. Let me see what I can figure out. There's got to be some kind of job out there for me."

Mother asked, "Hopefully something will open up, but how will you care for the girls while you're working?"

"First, I'll find a job, then I'll worry about the rest. One step at a time or it all becomes too daunting. Actually today, I plan to go into town and start applying." Looking down at my watch, I said, "I better collect the girls and get moving."

Janeen looked over at me surprised. "You're not applying for jobs wearing *that* are you?" I was wearing an old rough, heavy jacket of Sam's over my print house dress. "That might be fine for feeding the pigs, but for a job in town you better come upstairs and borrow my good dress-coat and hat. Just drop it off on your way home."

Driving away, my hands began shaking as I grabbed the wheel. I left home this morning filled with confidence. I knew it was time to move forward, but now doubt was creeping in.

Saturday morning, Main Street in Green Tree was lively with horse-drawn wagons, dusty black sedans, and trucks filled with families eager to do their marketing. After angling the car into one of the few remaining spots, I took a deep breath, closed my eyes, and prayed. Negative thoughts kept intervening. Why would someone hire me? Yes, I was a hard worker, but I was only good at one thing, being a farmer's wife. I really had few skills in business. Didn't Arlene tell me only this morning that twenty-five women had applied for one part-time position at Magee's?

But I had to try. There were so many stores and businesses on Main Street. They appeared busy with shoppers. Something had to be waiting for me. I tucked a quilt over the twins, gave them their dolls, and told them to stay put in the car while I went into a few shops.

The large red-brick courthouse was at the center, with stores and businesses skirting down both sides of the street, with the rail depot at the end of the business district.

I asked to apply at the Farmer's State Bank, Green Tree Mercantile, and the town's two cafés, but was told at each location there were no positions available. After each brief visit, I ran back to the car, smiling and waving at Sarah and Jo. After applying at stores at one end, I moved the car further down the street, going into the post office, the pool-hall, and the fabric store. Each time I came back to the car, my smile was a little thinner and my mood less enthusiastic. The twins would point and wave back, not quite sure what I was doing, but happy to see me reappear every fifteen minutes or so. After about an hour of going back and forth, the girls began whining. They were hungry and wanted to walk. Giving them each a sandwich I'd packed, I took them out of the car, and put a twin on either side of me. I continued going into stores and offices with strict instructions for Sarah and Jo to keep silent upon entering. I walked through the wooden doors, stood tall, put a big smile on my face and asked for the owner or manager. Many people I knew already by their first names and greeted them as friends, but friends or not, they all had the same response. No one was hiring.

Entering the hardware store, we stepped on the well-worn wooden floor boards, inhaling the mixed scents of sawdust and freshly oiled tools. I waved to the owner, Sam's Uncle Raymond. He was behind his counter, weighing a bag of nails for a customer. He wrote up the purchase on a receipt pad, collected twenty-eight cents, and returned my greeting.

"Good morning, Mariah. Haven't seen you three since the funeral. Terrible thing that."

"Yes. Thanks so much for attending and giving your support." I took a deep breath, willing myself to go on, and ask again for the fifteenth time this morning. "Raymond, I actually came by today to see if you possibly need a store clerk. I'm good with math, ledger books, and quite neat and organized. Or I could do sweeping, clean-up, anything really."

He listened to me patiently, as the girls stood smiling, looking up into his face, doing their best not to blurt out their excitement regarding the shiny red sled in the showcase window.

"No, so sorry Mariah, but as I'm sure you know, business is down. I'm doing everything I can just to keep my two assistants on the payroll. They've both been with me a long time."

"I see. Well, if you hear of anything, please let me or my parents know. I would really appreciate it."

He looked uncomfortable and coughed, saying, "Certainly, I'd be happy to put in a good word for you. And Mariah... I hate to bring this up right now, but Samuel's account hasn't been paid in a while. He owed sixty-five-dollars on the bathroom fixtures and pipe. He and I had a verbal agreement. I can show you the payment schedule in my credit book."

"Oh, I'm so sorry. I didn't realize we still had an open account with you. I'll do my best to settle that soon. Thanks for your patience, Raymond." He nodded, as I walked out embarrassed, hoping the other two customers in the store hadn't overheard.

After checking with all the remaining businesses up to the train depot, we turned back to the car. My early hopes had changed into discouragement. This morning, the long street of stores appeared loaded with possibilities, but now a sense of fear enveloped me. I nervously chewed on my lip, putting the girls back into the car.

My last stop was Whitmiller's Grocery, where I traded my fresh eggs for store credit, buying flour, baking powder, sugar, and coffee. I knew the Whitmiller's daughter from school. In the storeroom, she counted out and checked my eggs, as I made my final plea of the day for a position.

"Mariah, I'd be the first to ask my dad to put you on. I remember you at school; always so smart, but between you and me, business is down by half." She whispered this as if she was divulging top-secret information. "Farm families are just making do, buying less. Town folk are holding back too, keeping what they have in the bank. Nobody's adding new staff."

"Yeah, I see that."

"But your eggs are beautiful. You and Sam always have

some of the largest and best ones. You don't scrimp on your feed."

"I guess we all have our talents. Thank you."

The ride home was quiet as I tried to reign in my emotions, wanting to appear strong. Sensing my mood, Jo began singing a favorite: *Mary Had a Little Lamb*, which broke the silence, and cheered me up. I asked them both to sing another. Their repertoire was quite limited but Jo led the way with *Jesus Loves Me*, with Sarah joining in. Now at age five, it was funny how intuitive they could be, doing their best to keep my spirits up, attempting to make my earlier smile reappear.

# CHAPTER 22
# NANETTE

*C*larice banged on the door, waking her unfriendly neighbor, and asked to make the emergency call to the police station. When she returned to my apartment, she reminded me, "Nanette, if anybody asks, you bought the medicine from a lady on the street selling potions." I was in too much pain to acknowledge her, but I remembered the message. After that, everything was a chaotic, red blur.

I do recall lying in the backseat of a car, and being wheeled into a hospital. Then, I became incoherent. Twelve hours later, I awoke to find a nurse tucking sheets in around me. "Ah, you're awake. Last night was a close call. I'll let the doctor know you're conscious."

A young male doctor came in and pulled a white curtain around my bed, giving us some privacy from the numerous patients sharing the room. "How are you feeling, Miss Jorgenson?"

"I hurt everywhere," I said weakly, unable to lift my head from the pillow.

He nodded and took my temperature. "Fever's down. We've been in a big fight for the last several hours."

I squinted, looking up at him. "A fight?"

"For your life. Apparently, whatever you took wasn't very effective. From what your friend told us, it was meant to bring on your menses. The potion flushed out a partial fetus, leaving a mass behind." The doctor coughed, looking down at his clipboard. "Sepsis was inevitable."

Taking all this in, I was too exhausted to react emotionally. "What's sepsis?"

"A fast-moving bacterial infection, something that happens when your body turns on itself. Miss Jorgenson, if that policeman hadn't brought you in when he did, you wouldn't have lasted the night. You'd have gone into septic shock, with dropping blood pressure, eventually resulting in organ failure."

Nodding, I said, "I knew something was horribly wrong. I can't thank you enough doctor, but I'm incredibly weak and sore."

"You're young, appear to be healthy and strong. You should fully recover, but I need to tell you—something unexpected but unavoidable."

This didn't sound good.

"I had to perform a vaginal hysterectomy. It was the only way to clear the remains and infection. Unfortunately, with ovaries removed, you'll not be able to conceive. I'm sorry to tell you so bluntly, but the hysterectomy is a big part of why you feel so much pain and weakness."

"Oh my God." Even through my exhaustion, I felt a quickening panic. "Doctor, back up. When you say never conceive, are you sure? Maybe after a few years... a pregnancy might be possible? I'm only nineteen."

"No, I'm sorry. After a hysterectomy, it's simply not possible. These are difficult surgeries. We were in a fight for your life. You're truly lucky to still be here. Take comfort in that, Miss Jorgenson."

"Yes, a lucky girl." I turned my face into the pillow and began to cry, not wanting to prolong the conversation.

"You'll need to stay here for two days of observation, and then it's home for bed-rest for a couple weeks. A little walking is good; but no heavy lifting for a while."

I nodded with my face buried deep within the pillow, trying to make sense of what the doctor told me, contemplating my loss and future.

The next day I woke up to the face of Officer Olsen sitting in a chair next to me, reading a book. Looking around, I saw my room was filled with six other patients, all in bed, several with visitors. With so many people in one room, it was noisy. I was surprised I'd slept so long amongst all the commotion.

Still groggy, I cleared my throat. "Officer Olsen, I heard you're responsible for saving me. I'm so grateful."

"Happy to help out. But, Nanette, last time we spoke you told me you were going to stay out of trouble. And here you go, almost dying on us." He added a slight smile.

"Well, it certainly wasn't my choice. I'm sorry to keep you so busy."

He closed his book. "I need to ask you what really happened? Who sold you that potion?"

Although my mind was hazy, I realized he was not only here for a social visit. "Honestly, I have no idea. I'd missed my monthly, didn't know what was wrong, and went to the drugstore to see if they sold something to help. While I was checking the medications, a little old lady was in there and suggested I use her special tonic. I remember she was hunched over, white-haired, wearing an odd-looking knit cap. If I ever spot her again, I'll certainly let you know. I never expected this terrible outcome, but I'm grateful for you and the doctor."

"Hmm. Alright. So, you didn't catch her name and had no idea you were pregnant?"

"Absolutely not."

He stood up and stretched. "I wanted to follow up, make sure you're OK. Perhaps, one day, we'll get to have that slice of pie you offered me a while back. When are they letting you out of here?"

"Tomorrow, I think."

"I'll check with the doctor and come back to drive you home, if that's all right."

"I'm afraid I won't be good company, but the ride home is welcome. Thank you for everything."

I closed my eyes, knowing I needed rest, but my mind wouldn't allow it. Although the doctor had given me back my life, I understood something quite precious had been taken away. It simply wasn't fair. I pounded my fists in frustration on the thin mattress but then had a final thought, thinking of what Auntie always told me: When one door closes, another usually opens. I'd just have to keep kicking open doors.

# CHAPTER 23
# MARIAH

On the way home, I stopped at the Thomas' farm to invite the family to a special dinner, in appreciation for their kindness. Eleanor Thomas was delighted at the invitation. She and her husband, David, and Billy-boy, would come over Wednesday evening around six, after the evening milking.

The day after, David stopped by to give me my cattle sales results. From the snapped pocket on his overalls bib, he pulled out a roll of cash, and handed it to me. The heft of the bills felt good in my hand.

"Well, Mariah, it's about what I expected. Your cows sold between forty-eight to fifty-five dollars a head, giving you a total of four-hundred and eight dollars. Of course, barn repairs will take over a hundred of that."

"You're right. It's a far cry from prices of even a year ago. But at least I'll be leaving here with something."

"True enough, and I estimate next week you'll get about four-hundred-fifty total for the swine at auction." After handing me the cash, David kept his eyes on the floor, saying, "I best be going now." Then he left through the back door.

Conversation was definitely not his strong suit; I had to laugh comparing David to Sam, who was rarely at a loss for words.

The worry about my outstanding debt of sixty-five-dollars to the hardware store ate away at me. But later, while washing dishes, I realized I could leave Henry Anderson a sow and boar for breeding, in exchange for him paying off the debt. Afterall, it would be Henry and his new wife enjoying that new in-door bathroom. He might not like the deal, but it seemed a fair exchange to me.

I put a lot of effort in preparing my little dinner party for the Thomas family. It would be my final gathering at our house. I also invited my younger sister, Arlene, to join us. She was another big talker; someone that could keep up with Billy-boy. She also brought over a few borrowed chairs from our parents' house. Sarah and Jo would be eating early and sent to bed right after our guests arrived, which made Jo pout because she was always eager for more attention.

I plucked and cooked two chickens and made dumplings with gravy. From the cellar, I brought up two jars of pickled okra and stewed tomatoes, and again made the girls' favorite, freshly baked sourdough bread. With Arlene's help, we dragged the table from the kitchen into the front room, put a white embroidered tablecloth over the top, and placed the six mismatched chairs around. I believed every dish, glass, and piece of cutlery I owned was put to use that night.

When the Thomas family arrived, Jo and Sarah answered the front door, excited to see visitors. Seeing David first, Jo immediately took his hand and pulled him in. The twins were becoming comfortable with his frequent milk drop-offs. Billy stepped in right behind him. I was surprised that both men looked so different out of their baggy, well-worn, blue overalls. They'd been replaced with belted dark trousers and white shirts, with their hair brushed and slicked back. David and Billy both looked slightly embarrassed to be out of their comfortable uniforms. Mrs. Thomas, wearing a pretty full-skirted dress, admonished her gruff husband for insisting on wearing his overalls, but explained that he'd worn a clean shirt underneath.

As everyone inched into our small parlor, I thanked everyone for coming. "It means so much to Jo, Sarah, and me that you've become such good neighbors and dear friends, and we appreciate your family so much. Please, everyone, sit down."

I introduced Arlene, who handed out cold beers. She knew the Thomas family from church but had never really spoken much to them. Before sending Jo and Sarah upstairs, I asked them to perform a little ice-breaker. For the last three days I'd been teaching them, *Happy Days Are Here Again*, a wistfully ironic song being played frequently on the radio. They learned the words quickly and Jo taught Sarah hand motions and steps to go along. It was all Sarah could do to remember the words, but of course, Jo had her steps and motions down pat. As everyone got comfortable, I announced the girls had a new song to share.

Jo tugged on Sarah's hand, pulling her out of the kitchen, and whispered, "Just do what I do." Jo beamed toward her audience of six patient adults, singing out confidently as Sarah joined in following a step behind.

> *"Happy days are here again.*
> *The skies above are clear again….*

They were a hit. Everyone laughed and clapped. I wiped

away a proud tear, while Billy-boy picked Jo up and swirled her around, calling her, "A real natural."

Then Jo pointed at the admiring adults, "Now, everybody sings!" And we did, repeating the contagious song once again. Although I was fearful of what lay ahead, for that night at least, it was happy days for us all.

# CHAPTER 24
# NANETTE

*B*ack at home after my hysterectomy, I felt weak and tired. Not myself at all. An essential female part of me was missing and I grieved over that for some weeks. I knew a few women in Green Tree who never had children, my aunt included. They managed to have seemingly happy lives. Would I be able to do that? The thought of always being childless had never occurred to me, and now it was on my mind all the time.

Three weeks later, feeling physically stronger, I returned to my theater job, proud to see they had implemented my ideas at the concession stand. Mr. Grant had finally decided to use me full time, but after several months without a promotion, I knew I had to move on. I needed a manager who understood the value of my true potential. One could only eat so much free popcorn.

I'd also signed on to watch free movies to study acting. I'd taken advantage of that too, watching countless films, copying all the mannerisms of my favorite silent screen stars. I had their movements down perfectly and was certain most film directors would agree if they could only see me.

I bought a large mirror and I'd rehearse at home, raising

my hands all-a-flutter as I imagined the camera coming in close, then I'd open my eyes as large as possible, and scream—in silence. I also knew how to portray demurely, as I imagined my handsome co-star, leaning in for a kiss. Studying myself in the mirror, I'd learned which was my best side; a difficult choice. I'd taught myself to raise my chin just so and look off-camera, into the horizon, with sorrow. I felt sure, if I was ever discovered by the elusive Hollywood talent agent passing through Mankato, I was ready.

Romero became another issue. He stopped by about a week after my hospital visit to check on me. After I told him I'd been ill, he was at my beck and call. He was incredibly sweet and attentive, offering complimentary blocks of ice, chocolate, even flowers. Eventually, Romero took me to a family gathering where I met his gregarious four brothers, parents, and numerous nieces and nephews. All the family appeared to live together on a piece of land just outside of town, with a few small homes attached to one larger house in a haphazard fashion. All around me, people were speaking Italian with boisterous volume and lots of hand movements. After all my acting rehearsals, I was good at exaggerated hand and facial expressions, but couldn't really keep up with the conversation.

But I did recognize one word, which continued to come up, often in joking, nudging comments from his brothers directed towards Romero and me.

"Bambino," or "ahh molti bambini!"

Although Romero and I were only beginning a relation-ship, we seemed to be already in the midst of baby discussions with his family. Considering my hysterectomy, it was clear to me that Romero and I would never be a good match. I prob-ably needed to switch my prospects away from handsome, virile young men wanting big families to someone more mature. Perhaps someone with a prosperous business, and not necessarily looking for family. Albeit, a more challenging hunt, but I felt confident I was up to the task.

On a blustery cold day, on my way to pick up groceries for myself and Clarice, I ran into Obidiah Dawson, the dray-line delivery driver I'd met when I first arrived. I called out to him as he passed me by.

"Mr. Dawson, it's Nanette. Remember me?"

He pulled up on his horses and stopped to look down. "Nanette? Yes! Front Street Hotel. How are you?"

"I'm on my way to Alleman's on Van Brunt. Need to pick up a few things."

"Hop up; I'm passing right by. We'll catch up."

Up on the high seat, I glanced at the back of the wagon. "What are you hauling today? No produce, I see."

"It's a new tripod and camera for *Professional Portraits*, a photography studio. Owner's equipment finally came in. He's been asking me about it for days."

"Photography studio? I've never noticed one here in town. With new equipment, perhaps he's expanding?"

Mr. Dawson shrugged his shoulders. "No idea. It's located on Cherry Street."

"You know, I'd love to have my portrait taken. I haven't had one made since graduation. Maybe I'll just tag along with you. Do you know if he has an assistant?"

Obidiah again shrugged as he pointed out a few businesses recently closed. Pulling to a stop on Cherry Street, I observed the exterior of the building: a brick stand-alone on the corner, with two large showcase windows. Unfortunately, the windows were not being used to their full advantage, the door was weathered and unwelcoming, and an overhead sign was nonexistent. The windows had the name of the business painted across the front, but the windows should have been utilized to showcase his product, photo portraits… obviously. It was so clear this business owner needed my help and advice. And free photo portraits of myself might be just the ticket I needed for my movie career. I believe I'd just found my next career challenge.

As we walked in, standing behind the counter was a middle-aged gentleman in a suit, with thinning hair and glasses. As Obidiah and I walked in, I smiled at the studio owner and asked, "Mr. Dawson, will you introduce me to the manager of this lovely establishment."

The owner's eyes immediately twinkled with a smile; so different from the disagreeable Mr. Grant. He stepped in front of the counter and shook my hand, "Phil Greenly, proprietor. And you are… just delightful."

"A pleasure to meet you, Mr. Greenly. Nanette Jorgenson. Imagine, a young man like you with your own business? Impressive! I just have to say, I love everything about photography and find it absolutely fascinating."

# CHAPTER 25
# MARIAH

*I* was desperate to find employment. Janeen watched my girls a few times while I drove to surrounding towns within a thirty-mile radius. Again, I walked into every open store-front or place of business, but was told each time that things were slow or they preferred a man to fill the position. In a few towns, some retail operations were boarded up. I noticed the bank in East Point had closed. Newspapers were filled with stories of bank closures as depositors pulled out funds and closed accounts. The barrage of news was unsettling as I spent precious funds filling the car with gas, looking for work.

One morning, Catherine popped in for a visit while the twins were attempting to learn the art of drying dishes. Jo and Sarah crowded around their aunt, happy for her interest and small gifts. She brought them each a coloring book and a box of wax crayons to share. They were thrilled with this present as they went upstairs to color. I reheated this morning's coffee and offered Catherine a cup as we sat down at the kitchen table.

"Catherine, I'm so worried. I've been through every town within two counties. Nobody's hiring and my parent's house is filled to the brim. I hate to be a burden to my parents, moving back in."

"I totally understand. I was hoping to move out and be on my own this year but it seems impossible now. Mother is more dependent on me than ever. She's not able to do everything she used to, and lately we can't afford to bring in help like before. Crop prices are plummeting."

"I know. That's why I sold off my livestock."

"Yeah, Henry heard you sold everything and was miffed. Being Samuel's farm, he thought of your livestock as part of *our* family's business, but, in reality, it should be yours to sell. I think you did the right thing."

"Your family's business? What does the Anderson clan think I'm supposed to do? Just float away with Sam's kids and survive on thin air?"

Catherine took a sip of the coffee and stirred in some sugar. "Mariah, I know my parents have not been helpful. It's Samuel's death... They can't seem to shake it and seem to resent you for some reason. I know it sounds crazy."

"Not a day goes by that I don't think about the fire and wonder if I could have done something differently. If I'd only gone out to the barn a few minutes earlier, everything could have been altered. I've been living with guilt for months now, but I have to move on or I'll go crazy."

"Mariah, you can't blame yourself, *ever*. It was a freak accident and living on a farm... these things happen. We *know* they do. Anyway... I came over to tell you something I overheard yesterday. About a possible job. Are you familiar with the Martin family? Elliott Martin?"

"I've heard the name, but don't know him."

"He's a friend of Henry's. Elliott has a hundred-and-fifty acres north of us. He's about thirty, with three sons, but his wife is ill, can barely get out of bed. Some type of consumption, apparently even coughing up blood."

I shuddered thinking about it. "Sounds terrible... poor lady."

"Well, he's desperate for someone to move in and take care of her, keep up the household chores, feed the kids. Henry said Elliott's barely able to cope lately."

My eyes suddenly lit up. "Is there room for me and the girls to stay there? What's he paying?"

"I don't know the details, but you should go over and check it out. I know it's not much, but it might put a roof over your head and food on the table. In the past, when I visited Elliott and Rebecca, they were pleasant, friendly types. But I'm sure things are very different now."

"I'll be honest. I was hoping for something other than housework, but you're right. I should find out the details; it might be a good fit, temporarily."

"Trust me, I even considered it. I'm so ready to move out, but you know how mother is. And honestly, the work at the Martin's is probably tougher than at home, with three young boys, a sick woman, and all the other chores."

"Gosh, you make it sound so tempting," I said with a nervous laugh. "Anyway, I appreciate you letting me know about this, Catherine.

"You want me to tell him you're interested? Maybe you could go by in the morning. Their place is close to our main road."

"Yes, perfect. Please put in a good word for me."

"Sure. By the way, I heard Henry speaking with Dad. They're coming soon to inspect the farm and take the car back."

"I've been expecting that. The barn repairs are finished. I'll be leaving your brother with two breeder hogs. It's almost all Sam and I started with." I looked about wistfully. "I hope Henry and his bride will be happy here."

"Oh, they will, and eager to be in their own place."

"It was a good home to start a marriage. It wasn't easy, but I'll always remember this place fondly."

"Yeah, lots of memories here. Like the night the girls were born? Seems like yesterday."

I nodded, staring at the linoleum Sam had laid. "But maybe there's too many lingering memories. It's time to go. Initially I wasn't ready, but now the house feels so empty. Just standing in that mud room, thinking about Samuel lying there, or just walking past the barn still gives me chills."

We were both quiet for a minute, then Catherine said, "Oh, by the way, an old friend of mine, Nanette Jorgenson, is coming to visit tomorrow. After speaking with Elliott, you should stop by and meet her. She's so friendly. Now there's a girl that went out and found herself a good job. Moved to Mankato all by herself some years back, and seems to be doing well, running a photography studio. I've always envied her independence."

"Name sounds familiar. Wasn't she one of the Corn Harvest queens years ago?"

"She's the one."

Later, as Catherine headed for the door, I said, "Thanks so much for the job tip. I truly appreciate it. If I don't get this one, I don't know what I'll do."

## CHAPTER 26
## MARIAH

The following morning, we drove the slushy roads over to the Martin farm. With March approaching, temperatures were easing up. I reminded Sarah and Jo to be on their best behavior when I spoke to Mr. Martin. "Girls, his wife is ill and the family may want my help with housekeeping and nursing. This could be the job I've been searching for." I pulled up to a white clapboard two-story, not unlike ours, but with a large covered front porch with two lovely rocking chairs.

Wanting to make a good impression, I'd worn my winter church dress, a navy wool with a white collar, and a soft felt hat with a navy ribbon. I dressed Jo and Sarah in matching corduroy overalls, a Christmas gift from my mother. I was making an effort. I needed this job!

I patiently stood at the front door, holding my girls' hands, as they stood on each side of me. After knocking twice and waiting a few minutes, I was greeted by Mr. Martin who opened the door, looking disheveled and nervous. "Good morning, good morning. I'm Elliott. You must be Mariah Anderson? So sorry about Samuel, great guy. I know his older brothers well. Uh, come in... have a seat."

"Thank you, good to meet you, Mr. Martin."

As we walked into his front parlor, he looked about anxiously for a space for us. There was a small settee and two armchairs across from it, but everything was covered in piles of clothing, books, muddy boots, toys, tools, and dirty dishes. The house had a ripe, gamey scent about it. He grabbed a huge pile of stuff off the settee so the three of us could squeeze in. Then he pulled another pile off an armchair and sat down. Although distracted by the lack of any housekeeping, I kept a frozen smile on my face.

"Well, as you can see, we need a housekeeper... quite badly. I've got three sons: nine, eight and six. All in school right now, but they're a handful. Don't get me wrong, they're good boys. Already handy with tools and livestock, but not much help around the house, I'm afraid."

"Yes, boys will be boys," I said, a little shaken at daunting tasks that might be ahead of me. "So, Catherine Anderson tells me your wife has taken ill and you're in need of a caretaker. Is that correct?"

He spoke in a low voice, with his eyes on the floor. "Well, that and more. My wife, Rebecca, has tuberculosis. Was hospitalized for a couple of months but I couldn't afford to keep her at the sanatorium any longer. Her lungs are getting weaker by the day. And the coughing--it's terrible and the illness is contagious, so we've had to keep the boys away as much as possible."

"Well, that must be difficult for everybody."

He nodded, looking at me. "Yes, she stays in our room upstairs; the boys sleep in the basement and I stay in their room. Before, Rebecca was having her good and bad days, but lately things seem worse."

"I see. I'm so sorry...I know it must be terribly hard for you." Realizing I'd never introduced my girls, I said, "Mr. Martin, these are my twin daughters, Sarah and Jo. They've recently turned five. I was hoping for a position where we could stay together as a family."

"Well, that's not possible here. Even if I had space for them, it's not safe, health-wise. I was thinking I could set up a little bed in this room for a caretaker. The boys and I stay mainly in the kitchen or listen to the radio at night in the dining room. I guess I was hoping for someone that had grown children or none at all."

"Yes, I understand." Another *no*, I thought despairingly.

"But honestly, Mariah, you would probably be perfect here. I need someone that knows how to handle kids and under-stands farm life. I need a cook, cleaner *and* a caretaker—a woman that can do it all."

I smiled and asked, "What were you planning on paying this wonder woman with all the skills?"

"Honestly, I can't afford much. The position would be room and board and fifteen-dollars a month."

I immediately thought the wage was far too low. I knew Billy-boy, as a hired hand, was making thirty-five a month and this position would be as challenging as anything he did, but I also realized women were rarely paid an equivalent wage. I asked, "May I meet Mrs. Martin?"

"I checked on her right before you came and she was wide awake, so this should be a good time."

"Girls, you sit right here and wait. I won't be long." I could tell they were already getting restless and ready to explore.

I tied my handkerchief around my face as Mr. Martin and I climbed the stairs. He knocked lightly on the bedroom door. As we walked in, I tried not to show my surprise at the tiny, ill woman sitting in her four-poster bed staring right through me. I sat down in a wooden chair right next to her bed. Mrs. Martin looked twice my age, but was probably in her late twen-ties. She was rail-thin, almost hidden by the bed covers, and looked to weigh perhaps seventy pounds, with white, almost translucent skin, and dark circles under her eyes. Her dark hair, twisted back in a bun, was already streaked with several strands of gray. She held a white handkerchief near her mouth which was flecked with bright red blood.

"Mrs. Martin, it is so nice to meet another farm wife. I'm Mariah Anderson. We have a lot in common. I live south of Green Tree on a farm about the size of yours."

"That's nice," she whispered. "And children?"

"Yes, two girls, twins actually, although you'd never know it to look at them. Different as night and day. And I understand you have three boys, already farm-hands to their father."

She smiled weakly and nodded her head. "That's right. Three good boys. We're blessed."

"What can I get you, Mrs. Martin? Some hot tea and toast, maybe? I'd be happy to prepare something for you before I go."

"Hot tea would be welcome. Thank you." As she said this, a coughing spasm began and I exited the room with Mr. Martin, telling her I would be right back.

We went downstairs and he showed me the kitchen. It was, as I assumed, loaded with dirty dishes and bits of food on the work table and small counter space. There was a hand pump at a large kitchen sink and a filthy floor that needed a thorough sweep and mopping. A large shovel and pitchfork leaned against the kitchen wall and a pile of work boots, caked with manure, were strewn across the floor, landing wherever they'd been pulled off. The back porch and dining room were in a similar condition. The entire house was crying out for a thorough cleaning, organization, and a mother's touch.

"Mr. Martin, I see the kettle on the stove; if you could show me the whereabouts of your teapot and tea tin, I can heat up a nice hot cup for your wife before I go."

He started rummaging around the lower cabinets. "I'm sure it's around here somewhere. We really haven't had a need for a teapot lately." After a few minutes searching and much clanging about, he pulled out a dusty teapot and a tin of tea.

"I'm sure Mrs. Martin's throat feels sore after all that coughing," I said. "A little lemon and honey with hot tea really helps soothe the throat."

"Hmm, no lemons this time of year, but I bet there's a bottle of lemon juice down in the basement pantry, and I do know where the honey is."

As he headed downstairs in search of lemon juice, I filled a kettle on the stovetop with water from the pump, lit the wood under the burner, and waited for the water to boil. I took the shovel and pitchfork out of the kitchen and placed them next to the backdoor. The manure-splattered work boots had to go too. I matched up pairs and set them neatly against the back porch wall. I added two heaping teaspoons of tea leaves into the rinsed teapot, then grabbed a broom and started sweeping while waiting for the kettle to whistle. Growing restless, Jo and Sarah tiptoed into the kitchen, probably hoping to find a spare cookie.

"Mommy, can we help?" Sarah asked.

"Sure, Sarah. You hold the dustpan for me, and Jo, why don't you *carefully* bring me any dishes you can find in the other rooms. Bring one at a time and don't drop anything."

As the water began to boil, Mr. Martin walked up from the basement stairs with a smile and a bottle of lemon juice in his hand. "I found it!"

I poured the boiling water over the tea leaves and let it steep while I sawed off a few slices from a hard loaf of wheat bread. I rinsed off a sticky griddle, placed it over the hot stove top and toasted the bread, smearing it with a bit of butter I found on the cold-shelf, used for storing dairy, cheese, and eggs.

Mr. Martin stood awkwardly watching as we put a touch of tidiness into his unkempt house.

Picking up the cup of tea and plate of toast, I said, "I think

I've got it. I'll bring this up to Mrs. Martin, and then we'll get out of your way. You must have work to do before the boys get home from school."

"Actually, I'm going into town. Got to haul my milk to the dairy—although it hardly pays to sell it right now."

"True enough. Mr. Martin, I must say, I can see you're in desperate need of help. I don't know how we can make this work, but please consider me for the position and hold it open for a day or two."

"I can do that. I appreciate you stopping by and chatting with my wife. I'm sure she's lonely for some female company. Do you mind seeing yourself out? No need to lock up. It was nice meeting you, Mrs. Anderson."

"Yes. Thanks for your time."

As I entered the bedroom, Mrs. Martin seemed to use all her strength mustering up a grateful smile. Placing the items on a nightstand, I sat next to her, offering her a cup of tea. Her hands shook so badly that I edged the chair closer, and held the cup to her mouth for small sips. I found it necessary to break the bread into tiny pieces, then dunk them into the tea to soften the bites, almost like feeding a small, delicate bird. I continued to chat with Rebecca gaily, letting her know about news in town. I tried my best to picture her as she was before; a young, healthy, attractive mother and busy wife. Before leaving, I offered to help her use the chamber pot under the bed, and then emptied and cleaned it. I didn't want to show pity or fear around Rebecca, but instead, hoped she felt she'd found a friend.

After coming downstairs, I filled the sink with more hot water from the kettle and began washing the dishes. I scrubbed and washed; Sarah dried with a less-than-clean towel, while Jo stood on a chair and placed things on the dish shelf. The rooms were far from perfect, but better than when we arrived. I wanted to leave Mr. Martin a small sample of what I was capable of.

Walking back to our car, Sarah asked, "Mommy, is this our new home? It seems sad."

I felt defeat creeping in again. The job requirements seemed overwhelming and actually dangerous. My girls wouldn't be able to stay with me, and the pay was poor; yet, it was the only chance of employment I'd even had a shot at. I had three imminent needs: a roof over our heads within a week, a paycheck, and food. As we got inside our car which was on borrowed time, I dabbed nervous sweat off my forehead with my handkerchief.

## CHAPTER 27
## MARIAH

$\mathcal{W}$ith the Anderson farm close by, I decided to accept Catherine's invitation for a visit. As usual, the twins were happy to hear they'd be visiting their aunt.

On the way over, everything felt bleak. Stretching out in front of me, I saw fallow fields, dark with blue-black soil iced with white drifts of snow, still standing in patches among the rows. Although the winter had been bitterly cold, the snowpack had been light, which sent all the area farmers to speculate about possible drought in the spring. Farming was always a gambler's occupation.

Pulling up to the Anderson's, my anxiety grew. My mother-in-law and I hadn't communicated since the day I'd literally swept her out of my house with the broom. I almost smiled remembering my burst of defiance. Timidly knocking, I hoped Catherine would open the door, but no. Mother Gerta answered with her usual distant and formal demeanor.

"Well, this is a surprise. I don't believe we were expecting you, Mariah. And how are my granddaughters?" As she asked this, she reached down and gave them each a pat on the head.

"Sorry to disrupt your day, Gerta, but I was hoping to see Catherine for a bit. She'd invited us over to meet her friend."

"They're both in the parlor. Nanette's visiting from Mankato. I'll check to see if you're welcome to join them." In a moment she returned, finally opening the door wide enough for us to enter, making it clear the frost had not yet thawed.

The girls and I walked down the hall to the parlor, which had a fire blazing in the hearth keeping the space toasty-warm. The twins never liked this room. It had a furniture grouping upholstered in a stiff, shiny off-white brocade, which always resulted in a barrage of reminders for them not to sit, play, or eat near any of the furniture. Catherine jumped up, offering quick hugs, and introduced us to her friend.

Nanette was pretty, blonde, green-eyed and all smiles, as she announced that Jo was the spitting image of her father and the twins were just the cutest things she had ever seen. "Girls, your father was one of the most handsome boys in school and one of the smartest. Unfortunately, too young for me, but I certainly noticed him. It's such a tragedy he's gone."

This went over their heads, as the twins remained quiet, with Sarah hiding her face in the skirt of my dress, while Jo stood in the center of the room with her mind on more obvious things. There was a plate of muffins sitting on a highly polished round table between the two chairs Catherine and Nanette were sitting on. Jo walked over, speaking softly in Catherine's ear.

"Certainly," Catherine said. "You can each have a muffin, but no dropping of crumbs, *and first*, you'll need to sing for your supper."

Catherine's request seemed to confuse Jo. "Mariah, I saw Arlene at Magee's Saturday and she said your girls had learned the cutest song and performed it for company. Sarah, Jo… let's hear your song. I'm sure Nanette will love it."

Nanette shook her wavy blonde bob, clapping her hands. "Yes please, let's hear the song."

Sarah looked squeamish, realizing she had to perform again. I knew she remembered the words because she and Jo sang *Happy Days* in the car earlier today. But she was shy about performing in front of strangers. Sarah stared back at Nanette, pulling on my arm, and whispering "Mommy, I don't want to sing."

"OK, don't panic, Sarah. I won't make you. What about you, Jo?"

"Yes, I can," she said, eyeing the muffins. She stood front and center on the oval rug in the room, put her hand motions in place and belted out *Happy Days are Here Again*, in tune, remembering both verses.

Nanette looked thoroughly entertained with Jo's enthusiastic singing. "Wow, that's terrific. What a little doll! But I think you *both* deserve a muffin; don't you, Cath?"

"Absolutely. Girls, come to the kitchen to eat and I'll pour you some milk."

When Catherine returned, I said, "Sorry to interrupt your visit, but I just finished meeting with Elliott Martin and wanted to tell you how it went."

"Oh yes. Did you meet Mrs. Martin too?"

"Yes, and like you said, she's really ill. Looks like she's just wasting away; that consumption is a terrible thing and apparently highly contagious, so it won't be a safe place for the girls to stay. Plus, Mr. Martin has no space for them. If hired, I'd be sleeping in the front parlor. But, honestly, the family needs assistance so badly; the house was a disaster."

"Oh, that's so sad. I didn't realize she was that ill. And with the boys so young."

"I know. I'd really like to help, but I'll need to see if there's *any* way my parents can find space for the twins temporarily, until either his wife's condition improves or…" I looked up, shrugging my shoulders, not wanting to state the obvious.

"I remember Elliott Martin vaguely," Nanette added. "He was older; but always seemed pleasant enough."

"Yes, nice but definitely anxious and overwhelmed right now."

"You know, Mariah," Catherine said, "your parents have so much on their plates right now with Janeen's family there. I could take one of the girls for a while. My room upstairs is tiny, but we'd make do."

"What would Gerta think?"

"With Sarah so quiet and shy. I'm sure she'd be no problem."

"Honestly, they're good girls, but any five-year-old can be a handful at times. Although… if I worked at the Martin farm, I *would* be close. I could visit often, and if you kept Sarah, it might be easier for my parents to find space for Jo."

Then Nanette spoke up. "Mariah, this may sound strange, but I would love to take little Jo home with me temporarily. I have a small apartment to myself in Mankato and my landlady, downstairs, has three kids. I bet I could work something out and have her watch Jo while I'm at work. I realize you barely know me, but I'm crazy about kids. I would adore helping you out. Frankly, I could use the company and Catherine would vouch for me, wouldn't you?"

Catherine nodded in agreement, smiling. "Sure."

"Are you both serious?" I couldn't believe they were offering. "It's so incredibly generous of you both. I don't know though… We've become such a threesome lately, but it would give me a chance to take the job. Might only be for a few months while I keep looking for something better."

Catherine picked up a plate and muffin, handing it to me and said, "I'll discuss it with my parents, but it should be fine. After all, Sarah is their granddaughter. Nanette, are you really sure you're ready to take on a boisterous five-year-old?"

"I'm absolutely serious …Yes!" Then she turned her focus on me. "Just so you know a bit about me, Mariah, I help manage a photography studio. Love my job, but all I do is work and go home to an empty apartment. The last few years, I've wished for kids, but I seriously don't think that's going to happen. Little Jo and I would have so much fun together. I'm certain. By train, Mankato is only a hop, skip and a jump. Think about it, Mariah. You and Sarah could come to visit, and I can occasionally come to Green Tree. I think it would be a perfect temporary fix."

I felt overwhelmed with their generosity. "Well, you make a compelling offer, Nanette. This is all coming together so quickly; my head is spinning!"

The idea of sending my children away was heart-wrenching. But these were two good women that wanted to help. Catherine had always been Sarah's favorite aunt. It wouldn't take her long to acclimate if we were separated. And Jo was open and adaptable. She might enjoy living with Nanette and playing with the children downstairs. Catherine's old friend seemed to have everything I'd longed for years ago. Besides looking great in her stylish outfit, she had her own apartment in a larger town, and a good modern job. I knew I shouldn't be, but I was envious.

As the twins' temporary fates were being decided, they sat in the kitchen munching their muffins, unaware of the possible changes happening to our little family. Although I felt rushed in making a decision, it did make sense and seemed a good short-term solution. I decided I'd try negotiating terms with Mr. Martin for the position.

Within a few days, changes were put in motion. Mr. Martin agreed to hire me at a rate of twenty-three dollars a month, after hard bargaining on my part. Considering he was offering room and board, he felt this was a substantial salary. But in reality, he was not truly offering that. I didn't have a room at all, but a sofa in the midst of the parlor, and the board would be prepared *by me* for the entire Martin family. His so-called 'generous wage' worked out to a dollar a day because I would need Saturday afternoons and Sundays off to visit my girls.

I went to the town library and studied up on TB treatment and spoke with Mrs. Martin's local doctor about her home-care. When my mother came over, she noticed I seemed distraught with indecision, hating that I was breaking up my family, unable to hold things together and believing, in my heart, Samuel would be disappointed.

Mother consoled me saying, "Mariah, you're doing the best you can. It's just for a little while. Honestly, it's happening all over the county right now; families being sent every which-way trying to survive. We're all helping each other."

"I suppose that's true."

"Certainly. You're rescuing the Martin family in their time of need. Catherine is helping you and getting to know her niece better, and it sounds like her friend, Nanette, is thrilled to have a little one to take care of. At least the twins are staying with friends and family we know. I'm certain, it'll all work out."

"But I only just met Nanette. She seems nice enough—"

"Catherine knows her well and I traded with her aunt for years at the fabric store. You remember Miss Edwina at *Superior Fabrics*? She up and passed away last year. Caught a bad case of the flu, bless her heart. That poor girl, Nanette, is all on her own. Jo might be a good distraction for her, and you know Jo's always been more comfortable around strangers."

"Maybe you're right, Ma. I hope so."

Later, I sat the girls down in the kitchen and announced the disruptions about to take place. "Jo, Sarah… we're about to start a new adventure. We'll be leaving the farm soon so Uncle Henry and his new wife can take care of things here."

"Why can't we all stay, Mommy?" Sarah asked.

"When a new couple starts out, they usually want a place of their own, and soon they may need your bedroom for their own children. Remember Mr. Martin? I'll be staying at their home for a while and helping his sick wife get better. But the good news is, while I'm there, Sarah will stay with Aunt Catherine at Grandma Gerta's house."

"What about me, Mama?" Jo asked, looking scared.

You're going to have fun too. Nanette, Catherine's friend, asked that you come stay with her for a while. She's so excited. And you get to travel on a train!"

"No Mommy, I don't want Jo to go." Sarah started to whimper.

I grabbed both of their hands and knelt before them. "Girls, these changes are only for a short while. We'll all be together soon, I promise. I'm still going to be your mother and I'll come to visit often. This is a good thing; be happy. And I have a job now so I can earn some money." I hugged them both tightly and whispered, "Don't be sad, girls. It'll be like having an even bigger family to live with."

I was sure Sarah would find a welcome spot in Catherine's room and Jo seemed anxious but excited to stay with the pretty blonde lady who had lavished her with attention. But I knew, as much as Sarah liked Catherine, she would hate the idea of not seeing me and Jo daily. Her twin was her touchstone, her best friend, her other half.

Since our car had been driven away by Henry a few days before, it was up to our trusted horses, Buck and Shorty, and our buckboard to take us off the farm and on to our new homes. Key pieces of our household were loaded onto the hand-me-down farm wagon: two trunks, a suitcase each for Jo and Sarah, my carved wooden rocker, Sam's precious radio, two boxes of dishes, three boxes of preserves from the pantry, and our kitchen table and four chairs. Everything else had to stay; we were out of wagon space, and Mr. Martin had secured only a small corner of the loft to store my packed items.

I circled the wagon out of the backyard, with the girls sitting on either side of me. It was a cold, bright morning in early March and the girls were bundled up, silent with worry. They watched our large orange cat curiously look out, then scratch his paws on the rough wooden barn door.

Jo turned, staring at the cat as it watched us leave. "Mama, does Uncle Henry like cats too?"

"I'm sure he does, sweetie." I tried to remain cheerful and upbeat about what was waiting for us. But I knew my voice sounded forced and cracked as my heart was breaking. When we pulled away, I looked back on the only home the girls had known; the house in which Sam and I had worked so hard to make our own.

## CHAPTER 28
## MARIAH

"Jo, are you excited? It'll be a fun adventure, staying at a new home where there are other kids to play with."

She nodded knowingly. "I know Mommy. You told me Miss Nanette is nice."

Sarah had tears in her eyes. "Who will I play with Mommy? Jo will be far away."

I squeezed her shoulder. "Your cousins are nearby. I'll take you on the weekends and Aunt Catherine promises to play with you and help with your reading. That will be fun."

I struggled to keep up my happy banter all the way to the station. Nanette was meeting us and then she and Jo were taking the train to Mankato. I didn't want Jo to see how upset I was. Fear and sadness were contagious, especially around children.

Sarah was unusually quiet during the ride. Jo was her constant companion, the sister who often did the talking for the two of them. Even at their young age, Sarah was methodical and contemplative, while Jo was livelier and more free-spirited.

They succeeded together as a unit. And now I hated the idea of separating them.

But it was too late. Decisions were made which all seemed logical only a few days ago. Once Jo stepped onto the train with the beautiful Nanette, Sarah began wailing, covering her face with her red mittens, while I tried holding back my own tears. Standing on the station platform, I waved to Jo and Nanette at their window. As the train pulled out, I captured a picture which still lingers in my mind: Jo's golden halo of hair and her little cherub face staring back at us, with her hand pressed against the disappearing window.

Back on the wagon, it was a quiet solemn ride to the Andersons, interrupted by sniffles from both Sarah and myself. Once there, I held Sarah's hand as I chatted briefly with Catherine at the Andersons' front door. Then it was time to let go. Three times in one day, I felt my heart tear apart bit by bit, as I pulled a clinging Sarah off my skirts. I knelt down, hugged her, dried her tears, and promised I'd see her soon.

Although her Grandmother Gerta was firm and dour, I knew Sarah would be treated strictly but fairly under Catherine's care. I would see her as often as I could and I knew Catherine's temperament and fondness for her niece would be a perfect environment for Sarah to continue to thrive.

I finished the final leg of the day's journey to the Martin farm. I'd spent so much time preparing for our departure and studying up on tuberculosis, that I hadn't given much thought to the realities of living in someone else's home, while caring for three rowdy boys without usurping their mother's place. This would be a serious trial of skills.

As I arrived in the yard, I heard the Martin boys' voices. They seemed to be enjoying a Saturday afternoon of play among the trees. Mr. Martin came out from the barn, insisting I call him Elliott, and yelled for his sons to climb out of the Elms growing along their property line. As they emerged, he introduced me to Seth, his oldest at ten, Eli, eight, and Tommy, six.

"Boys, Miss Mariah is here to help your mother get better. She'll also be keeping up the house and preparing meals, so you help her out and do whatever she asks. Understood?"

They nodded their heads, but the oldest, Seth, looked a little dubious. "You're going to make Ma get better?"

"Well, I'm going to make her more comfortable and try to build her strength back, but it's in God's hands. Only he can make her better." At this comment Seth rolled his eyes, understanding that I wasn't promising anything.

"Do you make apple pie?" Eli asked. "Been missing that."

"Now that I *can* do and I'll make rhubarb too. It might not be as good as your momma's but I'll ask for her recipes." The thought of hot apple pie seemed to break down their defenses a little.

Turning to his dad, Eli asked, "Can we start sleeping upstairs again? The basement is too cold."

"That may be awhile. I've explained to you boys, time and again; your mother's contagious. I don't want to take a risk with you getting sick."

I added, "I do have a big thick quilt you can use. Also, have you tried heating stones? I warm bricks over the stovetop before bedtime, then rub them over the sheets and place them at the foot of the bed. It does wonders keeping toes toasty."

"I want toasty toes," Tommy, the youngest, said as he wiped his runny nose with the back of his hand.

"OK boys, Miss Mariah is going inside to say hello to your Ma. Eli, we need to get the milking started soon. You and Tommy get the equipment set up. Seth, unhitch Miss Mariah's wagon and get her horses settled in the back stalls of the barn with fresh hay, oats, and water."

When negotiating terms, Elliott had agreed to house and feed my horses as long as he had use of them. I introduced

Buck and Shorty to the boys and explained they were strong, good-natured horses who had been with our family for the last five years. As I rubbed Buck's nose, I said, "Seth, just like me, these horses are in a new home and need to be settled in with a little patience." Seth nodded in agreement. As Elliott and I walked to the house, he assured me, "Seth's good with animals, really takes a shine to them."

Stepping inside, I saw the cleaning I'd done a week before had disappeared. "Rebecca's been looking forward to your arrival. You made a good impression on her. She insisted I hire you."

Walking into her room, Rebecca was again wrapped up in blankets in her bed but appeared to be shivering. I began explaining my plans for her care to both Elliott and Rebecca.

"I spoke with your doctor and he explained the best-care procedures for you. Beginning tomorrow, I'll be washing all your sheets, blankets and bed clothes, and then clean your room with bleach. That way it'll be safer for all of us to visit you. Also, I've made several facemasks I'd like everyone to wear when near you. They should help protect all of us from spreading the infection."

Studying up on it from a book in the library, I'd read TB was caused by an infection of the lungs, often affecting relatively young adults, and was spread through the air from droplets when an infected person coughed, sneezed, spit, or even laughed. Although there was no drug treatment, some patients' conditions improved with fresh air, exercise, good nutrition and rest. Fever, loss of appetite, and aching joints were also reactions to the disease. The less Rebecca ate, the weaker she became and the stronger her infection raged with fewer antibodies to fight the disease. I thought it best to feed her small amounts of food throughout the day. Both Rebecca and Elliott nodded along with my suggestions and seemed in agreement.

Coming downstairs, I decided a good wholesome meal was the quickest way I could ingratiate my way into the family. There was little food in the pantry, but I found two chicken legs and a wing on the cold shelf. From the root cellar I grabbed an onion, three potatoes, parsley, and a couple of old, limp carrots. Adding salt and pepper, they all simmered down to a wholesome hot soup, served with fresh baked bread and butter.

From what Elliott told me, this would be the first meal the boys had shared with Rebecca in several weeks. I found a beautiful patterned tablecloth in the chest in their dining room, cleared the messy table, and swept the room. Back upstairs, I helped Rebecca change from her nightgown into a clean sweater and skirt and asked Elliot to carry her downstairs. We all sat down together, masks in place. At first everyone felt awkward, with the boys complaining, but when their mother began whispering questions to them about friends, pets, and school lessons, all three started clamoring for a bit of her attention as the unusual face masks were quickly forgotten. Later, I fed Rebecca in the kitchen, while the Martin boys removed their masks and ate their dinner. Although there was no time to make apple pie that night, I promised the boys it would be on the menu soon.

Once the kitchen was cleaned, I set up my canvas cot, placing it in front of the dying embers of the fireplace in the parlor. I covered it with sheets, a slim pillow and a quilt I'd packed in my trunk. A second larger quilt, a special wedding gift from an aunt, I took down to the boys in the basement. All three were sleeping on a thin mattress placed on bouncing rusted springs.

Lying down after a long emotional day, I contemplated how, in just a few short months, my life had gone from sleeping in my own comfortable home, embraced by a loving husband, to now—attempting to sleep on a stiff cot, surrounded by illness and a family of strangers. I tried to tell myself to stick to my goals and remain strong. Tears ran down my face in the dark as my stamina subsided while sadness and loneliness raced in. It seemed my sorrow helped my sleep come quicker, as exhaustion from an emotional day rolled over me.

Sunday morning, right before dawn, I began the start of a busy day: cracking eggs, frying up a slab of bacon, and baking biscuits. After breakfast, Elliott and the boys headed into Green Tree for church. There were so many tasks I wanted to accomplish on my first full day, I decided to forego this week's sermon.

Before leaving, Elliott brought Rebecca downstairs while I went to work laundering every sheet, towel, blanket, garment, and handkerchief Rebecca had used. While those dried on the line, I cleaned her bedroom, mopping and disinfecting floors, walls, window sills, night stands and bedposts. Although sunny, it was quite cold outside. I kept the windows wide open, wanting to push out the heavy scent of pent-up illness that had harbored for weeks in the closed room.

Because the Martins had an electric radio in the dining room, run by their generator, I brought my battery radio upstairs for Rebecca. I hoped to reconnect her with the world. Rebecca looked like she was just wasting away, so isolated, losing her will to fight.

While sitting together on the porch, I tried to engage her. "So, what would you normally be planting in the garden now, Rebecca? I want to make sure I plant some of the boys' favorite vegetables."

In breathy whispers, she said, "They're not too picky. Hungry all the time. Snap peas, carrots, green beans. Mariah, remember… a well-tended garden can provide year-round."

"So true. My mother taught me the same."

~

WITHIN A FEW WEEKS, life on the Martin farm began to fall into a pattern. Although far from perfect, the three boys and Elliott began following my requests for hanging coats and hats in the mud room, removing work boots before entering the kitchen, and leaving all tools in the barn or appropriate sheds. After serving Elliott lunch, he would carry Rebecca down and she and I would sit on the porch. We'd sit together while I mended clothing, and darned socks. She was often quiet, staring straight ahead, looking down the long driveway. I felt a big break-through one day when Rebecca smiled at me and then laughed out loud.

"That has got to be Seth's socks. Look at those. There are more holes than sock there. I swear his feet are going to outpace his height if they keep growing."

"You're right; this one may not be worth mending. How are your hands, Rebecca? Strong enough to hold a needle? It'd be a big help if you could take care of this knee patch, while I get the fish prepared for dinner."

"I can try, Mariah. Surely, I can hold a little needle again."

SIX WEEKS LATER, I could see the fruits of my labor in the garden. Already, early green shoots were beginning to curl around bean polls. I'd planted lima beans, radishes, carrots, and potatoes, all planted in neatly tilled sections. On good days, I allowed myself about two hours of work in the garden. It felt therapeutic as I worked the rich cold clods of earth with hoe and trowel. Often, I would have Rebecca join me, sitting off to the side, asking her advice on techniques and seed choices.

My official day off was Sunday. On Saturday, I'd prepare two Sunday meals for the Martins and then in the afternoon, Elliott would drop me at the Anderson's farm to see Sarah and catch up with Catherine, her parents, and brothers. My in-laws were thankfully, now, treating me more civilly. Sarah and I occasionally stayed over in Catherine's room or Janeen would drive over, pick us up, and we'd squeeze in with my family for Saturday night, and then spend the day together attending church and having family dinner at my mother's comfortable kitchen table. I lived for my Saturday nights and Sundays, when I could be a mother to Sarah again for a few fleeting hours. But it would be three long months before we'd see Jo again.

## CHAPTER 29
## MARIAH

*S*arah was adapting to living with Sam's family, but it was not perfect. When separating at the end of most weekends, she clung to me, begging me not to leave, always asking when Jo was coming back. The answer of "maybe in a few months," sounded infinitely long for a child. Sarah seemed happiest at my parent's farm when she could play with Janeen's boys and sleep next to me on Saturday nights when we stayed over.

To keep in touch with Jo, I mailed at least two letters a week to her and Nanette, filling them in on my time with the Martins and activities with Sarah and Catherine. I received a few letters back from Nanette which included drawings from Jo.

∼

THREE MONTHS HAD FLOWN BY. I'd been saving all my wages, combined with my livestock sales earnings, in hopes of securing a future home. But I couldn't wait any longer to see Jo. In early June of '33, I used sixteen dollars of that hard-earned cash for round-trip train tickets to Mankato. Sarah and I sat in our seats, watching foot-high fields of corn, grazing cows, and neighboring towns flash past us in window-sized pictures. From the little communication I'd received from Nanette, it seemed all was going swimmingly for the two of them.

As gifts, I'd stitched together two stuffed fabric dolls. I'd given Sarah hers a month before. Jo's doll had yellow yarn hair and a pretty painted face, with a dress made from scraps of matching pinafores I'd sewn for the twins a few years before. Sarah was charged with carrying the doll, excited to give it to her sister.

As we pulled into the Mankato depot, we anxiously stared out the window. Waiting on the platform, I saw Nanette and Jo standing hand in hand, speaking animatedly. Jo's normally feathery light hair was arranged in bouncing blond ringlets. She was wearing new patent-leather buckled shoes and a robin's-egg blue coat. I hardly recognized her. Nanette's light waved hair was partially covered with a small brimmed black hat and a stylish swing jacket over her dress.

I felt embarrassed about my and Sarah's appearance. We were so excited about visiting Jo that I hadn't given Catharine any special wardrobe instructions for Sarah. She was wearing her denim overalls with a red plaid shirt underneath. This was perfectly acceptable farm attire, especially for boys, but it suddenly looked out of place in Mankato. I pulled my old black cardigan over the tired print dress I'd been wearing for the better part of the last two years. I shook off my feelings of inadequacy. I was here to bring my family together for two days and wouldn't allow any negativity clouding our brief visit.

Carrying one small overnight grip in my left and holding Sarah's hand on my right, I rushed down the aisle, excited to see my Jo. Nanette and Jo waved back as we approached.

Giving big hugs all around, Jo and Sarah immediately headed off in front of us, holding hands, deep in conversation.

"Well look at those two; thick as thieves," Nanette said.

"It's natural; they've spent every minute of their lives together until three months ago. They have some catching up to do."

"Of course, you're right. Mariah, I can't explain how great things have been going. Jo-Jo has been such a joy to have around. Always laughing, singing, and her *dancing*... I want her to show you the new steps she's learned. She's taking tap and loves it."

"Tap dancing lessons?"

"She's a natural, Mariah. I'm telling you."

"More than anything, I'm so relieved the transition has gone smoothly. But it has to be such a change, suddenly having a child to care for out of the blue. I know my move to the Martin farm has been difficult. Although each day has its little rewards."

"Mariah, I haven't regretted a minute. Sure, I've had to make some changes, but all worth it."

"But the expenses for lessons and new clothes? I don't know how I can repay you right away."

"Oh, don't mention it. I noticed Jo-Jo was growing out of her coat, but I found a great resale shop in town. It's amazing what people are selling for almost nothing these days. And don't even think about paying for the lessons. When Auntie Edwina passed, I inherited a little savings with the sale of her house and business. I always wanted to learn to dance but never did; now I'll get to do it through Jo-Jo."

We stopped at a small café adorned with blue print curtains hanging in the windows, white cloth table covers, and miniature vases of flowers on each table. It was the type of restaurant I would have peeked into longingly until my practical side would tell me I had perfectly good potatoes and soup waiting at home.

"I thought you might enjoy the food here and the desserts are the best! Jo-Jo and I come here for their cherry pie and ice cream."

As the waiter directed us to a table, I said, "Well, this is certainly a treat, girls, isn't it? We so rarely go out for dinner."

Again, I wished I'd least worn a stylish hat. I was looking like the country bumpkin in the city. The waiter brought wooden booster seats for the girls and menus for Nanette and me.

Sarah said, "I want cherry pie too, Mommy. Can I have that?"

Then Jo announced, "Me too Auntie, I want pie."

I looked up; surprised Jo was asking *Nanette's* permission. I jumped in and said, "Well, silly. That's for dessert. Let's see what's on the menu for dinner."

Nanette said, "I hope it's OK for her to call me Auntie. I just thought Miss Nanette sounded so formal." Then she turned to Jo saying, "Now Jo-Jo, you know you love the meat-loaf here. Why don't you try that again?"

"But Sarah and I want the same."

I set the menu down and said, "Actually girls, both the meatloaf or pot roast sound very good. We can each try both, how does that sound?" Then Nanette ordered roast chicken to go with her cherry pie order.

I definitely felt I should pay for the dinner and was quickly calculating in my head if I had enough money with me for the meals and a hotel room. "Nanette, I asked around and heard there's a small rooming house not too far from your street. I thought the girls and I would stay there tonight. Are you familiar with *The Atkinson* on Main?"

"Oh no, you will *not* be staying there. Heaven's no. My apartment has a Murphy bed in the living room. It's not the most comfortable, but it should do for the night. Let's all stay together. It'll be fun."

"Are you sure? I thought you might like a little time to yourself."

"Absolutely not. I'm getting so used to having Jo-Jo with me."

Pointing to my menu, Sarah said, "Look they have p-a-n-c-a-k-e-s and e-g-g-s. Just like at home, Mommy."

"Yes, Sarah, that's what they serve for breakfast, but excellent job on reading that! Jo, your sister has been working on her letters and starting to sound out words. How's your reading going?" Jo just shrugged her shoulders and looked at Nanette.

"Oh Mariah, there's plenty of time for that. She's so young. Barely five. We'll start working on all that after I get her enrolled in school next year."

"Next year?" I said shrilly, and then lowered my voice. "Nanette, I'm sure I'll find a way for the three of us to get back together by this fall. I appreciate, so much, all that you're doing, but my plan is to find housing as soon as I can."

"Of course, but you know how time flies. Fall will be here before you know it."

"True enough. First, I need to see how Rebecca Martin's health progresses. Unfortunately, from recent doctors' reports, it doesn't look good. I've been making tentative plans with lots of *what-ifs*. I'm trying to save enough for a down payment on a small house. With all the bank foreclosures, there are some real bargains out there; but to buy a house, I'll need a steady job nearby. Maybe a teacher's position, which requires a certification exam."

"Great ideas, but it sounds like all that's going to take some time. Please don't worry, Mariah; I'll take care of Jo-Jo in your absence. I promise."

"Thank you, bless you." I patted her hand realizing she was turning into a good friend that was asking little in return except to care for my child. But I worried their bond was already strong. How would it be six months from now? Perhaps the novelty would wear off and she would be more than relieved to turn her charge back to me in a few months.

By the time we finished dinner, it was getting dark and the girls looked tired. We walked several streets over to Nanette's apartment, stopping at a small corner grocer to buy a few items and a bouquet of fresh flowers which Nanette admitted was her weakness. "My Auntie always had pots of flowers around the house. They remind me of her."

As we got to her place, she stopped downstairs, introducing me to her landlady, Clarice. Nanette brought her a sack of groceries. "Clarice is the best. She takes care of Jo-Jo when I'm at work, and I pick up most of the groceries."

I shook Clarice's hand. "Great to meet you, and thanks for all you do."

"No trouble at all. That little Jo is a trooper. My kids love her."

Nanette's apartment was small, clean, and cheerful with a decidedly feminine touch, with colorful coordinating draperies and pillows. Sitting on a small table, I immediately noticed a large framed studio portrait of Jo and Nanette, smiling together. She showed us her small bathroom, which had a shower stall; something I'd never seen before. It took up much less space than a tub and Nanette had decorated the tiny room with pink accessories.

"Beautiful place you have here, Nanette. I'd love to find an apartment like this." Saying this, I was reminded of my stiff portable cot set up behind the sofa. Quite a contrast.

"Oh, thanks. It's small, but convenient. It's my sixth year living here. I can't believe how time has flown since I left Green Tree. Now, here's where you will sleep tonight." She opened a large closet door and pulled down a bed that sprung from the wall. "Before me, a family of five was living here and they used this as a second bedroom at night. It's pretty handy."

Jo announced, "Auntie, Sarah and I want to sleep here. Can we please?"

"Sure, if you don't mind, Mariah."

"Trust me, I've learned to sleep anywhere."

Jo went into the small bedroom and brought out a new store-bought doll with curly blond hair, a smiling porcelain face, complete with dimples, teeth, and blue eyes which opened and closed. "Here; now we both have dollies to sleep with tonight," as she handed the home-made one back to Sarah. "This is Millie."

Watching that exchange, I felt a little chunk of my heart break off. But could I really blame Jo? As a child, if I'd had to choose, I probably would have picked the doll with the life-like face and curly hair.

That night, I was delighted to take a hot shower, after months of sponge bathing at the Martins. They had a small tub in the basement, but it took so much effort to heat the water and bring it downstairs, I hadn't bothered. I'd insisted on dunking the three dirt-encrusted boys in the bath on Saturdays, but I'd made due with rinsing off in the sink, after the boys went to bed for the night. After a cold sponge bath, I'd daydream about my long, luxurious Friday evening baths back at our farm. Nanette's little shower was a pleasant alternative. I insisted Sarah join me while we shampooed our hair together.

Clean and with damp hair, Nanette showed me how she was tying up Jo's hair in rags each night to keep the curls in place. Apparently, it had become a nightly ritual for the two of them. After tying up Jo's, Nanette did the same for Sarah. Although Sarah's hair was board-straight, she was happy to be treated like her sister.

"Mariah, when Jo and I walk down the street together, I can't tell you how many people stop her and tell me she's a ringer for Shirley Temple, that new little movie star. Have you seen *Stand Up and Cheer*? Shirley's adorable."

"Sorry, I'm afraid I don't get to the movies anymore."

After the girls dozed off, Nanette and I continued to chat on the sofa, with music from Guy Lombardo's orchestra playing softly on the radio. She explained that her boss had promoted her after a few months at the photography studio. She was originally hired to handle appointments and billing, but she'd expanded into promotions, going out to all the schools within a few counties, signing up contracts for student portraits.

"Mariah, no matter how tough times get, parents are willing to plunk down a few dollars for their kids' student portraits. And I've come up with the cutest backdrops for their sittings. It's been fun. Then, I thought about going to all the area churches to set up contracts for family portraits. And from there we expanded to weddings. Our business just keeps growing."

Nanette's success and clever ideas got me hoping that I, too, might have a chance of making something more of my life. I needed to keep trying and hope I'd catch a break. Samuel had always told me that we make our own luck. Nanette was certainly a good example of that.

The next morning, we all attended Nanette's church. The girls sat quietly playing with their dolls as we sang and prayed in the pews. By midday, the sun had snuck out between the clouds and Nanette showed us a little green patch of playground with swings, a see-saw, and merry-go-round where the girls ran wild. Unfortunately, the day sped by and we had to leave by two o'clock to catch our train.

This had ended up being the best two days I'd had since Samuel's death, but the leaving was bittersweet. At the station platform, we all hugged and Sarah began crying. Jo's eyes were wide and moist, as she held back tears. But I had to keep dabbing at mine to keep my composure.

I gave Jo a final hug before embarking. "Darling, I'll try to come back soon or perhaps Auntie Nanette will bring you to visit within a month or two." Then turning to Nanette, I said, "I can't thank you enough for all you're doing for Jo. I appreciate you stepping up and helping. You've been so great."

"Oh, don't worry about anything. The pleasure is mine."

Jo insisted Sarah keep the doll with the yellow yarn hair that I'd made, telling her, "Sarah, don't cry. I have Millie, you keep Betsy for now. You can hold her on the train."

It was a difficult ride home. I knew I was lucky that both girls had comfortable places to stay with caring women to watch over them, but I still felt conflicted abandoning my kids to others for an uncertain length of time. Arriving at the Green Tree depot, Catherine picked us up at the station and dropped me off at the Martin farm. Walking through their back door, and hearing the clamor of the Martin boys, I had to ask myself how much longer I could handle this separation?

## CHAPTER 30
## MARIAH

*U*nfortunately for Rebecca Martin, the July doctor's report was not good. I was hoping to hear there was improvement. Regrettably, he reported that her most recent x-rays revealed her lungs were deteriorating and the infection was spreading to her kidneys. I prayed things would turn around, but perhaps it was too late. Our drive back to the farm was quiet that afternoon. I know we both felt defeated.

Later, after putting two chicken-pot-pies in the oven, I came out to the front porch to see little Tommy kneeling on the floor with his head in his mother's lap, as she stroked his silky dark hair, humming an old hymn. I quickly stepped back inside, allowing them their private moment together, knowing this time was precious.

On a warm July morning, with white horse-tail clouds skimming across a blue sky, I walked Rebecca out to the garden and helped her sit on a blanket nearby. I was weeding a few rows of rhubarb and then planned on harvesting some dangling robust tomatoes. Suddenly, Rebecca had a coughing spasm causing severe bleeding through her mouth and nose. I ran over, helping her lie down, hoping it might slow the bleeding while I tried to clean her up. I pulled off my head scarf, wiping her face, while holding her head gently. Rebecca was so light that she felt like a shadow of herself, almost as if she was disappearing as I held her.

Grasping my arm, she whispered, "It's time, Mariah. Get Elliott; call the boys."

"Surely not, Rebecca." Tears began welling up in my eyes. "You've been feeling so much better."

I leaned into her, listening as she whispered, "I thank you, Mariah. You've been a good friend. Please...find them now."

I felt conflicted. I hated leaving her by herself while I went out in the field to find Elliott. I wasn't sure what section he was working in. I ran into the barn, only seeing my horses look up at me. I knew Seth had taken the cows into a pasture for grazing. I ran in that direction and found him walking back to the barn.

I shouted out to him, "Seth, where are your brothers and father? Your mother needs you, *now*! Near the garden; it's bad."

Taking off on a run together, he said, "Dad left for town with Tommy and Eli a while ago. Shouldn't be gone too long."

I knew if I took the horses and wagon to look for them, it would probably be futile. There was a desperation and finality to Rebecca's voice that I hadn't heard before.

Out of breath, with tears rolling down my cheeks, I told him, "Seth, you need to be strong. Sit next to your mother and comfort her—she may be leaving us shortly—going to God. This is your chance to tell her everything you've wanted to say."

"But I'm not good with words."

"Say what's in your heart. Just your presence will be a gift."

Rushing over, we sat on either side of Rebecca while she still had breath in her body, each of us holding one of her hands. Seth told his mother he loved her, begging her to stay with him as his throat choked up.

"Ma, I want to show you how I'm handling the horses; Dad calls me a natural. I want you to walk with me again in the pasture… It's beautiful right now. There are so many things we still need to do." Seth wiped his rolling tears off with the back of his hand.

Rebecca smiled weakly, grabbed his hand and whispered, "You're a good boy, Seth…A wonderful son… You are loved."

I felt her life escape with each ragged gasp, until it simply disappeared, leaving her limp and quiet on the blanket. She died quickly in her garden, surrounded by soft clover and a few scattered dandelions on a summer morning, with her eldest son and a friend next to her. I reminded myself that when death suddenly approached this was more than many could hope for. In spite of this, I still felt overwhelmed with grief. Emotion raced through me as I stroked her premature gray hair, and her soft, ghostly pale skin. Such a waste and tragedy for one so young and needed.

Coming home an hour later, Elliott, Eli, and Tommy, went quietly up to her room where Seth and I had carried her. Little Tommy was the most distraught and cried for hours. Everyone moved around in a daze during that week. Even though Elliott understood the seriousness of her illness, I think he and the boys had hoped things were taking a turn for the better, after seeing Rebecca out of her room and walking a bit the last few months.

Her funeral was attended by many neighbors and members of their congregation. I joined the pew where the Andersons were seated, with Sarah next to me. After the funeral, Elliott, at least, had seemed to make peace with Rebecca's death. It had been a long and difficult illness. I was sad to lose a friend and companion. Death had surrounded me too much this year.

The following week, I bleached Rebecca's room and

washed all her clothing and bedding. Elliott asked me to store her clothing in a trunk up in the attic. I took a lantern with me, knowing the attic wasn't wired for electricity. The floor was cluttered with boxes, a couple pieces of broken furniture, a few old toys, and two trunks. As I filled the trunk with Rebecca's clothing, I looked at the garret with a curious appreciation. The room was vaulted in the center, with low eaves on both sides, but was actually fairly spacious, with enough room for two beds under each eave and space for a chair or two with a rug in the center. It needed better light but I knew a window could easily be cut in the back wall and wiring could be brought up from the second-floor for an overhead light. This could be the space I needed to bring my family together, *if* Elliott still felt he needed me and was willing to take on two more young children in his house.

After Rebecca's death, we had not yet discussed my future employment. It seemed too soon and the wound too raw, but I needed to start planning my next move if my services were no longer needed.

I normally served Elliott breakfast with the boys after his milking, just after sunrise, but the following day I was up well before dawn with his coffee black, flapjacks frying, and eggs sunny-side up.

"Well Mariah, I'd be lying if I said my cows got me up this morning. The smell of those flapjacks was just too enticing."

"Glad you joined me. I have a lot to do today; I'll be cleaning up the boys' room and moving their things back upstairs."

"Good, it's time to get the boys resettled. I've been thinking; maybe we can fix the basement up for Seth, let him create his own space away from his kid brothers. He's getting older now, and three boys in that one small room is a lot."

"Sure; he'll probably like that idea. And Elliott... I wanted to ask if you still needed me to stay on here a while longer?"

"Actually, been thinking about it these last few days and I truly hope you'll stay, Mariah. I think back to those days before March; this household was in chaos. I know the boys are really missing their mom and I think it comforts them when you're around. They need a woman's touch. If I haven't told you before, we appreciate all you've done for us—from cooking, to keeping the house. We want you to stay."

"Thanks. I'd like to, but I had an idea yesterday that I wanted to discuss with you. I miss my girls *so* much and really need us to be together soon. When I was in the attic yesterday, I noticed there's enough space up there for two beds and a few pieces of furniture. Maybe with a window cut out and some power brought up, I could stay there with my daughters. I know it's a lot to ask, but I just can't live here much longer without them. And I have to say, sleeping in the front parlor, on the cot with no privacy…let's just say it's getting difficult."

We were sitting across the kitchen table staring at each other, and I think my request caught him off-guard. He stopped talking and looked over at the oven, rubbing his unshaved chin with his hand.

"Hmm, so that would be two more kids in this household, little ones at that. I don't know… How would the girls fit in with three boys? And that would be two more mouths to feed, problems to solve, and an attic to refurbish. Let me think on this for a while."

In a pleading tone, I said, "Trust me, Elliott; they're young but very good girls. They already know how to help with chores. And, regarding the attic, I could probably get my sister's boyfriend, Billy-boy, to fix the wiring and cut a window. He's great with building things."

"Now before you start tearing holes in my house, I *said* let me think about it. Having you here is one thing, having two more little ones underfoot is a whole other matter."

"Elliott, please give it some thought. Let's talk tomorrow about this. I know we can make this work."

"I'm not sure about that." He finished his breakfast in silence. After I took his plate, Elliott got up, slammed the door, and walked to the barn. I realized I'd thrown a monkey-wrench into his plans, but too bad. I *had* to ask.

After our discussion, I was on edge all day hoping Elliott would agree to my plan. I'd already envisioned the attic with the changes I could make. I'd move my radio there and bring up my old rocker and table from the barn. Maybe I'd have Billy build a simple set of bookshelves under my window which I'd frame with fluttering white lace curtains.

Months ago, after my dinner invitation to the Thomas family and Arlene, Billy and my younger sister had started dating, and now saw each other every available evening, both seeming quite smitten. Besides being a friendly guy, Billy and his carpentry talents could become a handy asset. Perhaps, I could even have him build a dollhouse for the girls. Then I reminded myself to slow down. In my head, I'd already revamped the attic. But in reality, nothing was decided.

I knew I wanted to eventually leave the Martin farm, possibly going into teaching. But first I had to take a qualification exam for a teaching certificate in my spare time. Having graduated from high school with honors, and being a widow would help put me in good standing. The school district was now refusing to hire young married women thinking they might get pregnant; so, as ridiculous as it sounded, being a widow or a man was an advantage.

So far, I'd saved all my monthly earnings, except for the money spent on my Mankato trip. If I could continue to save for a year, I calculated my nest egg would be enough for a sizable deposit on a small house. Checking the newspaper, I'd seen some decent houses in the area selling for as little as two-thousand-dollars, but there were so many hoops to jump through. Each time I felt discouraged, I'd hear Samuel's positive voice in my ear, pushing me to set a goal and work toward it, reminding me I'd eventually get there.

Seven months after his death, I still thought of Sam daily, especially at night. His motivation was something I'd cling to when exhausted after cooking and scrubbing the third cycle of dishes. I'd be hanging laundry on the line outdoors, and my heart would dance as I saw a tall lanky man in overalls come out of the barn walking toward me, only to realize it was Elliott, not Samuel. At night, though, I'd let Sam come to me completely. On my narrow cot, I'd lie on my side and imagine his strong, slender body right beside me, touching me, bringing his arm around my waist and pulling me next to him, whispering in my ear, *"It's going to be alright."*

I would think: What about Jo? She's so far away and Sarah begs to stay with me each time I see her."

*"You're doing all you can. You'll get there soon enough."*

I pulled him closer, feeling the heat of his body, comforted by his words. For now, this was enough to get me through another day.

The morning sun was well up in the eastern sky when I awoke. I jumped up abruptly, having never slept this late at the Martin's. Everybody would be up and nobody had been fed. What a terrible impression I was making after begging for more space for my daughters. Grabbing from my bag I kept behind the sofa, I pulled a brush through my hair and twisted my locks up in a bun. I ran through the kitchen and used the outdoor privy, then threw some water on my face from the pail at the kitchen sink. Glancing around, I noticed a few slices of yesterday's sour-dough loaf had been cut off and the butter and jam were sitting out on the table. It appeared they'd each had one crusty piece of bread. I started the coffee, poured up the last bottle of milk, and made a pot of oatmeal. I knew Elliott and the boys would soon come in hungry from their early morning work. Perhaps Elliott thought I was on strike until my demands were met. Of all days to oversleep!

I went out to the yard and saw little Tommy sitting on the fence which enclosed the swine. When I approached, he was crying. I patted his back and asked, "Tommy, what's wrong?"

He pointed down to the muddy ground, where a small piglet was dead, presumably crushed by the crowd of feeding piglets lying by their mother. It occasionally happened with runts of the litter. Through his tears, he asked, "Miss Mariah, why do things have to die? He was my new favorite."

"Accidents happen, Tommy. Life is far from fair. Sometimes the littlest ones get pushed aside, but occasionally they become the smartest and strongest in the end. Shall we bury him? Come along and help."

He nodded his head and I went into the garden shed and retrieved a spade and an old flour sack which we wrapped the piglet in. Tommy followed me to the side of the garden, where we shoveled the soft black earth, put the piglet in the hole, and covered him.

"You know Tommy, with lots of livestock and pets around here, you'll see more deaths over the years. It's a part of the cycle; this little pig can eventually make the soil richer. Livestock is raised for food. Most are killed eventually. It gets easier with time."

I hugged the little boy as his tears poured out. He had already suffered a great loss and I knew the tears were an extension of his grief over Rebecca's death.

"I'm the littlest here. Do you think I'll die soon?"

"Of course not, Tommy. A smart, strong boy like you? Certainly not, although some of us leave this earth earlier than others; but I know you'll be around for a long time."

As he wiped his tears again, I said, "Tommy, your mother loved you *so* much. She was so proud to see you finish first grade."

"Really?"

"Absolutely. Rebecca was proud of you and your brothers. She loved having you read your primer to her. You know, in the afternoons, when you'd come rushing through the door after school? That was her favorite moment. You were so special to her."

"Do you think some boy in heaven will read to her?"

"Probably. Tommy, I know you only had your mother a short while, but she'll be watching over you and sometimes, if you're really quiet at night, she may talk to you and give you advice. She'll always be with you. Just listen carefully."

Dusting off his hands from the garden soil, he said, "OK. But don't tell Seth and Eli."

"Sure, it'll be our secret."

"And don't say I was crying about the pig. They already call me a cry-baby."

"Won't say a word. Hey, I know you must be hungry. Breakfast is ready. Where are your brothers and dad?"

"Dad's walking the oat field this morning, Seth's in the pasture, and Eli's in the hen house. I'm supposed to be helping him."

"Let's get them now and we'll all have breakfast together."

Within thirty minutes, everyone re-gathered at the table for a meal. I apologized for sleeping in and nobody seemed to mind once they were munching more toast and jam, oatmeal, and sliced melon. After breakfast, the boys went to baseball practice and Elliott stayed for a second cup of coffee and cleared his throat.

"Mariah, I've been thinking about your attic idea and I've got a proposition for you." I became excited; he had actually considered my request. "I think we should start with *one* of your girls staying here and then see how it goes."

Angrily, I rapped on the table abruptly. "Only one? How can I choose, Elliott? Don't make me do that."

"Look Mariah, I'm up to my eyeballs in debt with the new tractor I bought last year and Rebecca's funeral. I simply cannot take on too many expenses right now. Let's take it one step at a time. Remember, I wasn't planning on having *any* extra children here."

"I understand, but this separation from both girls is extremely difficult. What about the attic space? Can I convert that?"

"I don't see why not. I'll help pay for the wiring and window for the attic, but I say we go fifty-fifty on that. I can take it out of your wages if you don't have the cash."

I was disappointed. His proposal was an offering of a glass half-full, but it *was* something.

"You're right, Elliott; it's not what I was hoping for, but I appreciate the offer. It's just so difficult to choose who to bring over." I considered for a few seconds, then said, "Maybe Sarah? There're no other children for her to play with at the Anderson farm, while Jo and Nanette are doing so well together in Mankato."

"Makes sense. And hey, maybe by late fall things will turn around. Everybody is saying President Roosevelt is the man to do it. Making lots of policy changes. Who knows? We'll take this one step at a time. Start with moving Sarah here."

I stood up from the kitchen table and began picking up breakfast dishes. "All right, Elliott. Thanks. I'll speak to Billy-boy and see what kind of price he would charge for the attic changes. I don't think it'll be all that much."

"Good, because *not much* is all I seem to have. And damn, I was actually thinking of adding indoor plumbing for a new bathroom, but that'll have to wait. Every winter, once it gets near zero, I make a morning run to the privy telling myself, I'm adding that dang bathroom." Elliott breathed out a deep sigh and added, "We'll see…maybe next year."

"I'd certainly be on board for that and willing to help build it. Sam and I laid and fitted every pipe and plank ourselves. Actually, I still owe money for supplies from the hardware store for that bathroom. Sixty-five dollars. I hate having an account way past due."

"Isn't Henry over there now? He should take over the payments. He's enjoying the fruits of your labor."

"He was supposed to take over the account when I gave him two breeder hogs, but I found out recently he hasn't made any payments. But I hate to make waves. I've already upset the Anderson family enough."

"Doing what? That barn fire was no fault of yours. Henry and his wife will enjoy that bathroom far longer than you ever did. I'll speak with him about it next time I see him. We've been friends for years."

I was thankful for his generosity of spirit on this issue, at least. "Thank you, Elliott. That would ease my mind considerably."

That evening, I laid down on my cot as the boys listened to *The Lone Ranger* on the radio in the next room. My glass-half-empty attitude was turning around. I was happy that Sarah could join me. She seemed the most emotionally vulnerable at this point, and would benefit by coming here. I explained all of this in my head to Sam.

Also, the prospect of creating our own special place in the house was exciting. I would finally be able to regain some privacy. Knowing Sarah's shyness, bringing her into the house with three rambunctious boys might be difficult at first, but she would acclimate. She was a quiet, polite child and shouldn't rankle Elliott's temper too much.

Then, getting Jo moved here was my next big goal. "*Yes, Sam, I remember. One step at a time.*"

# CHAPTER 31
# NANETTE

$\mathscr{I}$ wanted to close the studio quickly before Phil Greenly finished in the dark room. I'd totaled the day's receipts, counted the cash drawer, and wiped down the photo sets. I was tired of his mutterings of undying love, sideling over to me, begging for a kiss and embracing me once the doors were locked. He'd had plenty of opportunities to make our long-running affair legal, but up until now, all he'd offered were four years of tired excuses. For me, it was definitely over.

I admit, initially, my clandestine relationship with Phil, along with my career at his photo studio, was exciting. The sex was good and the work was challenging. Together, we had become an integral team building his studio's business. We were the perfect combination in that regard. But, for years, Phil had promised me he was leaving Gwen, his boring nag of a wife. Unfortunately, there was always some excuse about bad timing. First, it was not a good time because Gwen's father had recently passed. Later Phil said we should wait until his son was doing better in school. Then, his mother-in-law had moved, and where would Gwen go if he left her? Every six months there was always some ridiculous justification.

I was done; the attraction was over. I could certainly do better than Phil Greenly, for heaven's sake. I was only sorry I'd wasted my prime years on him waiting for his divorce and our marriage. I was now twenty-six, almost spinster material!

Phil hired me the first day I came in with Obidiah Dawson, helping carry in his new photo equipment. I told him I was interested in photography and mentioned I was thinking of leaving my position at the Mankato theater. I remember telling him, "I've always wanted to work in a photo studio. It must be fascinating, Mr. Greenly. And looking around here, I see the potential for a great business."

Phil looked at me with interest. "What do you mean by potential? I do pretty good here. I get by."

"But who really wants to only get by, Mr. Greenly? Hire me and we'll do so much more together." As he stepped closer, misconstruing my intentions, I immediately suggested ideas about sprucing up the shop's image with signage and exciting window displays. After discussing several ways I could earn my keep as his full-time assistant, Phil hired me, caving in quite quickly.

Initially, I'd had no attraction to Phil, with his receding hairline, thinly budding mustache and thick eye glasses. Just not my type. But he was pleasant and eager to make improvements in the business and we became an effective team. But eventually, sexual attraction snuck its way into the mix and muddied things up. After he'd made a few meek but obvious advances, I thought long and hard about how I could improve my standing in the community by being married to a successful business owner. Unfortunately, all that had never materialized and I was tired of waiting.

I called out through the closed darkroom door, "Phil, I'm leaving. The books are finished. Have a good evening."

Through the closed door, I heard, "Nanette, wait just a moment. I need to speak privately with you."

"Sorry, I have to leave now. Jo-Jo has dance lessons." I turned to go, wanting to dash out before he could emerge from the darkroom. I flipped the closed sign, turned the key in the lock, and then waved as I saw him rush up to the front. He simply could not comprehend the meaning of: It's over!

Imagine, allowing myself so many intimate moments with him in the back, while inhaling the sour chemical scent of developing fluid. The thought now turned my stomach as I hustled home across the downtown sidewalks. I could never develop another photo again without thinking of Phil Greenly's hot breath on me, steaming up his eyeglasses.

I walked past the recently opened JCPenney department store, admiring the new fall coats in their store window. Perhaps I should splurge this year? But who was here to admire and appreciate something fashionable? Nobody of note. I laughed to myself, remembering when I first arrived in Mankato; the town had seemed such a big step up from Green Tree. But now it felt small.

I dashed into the corner market, swinging the screen door behind me, inhaling the scents of saw dust on the floor and freshly baked bread. I offered a friendly greeting to crabby store owner, Elsa Brown, as I grabbed a few items for myself and Clarice.

"Evening, Elsa. How is your day going?"

"Same as any other, I suppose. Did you bring your bottles for a deposit return? I'm not discounting unless you bring the milk bottles."

"No, just these items today. Thank you." My goodness, she was an unhappy person. I then rushed home, knowing Jo-Jo would be waiting, excited to see me with a smile on her face. How precious that little girl had become to me. And me to her. Like two peas in a pod, and I rarely corrected people anymore when they remarked, "Well, your daughter is just the spitting image of you, isn't she?" We had the same light hair, light eyes, and long legs. Jo-Jo seemed nothing like Mariah, who was pretty enough in her own simple way, but honestly kind of boring. And those pathetic clothes of hers! I'd often asked myself what Sam Anderson had seen in Mariah. I certainly couldn't see it.

Knocking at Clarice's door, I smiled as Jo-Jo opened it. "Hello there, baby girl; let's have a hug from my angel."

"Hi, Auntie." She then took my hand and said, "Let's go. Dance class tonight. Hurry."

I put Clarice's groceries on her counter and yelled out, "We're leaving, Clarice. Milk, bread and apples are in the kitchen."

I heard her yell, "Thanks, doll," through a bedroom door, as I checked my mailbox, and then followed Jo-Jo upstairs. There were two bills and another letter from Mariah. My Lord, did that woman have nothing to do except write us letters? And they were always so dull.

"Jo-Jo, put on your rehearsal clothes and I'll heat up some soup for supper." As I waited for the canned chicken noodle soup to boil, I scanned Mariah's letter for anything interesting. Seemingly more of the same drivel: *exploits of the Martin boys, Sarah's amazing reading talents, news about Catherine Anderson...* Now here was something different... *Mariah was having Sarah move in with her at the Martin place. Mariah had cleared an attic room, and Jo might be able to join them in a few months!* Of course, she'd often said similar things like this in her letters, but this time it sounded like it might really happen.

As precious Jo-Jo came out of the bedroom, dressed in her leotard and shorts, carrying her shiny tap shoes, my heart gave a lurch. It was too soon for her to leave me. I couldn't let this happen. We were like mother and daughter. Mariah had no idea how talented and vibrant her daughter was. She'd never know how to develop Jo-Jo's full potential. My heart and brain began to panic, sending quick palpitations through my body, as I overheated. I opened the window and drank a glass of water, trying to calm myself. A few minutes later, we sat down to a simple meal of soup, crackers, and fruit, but I could hardly bring myself to eat as worry set in.

When I'd offered to care for Mariah's daughter, I never imagined the bond Jo-Jo and I would develop. It was as if she was the embodiment of the child I'd lost with my abortion years ago. Had I continued with my pregnancy, the child would have been just a few years older than Jo-Jo was now.

Throughout the night, concerns continued to roll through my mind; by the next morning, I put a plan in motion. For years, I'd wanted the chance to catch the eye of a famous Hollywood talent agent, but I realized the time for that had probably passed me by, but it wasn't too late for my little protégé. I was confident Jo-Jo had the goods in the talent department, a triple-threat singer, dancer and perhaps actor? Besides, with the huge growing popularity of Shirley Temple, every movie mogul must be hunting for another shining child-star that would be a bankable box-office bonanza—at least that's what my *Silver Screen* magazine was reporting.

I arrived at the studio early while Phil was out shooting class photos at a near-by elementary school. I printed up ten copies of Jo-Jo's latest photo which I'd taken after her dance recital. She was adorable, wearing her sequined tuxedo jacket, tights, top-hat and a cane. Earlier, I'd checked classified ads in a back copy of my subscription to the *Hollywood Reporter*. I'd seen the listings of several talent agents seeking child actors and entertainers. That morning, I mailed ten agents a copy of Jo-Jo's picture with her list of talents. Now, I had to sit back, be patient, and hope one of them would call me and want to sign her.

A few weeks later I got a call from an agent. I remembered

his ad: *Talent Agent, James Diamond…your shining connection to stardom*! *Represents adults, children, and dogs.* Luckily, Phil was in the darkroom when I received Mr. Diamond's call. I didn't want him, or anyone else, knowing my plans.

"Nanette Jorgenson? James Diamond here; but you can call me Jim. So good to speak with you. I don't usually encourage out-of-state clients, but I got a real feel for your little girl here, Jo-Jo…Love the photo, by the way. Seems spunky, bright, really swell."

"I'm excited to receive your call. Jo-Jo is all that and more, Mr. Diamond."

"Let's see… I'm reading her bio here. Tap-dances, sings, can memorize lines, cute as a button. She's got the goods, Mrs. Jorgenson. Believe you me, I can read a lot from a photo. How soon can you two get to Hollywood?"

I was over the moon, but tried to tamp down my emotions, trying not to sound too excited. "Well, we should be able to come soon. Now, what kind of cash guarantee would I have with you, Mr. Diamond?"

"That's not the way it works, ma'am. I can try and get her in to see casting agents for parts, but there's never a guarantee. I make fifteen percent on anything your girl earns. Trust me though, I know everybody in the business. I'll get your girl in front of the camera, one way or another. Decide on a date and time and I'll meet you at the Los Angeles train station and get you two set up. What do you say, Nanette? James Diamond, your connection to stardom… at your service."

He was a fast talker, perhaps over-promising, but sometimes you had to take a leap of faith. "I believe I'll say *yes*, Mr. Diamond. I've got a real jewel of a little girl to add to your client roster. Can't wait for you to meet her in person! Uh, you reached me at my work number, but it's best not to contact me here. I'll call you later with our travel details."

After hanging up, I stood stock still, not believing our luck. Was this really happening? Could I finally move to Hollywood and start my life over? I'd dreamed of this day but never believed it would happen. It had always been my fantasy, but did I possess the courage to make it a reality? True, nothing was guaranteed for Jo-Jo, but at least we had a path to follow, someone to show us the ropes. She had the talent. I had the drive and imagination. By God, we'd be unstoppable.

THROUGH THE NEXT FEW WEEKS, it was difficult keeping my mind on anything but the big move. I knew everything had to be done in absolute secrecy without revealing my plans to anyone. Jo-Jo and I would have to simply disappear. I would be leaving Phil, my former lover and business partner. Clarice, my good friend and landlady, would be hard to leave behind. I'd developed strong friendships and relationships throughout Mankato. Even my old gang in Green Tree, especially Catherine Anderson, could *not* be made aware of my plans. I needed to find the courage to throw all of my past out the window. I could no longer look back, only forward. This was a huge step.

Another wrinkle; spending habits. I'd always been more of a spender than a saver. It was quite an eye opener when I checked prices for coach-class tickets and sleeping berths from Mankato to Chicago, and then on to Los Angeles. I cleaned out my banking account, paying one-hundred-and-sixty-dollars for the two of us, plus extras such as food and tips for porters. That left me with a hundred dollars remaining to get us settled. Beyond that, we'd be relying on blind luck. It was a bold step, but it was a move I felt compelled to make. It was really all for Jo-Jo, for her development, for her future, and to keep us together. That, I knew, was essential. If Jo-Jo went back to live at the Martin farm, her talents would be wasted on picking eggs and weeding the garden. My girl had the possibility of an amazing future and I needed to help guide her through those shiny golden doors.

# CHAPTER 32
# MARIAH

*M*y mind eased considerably when Elliott allowed me to bring Sarah to his farm. Her move brought me one step closer to having my little family back. After seeing how easily Sarah fit in with the household, I figured that within another month, Elliott would also agree to let me bring in Jo.

Sarah and I loved our refurbished attic. Billy-boy helped me install a large window, in addition to painting and extending the wiring one floor up for electricity. While painting, he kept asking me all kinds of questions about Arlene. It was obvious he was crazy about her, or perhaps in love.

Our new window was on the south wall which looked over the vegetable garden and the extended green fields of the Martin farm. The first morning Sarah stayed with me, she dragged a footstool over to the window and stared down, watching all the activity of the farm, and studying Elliott's three sons.

"Mommy, it's pretty here. I can see everything; like being up in the sky." From that point on, I no longer referred to it as the attic, usually reserved for servants and old discards. Instead, we told everyone we were living in the *sky room*. Much more elegant.

I brought over my radio, kitchen table and chairs, and placed my rocker between the two twin beds under the eaves. Between the furniture I'd stored in Elliott's loft and the bed frames and mattresses I'd picked up at a second-hand store, I finally felt like I had a home for the first time in months and I relished it, feeling Sam's presence as I rocked in the evening listening to music coming from his precious radio.

It took a few weeks before Sarah overcame her shyness with the Martins, but eventually the youngest son, Tommy, became her protector and closest friend, as they shared chores together. They bonded, gathering eggs, feeding the chickens, and sweeping out the coop. I also convinced the teacher at the rural school to allow Sarah to start classes, once I explained her early reading talents. It made Sarah so happy to attend school with Tommy each weekday, almost like being part of their family.

One dark, humid morning as I prepared breakfast, Elliott came in with a smile on his face. This was unusual. He wasn't the happiest of men. "There's rain in the air. I can taste it and feel it. It's gonna be a big one."

I sniffed the air. "You're right. I feel it too. Something to tamp down this blowing dust, and hopefully enough moisture to get us through harvest. What day is the harvesting machine scheduled?"

"Next Wednesday. Should be a good haul," he said. "Too bad the corn price is hardly worth the effort. But there's talk of crop subsidies coming. Let's see if Roosevelt gets it all sorted out".

"Can't be worse than Hoover. He did nothing."

I thought about all the recent after-church chatter. Hopefully a long drenching shower would subdue all the worry about lack of rain. The drought had already plagued states west and south of us. Our winter snowpack always helped, but this past winter the snowfall was lighter. Clouds of blowing brown dust from eroded soil and abandoned farms in the west had already hit areas in Iowa just south of us. The newspaper was filled with stories of the sky turning dark mid-day as a thick blanket of fine earth blew across, seeping through cracks and crevices of homes and barns, creating havoc with the health of livestock and people. We'd had a few days of it, but nothing as relentless as some lower states.

After rinsing dishes, I stood out on the front porch watching the churning black clouds bearing down. Then, fat large drops began plopping on the front steps; often these big ones would quickly peter out, and the storm would blow over. But within a few minutes, the juicy drops formed into a sheet of rain, quickly saturating the ground in front of the porch.

I called into the kitchen, "Elliott, it's coming on strong."

He stepped out, standing next to me, grinning. I could tell he wanted to stand out in the yard and jump in the puddles for joy, just like I could imagine Sam doing. But instead, he grabbed his oiled coat and said, "Best get on with the milking."

The following Saturday, after a successful harvest, Elliot popped into the kitchen in the afternoon with a surprise request. "Mariah, why don't you and I head into town this evening and try out the pork chops at the new *Comfort Café*? My treat."

"Sounds wonderful. What's the occasion?"

"It's time you went somewhere besides church and the grocers. Lots of the men have been talking up the food at the new place. Seth can watch the kids for a couple hours. Besides, it's Saturday. They'll all be listening to *The Lone Ranger*."

"I'd love to, thanks." This was highly unusual because neither of us ever spent money on outside food. I looked down at my spotted apron, my dowdy print house dress and wished, again, that I had better clothes. "Just give me a little while to get dressed."

"Sure. It's nothing fancy; take your time. Maybe I'll even get out of these overalls."

I put on my navy church dress, and made a promise to myself to take the time to sew a few dresses for me and the girls this fall. Elliott came downstairs dressed in a white shirt, brown trousers and a neck tie I'd never seen.

"Well, look at you Mr. Martin. Looking mighty spiffy tonight. Love that tie."

"You do? Had it for years but never wore it."

The kids were fed; I put Seth in charge and everybody, except Seth, was on a strict bed-time curfew for 8:30. I was pleased to be going somewhere… anywhere. Life on the Martin farm was always busy, but also isolating. I hadn't been to a restaurant since my trip to Mankato last June. At times, Elliott, prickly and silent as he was prone to be, was almost a friend, not just my employer. We had so many shared responsibilities. I was hoping, during dinner, that he'd announce that Jo could move in.

After parking, we took a leisurely stroll down the busiest section of Main Street, checking out window displays. Although many stores were closed for the evening, the sidewalk was busy with people going to the pool hall, the V.F.W. bar, and the two restaurants.

Arriving at the café, Ellott and I waited several minutes for a table. Apparently, word was out about the new restaurant and every table was occupied; surprising for a community of tight-fisted farmers during a terrible economy. The heavy rain must have cast a spell on them. But Elliott assured me the prices were low and the portions plentiful. Between the two of us, we knew about half the people in the restaurant. We stopped and chatted with many on the way to our table situated next to the window.

As I sat down, Elliott was waylaid by a neighbor who wanted to discuss the merits of the latest gasoline-powered tractor. Waiting alone at our table, I noticed my old neighbors, David Thomas and his parents pass by outside. I knocked on the window and waved, as they came in. The Thomas crew came over and Eleanor reached down, giving me a quick hug.

"We've missed seeing you, Mariah. How are you and the twins doing? It's been months."

"I'm good. Been attending the Lutheran church in town lately. Elliott drops me off while his family attends the Methodist service. It's easier that way. And Sarah lives with me now at the Martin farm, but Jo is still with a friend in Mankato. Hopefully we'll all be together soon."

In his soft quiet voice, David looked down at me and said, "I sure hope so. Hate to see the three of you separated. Mariah, would you care to join us for dinner?"

Just then, Elliott walked up as I explained that he and I were eating together. David looked embarrassed, mumbled something, and walked back to the door to wait with his parents, as Elliott sat down.

We shared a good meal of green vegetables, mashed potatoes with gravy, and I tried the fried chicken while Elliott sampled the pork chops. We split a generous slice of chocolate cake with ice cream, as I anticipated some sort of discussion regarding Jo. But Elliott continued speaking about machinery needing repair, a new type of feed he was looking into, and which farm had the biggest harvest. I was up to my eyeballs in farm talk. I wanted to discuss my family, new songs on the radio, the latest movies, politics, even the boy's homework, anything... besides farming headaches. But we didn't.

As we strolled down the other side of Main Street, walking past the courthouse, bank, and crowded pool hall, I decided to broach the subject. "Elliott, hate to bring this up again, but have you considered allowing Jo to move into the sky room with Sarah and me. As you've seen, Sarah is no problem..."

"Mariah, I told you already, I need time to *think* about it.

Don't push me on this. Sarah just recently arrived. I'm not ready for one more child in the house. There's some commodity bail-outs coming. I need to see how things will go."

I'd had enough excuses and blurted out my frustration. "Sarah's been here two months, Elliott. What do politics have to do with adding one small child to my little room upstairs? Jo is no longer a baby. She's five, very verbal and so helpful. She'd be a nice addition to the household, and honestly, *all* the kids have been *my* responsibility." As my anger built, my voice became shrill. "I take care of the feeding, cleaning, mending, drying tears, breaking up fights, and checking homework. Elliott.… *please*?"

I knew I'd said too much. Elliott could be pleasant but was also strong-willed and didn't like his opinion questioned. He stared at me with a scowl across his face, and then simply shut down. We drove back to the farm in a chilled silence. This evening's unusual dinner request may have been a trial run, as Elliott considered me as future wife material. Well, I'd squashed that idea. I didn't care. I had *no* romantic interest in Elliott Martin.

Returning to the farm, I curtly thanked him for the dinner and walked into the house. I then looked in on the younger boys in their bedroom, and climbed the steep stairs to the attic. Following behind, he said nothing, slamming the door to his room.

## CHAPTER 33
## NANETTE

*T*he following morning, Jo and I knocked on the door downstairs and Clarice swung it open and announced, "Hi ladies. Jo-Jo, the kids are playing out back already."

As Jo-Jo ran out the back to join them, I mentioned, "Big news. A cousin from Chicago has invited us to visit her. I'm taking two weeks off for our trip. It's coming up next week and I'm so excited. Never been to a really big city before. Have you?"

"Lucky girl and no, I've never been. So, no need of me babysitting for those two weeks then?"

"That's right. I'll send a postcard though. Keep you updated on our shenanigans."

"Alright, and make sure to bring me back something delicious. Maybe chocolate?"

"Best remind me before we leave. Gotta go. I'm running late for work. I'll see you this evening, Clarice."

When planning our disappearance, I only wanted to tell Clarice that we were taking a trip to Chicago. Later, I would mail a letter, letting her know I decided to move there permanently for a better job. I wanted to eliminate any questions asked before we left and not leave any trail leading to Hollywood. I did feel a little down though, knowing I'd miss her friendship, advice, and my apartment.

For Phil, I said the same thing. I hated leaving all the studio business on his shoulders, after all we'd built together, but there were a lot of people in Mankato looking for work. He'd find somebody. Without me as a distraction, Phil could mentally go back to his family and live a less complicated life. It was all for the best.

Jo-Jo also understood we were going on a trip, but I planned on telling her our actual plan once we were on the train. For our journey, I sewed myself a light-weight robin's-egg-blue coat which matched Jo-Jo's coat perfectly. I bought a new angled hat with a feather that looked rather fetching, and a large blue bow for Jo-Jo's hair. Before departure, I was admiring our travel costumes in the mirror.

As I tweaked her hair bow, I reminded her, "Don't forget darling, if you want a good life, you always have to look good. My dear auntie always told me that. It's quite important."

"Do I look good?"

"Yes, absolutely adorable, although that coat is already getting a little short for you."

I still had the three suitcases I'd brought to Mankato six years ago. But now, I had so much more, including all of Jo-Jo's things. I purchased a large trunk and asked my friend, Obidiah Dawson, to take us to the train station to begin our four-day journey. It was only fitting that the man who had picked me up and introduced me to Mankato should be the one to help me make my exit.

The day of our trip, Jo-Jo and I climbed up on the springy seat of his horse-drawn wagon and looked over the downtown streets we were leaving. On the station platform, I hugged Mr.

Dawson and got unexpectedly emotional for all I was leaving behind.

"Mr. Dawson, thanks so much. You're a true good friend."

He patted my back saying, "No need for the misty eyes, Nanette. It's only a little vacation. We'll see each other soon enough. You and your girl go have a big time in Chicago. Went there myself about fifteen years ago and had the best hot dog and beer a man can buy."

"You hear that Jo-Jo? Wonderful restaurants there!" Jo-Jo simply smiled up at Mr. Dawson.

"Well, I best be going. Got cases of tomatoes to pick up. Be careful now; that's a big city you're heading to. Stick to the main streets downtown." He handed down our suitcases and trunk. "Great God, why so much luggage, Nanette?"

"Oh, I'm bringing a lot of old clothes to a cousin we're visiting. Mr. Dawson, thanks again for everything."

After having a porter stow our luggage, I located our coach-class seats, putting Jo-Jo next to the window. After we pulled out of Mankato, I decided to explain my plan to her. "Jo-Jo, do you remember your first train trip last March? When we came here from Green Tree?"

"Yes… I remember looking out the window. Sarah had on red mittens and my mother and Sarah cried as our train left; I remember because Sarah was holding up the mittens hiding her face." Jo-Jo turned her face to the window and wiped away a tear. "Look, there's a pretty horse and lots of cows in that field."

I grasped her little hand and squeezed it tight. "Jo, there's something I want to talk to you about. I hope you'll understand and think it's for the best. It's probably time you called me *Mother*, instead of *Auntie*."

Turning her head away from the window, she looked at me curiously and asked, "Why?"

"You remember when your father passed away in the fire?"

She nodded and said, "It smelled very bad that night and Mommy cried for a long time."

"That's right. Well, Mariah's had a difficult time trying to find a new home and job. She makes very little money and can only afford to keep one child with her. She chose Sarah, because you and I are doing so well together. And she knows I wanted a little girl just like you to take care of. Your mom asked me to become your *permanent* mother. She's been busy working on another farm, serving another man's family and doesn't have time for two girls. But I want to care for you and want you to stay with me *always*. Would you like that Jo-Jo? Would you like me to be your mother?"

Jo-Jo had a scared and confused look on her face with tears running down her cheeks. "She wants Sarah but not me?"

"Well, let's say things have been quite difficult. She knows I can provide for you. I'll always be there to protect and love you. And never send you away."

She looked down nodding, and then asked, "And Sarah? Can she stay with us too?"

"No. Mariah will keep Sarah. But you and I will be starting a new life together in a wonderful place called California. That's where we're headed. No more snow; imagine that! It's gonna be blue skies and oranges, and you love oranges. Also, theaters, restaurants, movie stars. I think we'll both love it. What do you say?"

She tried it out on her tongue. "Cal-i-for-ni-a. I do like oranges and going to the movies, but Sarah's my best friend, and what about Miss Clarice and Jonathon? Who will I play with? Won't my mommy miss me?

"I promise you; you'll make new friends. There'll be lots of new children to meet in Los Angeles. You'll have no trouble in that regard. Understand that I want what's best for you. You'll get to do your tap, singing; all those things you love. I care for you very much, and know we'll make a formidable twosome."

"What is for-mid-a-ble?"

"Strong together. It's us against the world, kid, and I think we're gonna be OK. But enough about all that. Guess what? There's a special car on this train for dining, with fancy tables and chairs. Shall we go and have lunch soon? Whatever you want to eat Jo-Jo. Let's go exploring."

Walking down the aisles of cars, we hung onto the seat backs, trying to balance with the swaying motion of the train. After locating the dining car, we were seated by one of the waiters. All were dark-skinned men, dressed in white coats and black trousers. I'd seen pictures but had never seen a negro before in person, and now, here were three men, offering polite, impeccable service. As our waiter greeted us, offered menus, and filled our water glasses, Jo-Jo couldn't stop staring. As soon as he left the table, she tugged on my arm.

"Auntie...Mother, why is he so dark? What's wrong."

I whispered back, "These men working on the train are called negros. They look different from you and me but I'm sure they're quite nice, capable men, so don't stare. That's rude. As we travel, we'll see people from many different places and learn lots of new things. That's what makes travel interesting; exhilarating isn't it? Now let's decide on our lunch."

As we were eating, a smartly-dressed gentleman in a suit and bow-tie stopped at our table, leaned over and said, "Excuse my forwardness, but I have to say, you two must be the loveliest creatures on this train. Just delightful. If you would allow, let me take care of your lunch bill." He handed me his card. "I'm Willard Williams, territory manager for the Wonder Toy Company. I'm on these trains all the time for business."

I studied his card, "Well thank you for your kind offer, Mr. Williams. I'm Nanette Jorgenson and this is Jo-Jo."

"And Mr. Jorgenson? Not hungry today?"

"That's none of your business, is it Mr. Williams?"

"No, don't suppose it is. If you're interested later though, several of us meet in the club car for afternoon drinks around four?" Tipping his fedora, he added, "You lovely ladies have a good day."

Jo-Jo giggled as he walked away. "He called me a lady, that's funny,"

"Yes, a lovely little lady. Now finish your sandwich, sweetie." Imagine that, a cheeky guy flirting with me right in front of Jo-Jo. Although, honestly, I wouldn't mind meeting some lively new people for drinks. I'd been hanging onto the idea of marrying Phil for far too long. It was time for me to live a little. Perhaps I could make a brief appearance in the club car while Jo took her afternoon nap.

After returning to our seats after lunch, I read for a while and Jo-Jo worked on her coloring book. The shifting train motion worked like magic, eventually putting her to sleep. I put a blanket over Jo-Jo and set her doll, Millie, next to her. In the ladies' room, I adjusted my hat, refreshed my lipstick and cologne, and made my way up to the club car which was close to first-class. As I walked in, the haze from cigarette and cigar smoke was so heavy I could barely see. There were a few other women in the car, but it was predominantly men, sitting in rounded leather booths, playing cards, talking and laughing loudly, clinking glasses. From the end of the car, I heard my name.

"Mrs. Jorgenson, back here. Step aside, gentleman."

There were four men seated and they all stood up as I approached. Good. They had manners at least.

I smiled, reaching out my hand to shake, as Mr. Williams introduced me to his three friends, all traveling salesmen familiar with the route. "Thanks for your invitation. Thought I'd pop in for a refreshment while my daughter was napping. Hope I'm not interrupting anything, Mr. Williams."

"Call me Willard. No, not at all. There's room in our

booth. Scoot over Daniels. How are you at pinochle? We'll deal you in on the next hand."

"My auntie taught me, but I haven't played in years." In reality, Clarice and I played often with our neighbors on my days off. I thought acting the novice might work to my advantage.

"Don't worry. It'll all come back to you. What can I get you to drink, Nanette? May I call you Nanette?"

"Certainly. A sarsaparilla would be lovely. Thanks"

"Coming right up." He waved to a waiter who quickly brought my drink which was sweet and delicious. "Boys, you should see Nanette's daughter. Looks just like her mom and cute as a doll. Thompson, pour a little spirit into Nanette's drink. You want him to liven it up for you, right?"

A silver flask slid from Thompson's jacket. "Oh, why not. I'm on vacation after all."

They dealt me in on the next hand but they were playing for nickels, so I didn't think I could get into too much trouble. The men were entertaining, exchanging road stories and client interactions. They seemed impressed when I explained I worked in a photo studio. The time flew as we exchanged jokes and I continued to have winning hands. I was having fun and had almost forgotten what that felt like.

In the middle of another hand, Willard announced, "Uh-oh. Nanette, seems somebody is looking for you."

I turned and saw Jo-Jo walking toward me, hanging on to Milly, with tears running down her face and her thumb in her mouth. I was sitting on the end of the booth and quickly stepped over and hugged her. "Don't cry sweetie. Mother's here."

"You said you wouldn't leave. Were you running away?"

I grabbed my linen napkin from the table and wiped her tears. "Don't be silly. You were sleeping and I decided to visit Mr. Williams for a drink. Would you like a root beer or

Sarsaparilla? Come sit on my lap." She nodded as I dried her tears.

"Gentleman, this is Jo-Jo."

Looking at her doll, Willard asked, "Who you got there, Jo-Jo? May I see her?"

"Milly. She's my favorite."

"She is? I can see why. Actually, I believe she's one of ours, made by Wonder Toys. Yup, Curlie Cutie, number 2412, definitely. Now look at this, boys: This doll, held by a little girl, held by her mother, all mirror images of each other. Is this the ad of a lifetime or what? That picture is priceless."

My ears immediately perked up. "How priceless? I've got a Kodak camera in my bag. Willard, why don't you take the shot? Your boss may want it for an ad campaign."

"That's using your head. Show me how to use it." The other guys grumbled as their card game was interrupted and they had to climb out of the booth, while I cleared ash-trays and drinks out of the shot. I showed Willard how to operate the little box camera, a birthday gift from Phil. We quickly took several poses with Jo-Jo being the perfect model; she'd gotten used to being around cameras, staying at the studio with me occasionally.

I promised to mail Willard our best prints once the film was developed. After Jo-Jo finished her root beer, I took my winnings and left. I'd interrupted their little men's club long enough and walked away with a buck and a half in winnings.

After eight hours of travel, we switched trains in Chicago. Jo-Jo was the only person I'd talked to about the California stretch of our trip. Stepping out on the Chicago station platform, we located our luggage, hired a porter, and then purchased tickets to continue on to Los Angeles. I was amazed by the enormity of Union Station, and held tight to Jo-Jo's hand as we bumped into crowds of people scurrying in all directions. Trying to follow closely behind our porter, I was distracted while staring at sleek marble floors, lit by ornate brass lamps, and high classic columns throughout the impressive station. Chicago was definitely on a whole new level.

It was late as we climbed on board our second train. A Pullman porter directed us to our sleeping berths. Jo-Jo was exhausted but excited to sleep on the top berth with Millie, while I stayed below. As my head sunk into a comfortable pillow, I looked out my small window as we zipped past the golden lights of several campfires scattered near the dark tracks. Looking like little matchsticks burning around the shadows of shanty towns, as the darkness hid the collapse of so many people's dreams. The papers now referred to them as Hoovervilles. Almost like small towns, these camps had sprung up around the passing trains; places where countless numbers of the homeless congregated.

Turning away from the window, I reflected on what we were doing and considered my regrets: the lies I'd told friends who I might never see again, my career in Mankato, how Mariah would react when she discovered we'd left, and then, of course, the uncertainty of success in Hollywood. My mind now swirled with doubts.

But every now and then, you know when wrong is right. I knew we had to make that right turn and keep moving.

## CHAPTER 34
## NANETTE

$\mathcal{A}$fter three days of stops, starts, and seemingly endless vistas of dusty plains, mountains, valleys, and fertile fields, we arrived at La Grande Station in Los Angeles, located at Second Street and Santa Fe Avenue. We walked out rubber-legged, stretching, with tired eyes. We both squinted at the light, attempting to take in the bright afternoon sky, the green grass, bricked walkways, and odd-looking palm trees land-scaping the grounds of the busy terminal. It smelled different, felt different, looked different. Like we'd arrived in some exotic foreign country. The station had rounded domes, red-clay tiled roofs, with a hint of Spanish architecture which I'd only seen in books. Deeply inhaling the fresh air, I felt a coolness to it, but at the same time, the sun warmed my skin. Then I caught a scent wafting on the breeze… oranges. California!

I searched for our luggage deposited along the platform and hired a porter from the line-up of several standing in the depot ready to help. Once inside the terminal, Jo-Jo and I began looking for James Diamond, the agent who was about to change our lives.

After nervously waiting about forty-five minutes, a young

gangly man in a pinstriped double-breasted suit walked quickly toward us. With his hand outstretched, he said, "I recognize you from your photo. You must be Jo-Jo, and you must be Nanette Jorgenson. So glad we can meet in person. Hope you haven't been waiting too long?"

"No, not too long, Mr. Diamond," I said, trying to keep the impatience out of my voice.

"Great! And you, Miss Jo-Jo, are prettier than your picture. Let's hope you can act as well as your mother says you sing and dance."

She looked right back at Mr. Diamond, gave him a large smile and said, "Yes, you bet-cha, Mr. Diamond." It was a phrase she'd picked up from one of the salesmen on the train and I'd heard her testing it out a few times already.

"Oh, Mrs. Jorgenson, I got a good feeling here! Got the two of you set up in a swell hotel; not too expensive, of course, and close to my office. If we get some contracts negotiated, you can shop around for apartments. You may need to get yourself a car. Everybody drives in Hollywood."

"I can assure you Mr. Diamond, a car will not be in my budget any time soon."

He continued to talk rapidly as we followed behind him, with our porter trailing us with the three cases and the trunk. Jo-Jo eventually squeezed in the back seat of his car with the three cases, and the porter had to tie the trunk to the bumper. I tipped and thanked him, as Diamond sat in the front seat and waited.

Driving away, Mr. Diamond continued to talk without stopping for a breath. "Well, it looks like you girls packed to stay a while. I like that! Optimistic! But this movie business isn't easy, girls. You gotta be ready to take rejection. Lots of talent out here. Everybody thinks their kid is the next big star, but we'll run a screen test on you Jo-Jo and farm it out to the studios. I know a lotta people in this town. We'll get somebody to take notice. You'll turn heads, no doubt. Now Mrs. Jorgenson, may I call you Nanette? Nanette, those screen tests I was mentioning…they're not cheap. They'll cost you about seventy-five-dollars to shoot, but then we'll be able to show it to several casting directors. In addition, we need a good headshot to put in Jo's press kit. That will be about thirty bucks to get us started and we'll talk about my fees later." He had pulled to a stop in front of a hotel.

"That's a lot of money, Mr. Diamond. Is this standard?"

"No, it normally costs more, but I'm getting you a good deal with some friends I know in the business. OK, I'm going to drop you off here at the hotel and tomorrow I'll pick you both up at ten o'clock sharp and we'll get started. I'll need that money now, Nanette, to get those appointments set up for tomorrow."

I leaned in to him using my most determined voice. "Mr. Diamond, I may be a rube from the Midwest, but I'm not a fool. We'll meet tomorrow and I'll be happy to pay your associates *myself* when I see samples of their product. If I don't like the quality of their work, we'll find someone we like better. I'm quite familiar with value and costs at a photography studio, and those prices are sky-high. Thanks for picking us up today and we look forward to working with you tomorrow. Say good-bye, Jo-Jo."

"Well… OK then. I may not be able to make those appointments without prepayment. Not sure about that, but I'll check around."

"If they're reputable business associates of yours, as you say, I'm certain they will accommodate you, Mr. Diamond."

I may have had stars in my eyes, but my feet were planted firmly on the ground, and I could smell a scam from fifty feet away.

Diamond had stopped in front of the Palms Hotel in Holly-wood. I stared up at a six-storied white stone building with ornate carvings on the corners, and a dozen stairs leading up to decorative double doors. There were two uniformed bell-hops waiting at the curb and I immediately started worrying about how much this was going to cost me.

Bags ma'am?"

"Yes, please. Three cases in the back and the trunk behind."

After they quickly unloaded, Diamond curtly nodded, saying, "See you ladies tomorrow," and then drove off.

Jo-Jo looked up at the impressive building with a huge smile. "Is this a castle?"

"Not a castle, darling. But a nice hotel. Let's go inside."

I was remembering my first hotel stay at the disappointing *Front Street* in Mankato. The Palms looked far more promising. Hopefully, I wouldn't be ejected from this one. Walking in, I saw four deep-green velvet sofas with fringe trim, patterned matching side chairs, well-worn oriental carpets and beaded table lamps.

I checked in at the desk, telling the clerk we needed a basic room with a double bed. After signing the register, I was given a room key. Good! No trouble checking in as a single woman. Having the child next to me probably helped.

There was an elevator, but it was so narrow that it took the bellboy three trips to get everything into our fourth-floor room. Jo-Jo was so excited to ride the elevator that she insisted on taking it all three times while she and the bellhop, Rupert, became fast friends.

The room was very small. Between the trunk, three cases, one double bed, night stand, window and lamp, there was no place to stand in the room unless you stood on the bed. Jo-Jo immediately climbed over the cases and began jumping on the bed.

"I think I like Hollywood, Mother. It's exciting."

"Good! Now stop jumping and let's get cleaned up."

There was a bathroom down the hall which we quickly made a grab for, locking the door behind us, while we enjoyed a much-needed hot bath after our four-day train journey.

Relaxing in the sudsy tub, I discussed my plans with Jo-Jo. "You know kiddo, there's a lot of movie executives looking for a child star like you; someone outgoing, that sings and dances. Remember when we saw King Kong, and there was a short movie that came on before? It starred a little girl, Shirley Temple. Just about your age. According to Silver Screen, she's already been in five movies *this* year. Can you imagine?"

"I like Little Rascals. They're so funny."

"Well, who knows? Maybe you can become part of that gang. That would be fun."

As I shampooed her hair, Jo-Jo asked, "What's a child star?"

"Oh, a child that's the main character in a movie. Someone who can capture the audiences' attention. They have a special spark."

We were interrupted by knocking on the door and a gruff voice, "Let's move along. There's other people staying here too."

I called back to the impatient guest, "Give us a minute. Almost done." We wrapped up in robes, walked down the hall to our room, and dressed for dinner.

That evening, we stepped out on the sidewalk feeling fresh and excited to be in the thick of things within the movie business. We walked a few blocks, hunting for an inexpensive diner, but instead found a take-out Chinese restaurant, *Hung Fong*. It had a few tables and chairs set up on the sidewalk. I was hungry, tired of looking, and said, 'Let's give this a shot. It's time for us to try something new." We both had our first taste of won-ton soup, chop suey and egg-rolls. Delicious, and the price was ideal. We both ate, stuffing our hungry stomachs, for a little over a dollar. It quickly became our favorite place to eat.

In the morning, we dug through Jo's trunk, searching for the perfect screen-test outfit. We decided on a short purple and white polka dot dress with a pleated skirt, and I finger-combed her hair into blond ringlets. We then parked ourselves near the street watching for Diamond's car. But after thirty minutes of waiting, we took turns sitting on the front steps. After an hour, I called his office and was told by a receptionist that Mr. Diamond was in a meeting and he wouldn't be making any other appointments for the day. Apparently, our Hollywood ambassador to the stars had abandoned us. We might be navigating the winding roads to movie success on our own, and it was up to me to figure something out.

# CHAPTER 35
# MARIAH

*I*n addition to Elliott, someone else had been frustrating me for the last few weeks. Daily, I made the long walk to the mailbox, expecting a letter from Nanette, but each time I came back empty handed. While I continued to send her bi-weekly updates of activities, she'd sent me nothing lately. Was she so busy she couldn't drop me a few lines? I waited each week in anticipation to hear how Jo was doing. But nothing came. Nanette didn't have a phone, but I knew I could reach her for important things at her job. The next time I went into Green Tree, I used the drugstore payphone and called the number for Professional Portraits in Mankato.

The phone rang several times before an unhelpful woman finally picked up.

"Hello, this is Mariah Anderson. I need to speak with Nanette Jorgenson please."

"Nobody here by that name."

"But she works there…has for years. What about Mr. Greenly? Is he available?"

"He's in the studio with clients. Best not to interrupt. Maybe try back around five."

"Five? Please ask Mr. Greenly if I might just have one minute of his time?"

"No. Doesn't like to be interrupted. Goodbye ma'am."

I had dinner to prepare, kids to supervise and couldn't hang around Svenson's Drugs another three hours to call back. Surely Nanette would have told me if she'd changed jobs. I was surprised she'd leave the studio. She was so involved with every aspect of the business and had talked my ear off about it when I visited. Maybe the girl answering was new and didn't know her. Or perhaps Nanette had received a better offer. She was such a go-getter.

I needed to see my Jo. It had been too long. Leaving the drugstore, I made an impulsive decision. I went to the train station and bought tickets for the Saturday morning train to Mankato. Sarah and I would go together and bring Jo home for a brief visit, and I couldn't care less what Elliott had to say about it.

Anticipating our trip, Sarah and I counted down each day as Saturday approached. After buying my tickets Monday, I'd mailed Nanette a letter with news of my trip, but, as usual, I'd not received any word back.

I wore a new burgundy dress with white trim, which I'd finally sewn and added to my dismal wardrobe. I wanted Jo to see me as she was used to seeing Nanette, well-dressed, happy, and confident. I didn't want to feel as if I were competing, but after our first visit, I wanted to make a better impression. Nanette had a way of making me feel shabby.

As Sarah and I stared out the window during our three-hour train ride, my mind tried to push away the guilt. It had been almost seven months since Jo had left. Sarah and I had only visited her once last May. Where had the time gone? Nanette had promised to visit Green Tree with Jo a few times, but that had never materialized. Surely though, I should have tried harder. But there were always obstacles: money issues, Rebecca's TB, or someone else needing attention. I had to keep telling myself, the three of us would soon be starting a new life together. Something would have to break my way.

The noon train eventually pulled into Mankato for a quick stop. My plan was to visit briefly with Nanette, eat some lunch, and take Sarah and Jo home on the four o'clock train back to Green Tree. I wanted Jo to stay with me for at least a week and then I'd return her to Mankato, until Elliott changed his mind and allowed her to move in permanently.

Sarah began looking eagerly out the window for her twin. "Mommy, I don't see Jo. Where is she?"

"They're probably waiting inside the depot. Let's go in and check." There were a few people leaving the building, but no sign of Nanette and Jo. "Sit on the bench, Sarah; I'll check the toilets." Coming back, I patted her hand and said, "Not to worry sweetie, we'll wait here a little while. Maybe Miss Nanette had to work. We can walk to her place if they don't come soon."

Tears started to well up in Sarah's eyes. "Where's Jo, Mommy? You said she'd be here."

"Be patient, Sarah. How about some apple slices? I packed some for you. Maybe they're waiting for us at Miss Nanette's place."

I vaguely remembered the way, but had to stop and ask directions to Nanette's address a few times. I eventually found the two-level duplex and rang her buzzer. There was no answer and I noticed a man's name now on the mailbox slot next to the door. That's when I felt a chill go through my body. I knocked on her neighbor's door, hoping for information. She and her landlady had seemed close. What was her name? Carla? Clara? Clarice... that was it. Thankfully, she answered the door, with a son peeking out next to her, as she eyed me suspiciously.

"Hi, I'm Mariah Anderson, Jo's mother. I met you briefly back in May. Are Nanette and Jo still living here?"

She squinted at me. "What's your name again?"

"Mariah Anderson. And you're Clarice. I remember Nanette always speaking so highly of you. I came to pick up Jo and take her back to Green Tree for a visit. I sent Nanette a letter about it on Monday."

Clarice stepped out of the door a bit further. "Hate to tell you this, but Nanette moved over three weeks ago. Left me in the lurch with the apartment and our child-care arrangement. My kids really loved Jo-Jo. Nanette said they were going on vacation to Chicago, but then later sent a letter saying she had a job there."

"In Chicago! Why wouldn't she have told me? That's preposterous. What's her forwarding address?"

"Honestly, the letter didn't have one. Just said I could have the stuff she left in the apartment. Rented it right away. Look…I don't know who to believe here. But recently, Nanette told me she now had full custody of Jo-Jo. And I can assure you, she really loves the kid. Took great care of her. Maybe her old boss, Phil Greenly, has more information. They were pretty close. Uh, I'm in the middle of baking though. Need to get on with it."

Feeling desperate, I put my hand in the door as she stepped back attempting to close it. "Please Clarice, I assure you, I *am* Jo's mother. Nanette was only helping me out after my husband passed away. May I leave you my address if you hear anything?"

"I suppose so. No harm in that, but I don't want to get between the two of you. I don't know the full story here. I will tell you this, though. Nanette and Jo-Jo were like peas and carrots. Always together, and the spitting image of each other. She loves her like a daughter, even if you say she isn't."

As she spoke, Sarah grew more anxious and asked about Jo again. Why would Nanette do this—a close friend of Catherine's, growing up in Green Tree, and then abruptly leaving her friends here in Mankato? Surely there had to be some logical explanation.

As Clarice slammed the door on our disturbing conversation, I walked away wondering why Nanette told her she now had full custody. We'd never discussed that. Nanette's outright lie made me so angry I could spit. I'd even sent her a letter a few months before explaining that Sarah was moving in with me at the Martin's farm and I was sure I'd be able to bring Jo home before long. Oh my God... maybe that was it.

It slowly dawned on me. She must have thought Jo would return to Green Tree soon and decided to disappear. Would she really do that? That would be horrid! Could she be that devious?

We found ourselves on another lengthy walk to the photo studio where Nanette had worked. I desperately hoped Mr. Greenly knew something about Nanette's absence. Working together for six years; surely, they'd grown close.

Sarah was growing hungry, tired, and upset. Along the way, we stopped at a green-grocer. Opening the screen door, I stared at a tin bread sign featuring a smiling young blond girl biting into a slice of buttered bread. Reminded of Jo, I became upset. I bought Sarah a bottle of milk and a roll, and asked to use their restroom as I tried to pull myself together.

Eventually locating the photo studio, we walked into the small lobby, seeing a couple dressed in their Sunday-best holding an infant. I asked the young woman behind the counter for Greenly.

"You got an appointment?"

"No. No appointment. I'm here to ask Mr. Greenly some important questions, and I'm in town for only a short while."

"He's preparing for a shoot right now. Should be out shortly."

"Please, it's imperative that I speak with him."

"Ma'am, he'll be out soon. Have a seat."

Eventually, a man with thinning hair and glasses came from the back and ushered the seated couple into the studio. I quickly followed behind him, before his desk clerk could block me.

"Mr. Greenly? I'm Mariah Anderson; looking for Nanette and my daughter, Josephine. It's important that I locate them. I know the two of you worked together quite a while. Can you tell me where she is?"

With a handkerchief, he wiped his brow, shook his head, and appeared to dab away a tear. "Wish I could tell you. She and her little girl decided to take a vacation to Chicago three or four weeks back. Business was slow so I agreed, then she sent me a letter saying she'd found a new position. I was shocked. Haven't heard another peep outta her. Tell the truth, I'm pretty worried. Not at all like Nanette to leave her job without a word. But miss, sorry, I have clients waiting. Leave your address with Sherlene at the desk. If I hear anything, I'll let you know."

I couldn't let him go without speaking my mind, as I placed my arm on his. "First, Mr. Greenly, let me assure you, Jo was *not* her daughter. Nanette *never* had custody of her. Jo is *my* daughter and now they both seem to be missing. But I'd appreciate any help you could offer us." My worst fears were solidly confirmed. As he retreated to the studio, I left my name and address with the surly Sherlene and asked for directions to the police station.

The station was only a few blocks away and we had ninety minutes before our train left. Walking briskly into the station, I asked Sarah to sit down on a chair, while I approached a uniformed policeman at the central desk. As my mind was imagining all kinds of scenarios, my voice verged on hysteria, and I had my hanky in hand for emerging tears.

"Officer, my daughter is missing." I took in several deep breaths before trying to speak again. "I'm sorry, I can't believe this is happening." I wiped my eyes and nose. "It's probably a case of kidnapping. What should I do?"

The middle-aged officer remained calm, leaning forward on his elbows, behind the cluttered counter. "OK, let's calm down, ma'am. You say kidnapping?" He picked up his pen and clipboard, then started shaking his head. "Ever since that Lindberg baby, everybody thinks their missing kid is a kidnapping. Let's start from the beginning, shall we?" The doubtful officer began writing. "Who are we looking for? Who's missing?"

"My daughter, Josephine Anderson. She's only five... so pretty, so young." Then my tears began again.

"OK, Mrs. Anderson, let's get this report finished. I need to write down the facts. So, you live here in Mankato?"

"No, we live on a farm near Green Tree, Iowa. About a three-hour train ride. But Jo was staying here with a friend of ours. Nanette Jorgenson. This was her address." I handed him a crumpled envelope with Nanette's return address, which he copied down.

"So, did this Nanette have your permission to let your daughter stay with her?"

"Yes. Jo's been with her since early March. My husband died in an accident and we had to move from our farm and... well... things have been difficult."

"I get the picture. So, the Jorgenson lady was doing you a favor? Taking care of your daughter?"

"Only until I could find a place to accommodate the three of us." Pointing to Sarah, I added, "That's her sister over there, her twin. But I *have* a place now. I came to pick up Jo for a visit."

"Any money involved? Were you paying Miss Jorgenson a fee to take care of your daughter?"

"No. She offered to take care of expenses. Why does that matter?"

"Just getting the whole story here, Mrs. Anderson. Go ahead."

"I wrote Nanette telling her when I'd be up to get Jo, but it seems she's suddenly gone somewhere with my child. Her land-lady and her boss both say she left about three weeks ago without notice and later told them she'd moved to Chicago. She never mentioned a word about this move to me. I'm so afraid she's kidnapped Jo."

"Well, let's not jump to conclusions, Mrs. Anderson. Maybe she's mailing you a letter with her new location? Perhaps she transferred for a better job? Lots of people moving around looking for work right now. We just don't know, do we? Now, do you have documentation of when she took charge of your daughter?"

"Well, no. It was the first of last March. I had to leave our farm, with no idea how long the separation would be. At first, I thought only a few months, but it's been over seven. Things have been quite difficult," I said as I dabbed my eyes dry. "We visited here last May and everything seemed just fine."

"Only once? Green Tree isn't that far," he said in an accusatory tone.

"Well, I kept planning on coming again, then Nanette said she was coming to Green Tree, but changed her mind. You know how that goes? I tried. I really tried."

""Uh-huh. Did you give her any custody papers, Mrs. Anderson?"

"Only for medical records. Jo had a bad cough. I sent a form giving her temporary permission to sign as her legal guardian. But she always knew I was coming back to get Jo. It was always understood."

"OK. I'll give this report to my Captain, but unless this Nanette is living in the area, there may be little we can do, locally. You willingly let her take care of your daughter at her expense for over seven months and now Miss Jorgenson has moved. I don't think we have much of a real case here, Mrs. Anderson. Best go home and see if you can locate her, and *then* you let us know if she gives you any trouble handing her over."

"That's it? That's all you can do?" I looked around the quiet station in a panic, hoping anyone else could help. There were two doors on either side of the back wall, both were closed.

"I'll file your report. I'm writing down the details. We'll put out a search, make sure she's not still in the area. If she is, we'll let you know. You're not really sure she got your letter about picking your daughter up, right?" I nodded back. "At this point I can't make much of an official complaint. To me, it sounds like poor communication."

I was mad, heartbroken, and confused. "Trust me sir... When your child has been taken without notice, a mother does not want to hear it's a case of *poor communication*." Then Sarah came over, taking my hand and asked: "Is Jo here, Mommy? Can she come home now?"

At her question, I burst into tears again, stuffed a copy of the officer's report in my bag, and left the police station in despair. Exhausted, with little resources except our return tickets, we headed back to the depot for our four-o'clock train. It was a quiet, colorless ride home, as I sat next to Sarah, holding her tight as she fell asleep to the rocking motion.

Catherine Anderson was there waiting to pick us up at the Green Tree station, excited to see Jo after so many months. But she was shocked to hear that Nanette, one of her oldest friends, had left Mankato with Jo, without a word to any of us.

# CHAPTER 36
# NANETTE

*I* slammed down the phone after hearing that James Diamond was not coming by. I was furious but not totally surprised.

Walking back outside, I sat down next to Jo-Jo on the hotel stairs. "Well, it appears Mr. Diamond will *not* be your agent, darling. Definitely not a reliable character. I made a mistake trusting him. Thank God we never signed any client contracts with him."

Jo-Jo put her arm around my shoulder. "Don't be sad. I didn't like him anyway. He talked too much."

"Actually, this was probably a good thing. There must be a hundred agents in this town and I know once they see you, darling, they'll be rushing over to sign you and get you in front of the cameras. You know, Jo, perhaps I haven't approached this correctly. I think we need to take our time and find the right agent; someone honest, who's well acquainted with the studios and not just after a quick buck."

"Okey-dokey." Although Jo-Jo looked concerned, I knew she didn't fully understand what I was talking about.

"Our room costs four dollars-a-day, plus there's food

expenses, and with no money coming in, my savings won't last long. Maybe I should find a job before we find you an agent. This acting business might be more complicated than I thought. Do you think that's a good idea? Me looking for work?"

Jo-Jo nodded her head. "I do like this hotel. Can we stay for a while?" She already thought of the big lobby as her own personal parlor.

"We'll see. I'm going inside to look up addresses of photography studios near us. Maybe somebody's looking to hire."

"Can I stay here and keep helping the boys with luggage? Rupert says I can carry the little bags."

"I suppose."

I asked for a phone book at the registration desk and began looking up addresses of photography shops in the yellow pages. Then I walked to a drugstore down the block and purchased a city map. I located the studio addresses, circling them on the map. As Jo-Jo and the bellhop came trooping in with a guest's luggage, I told her we were going on a job hunt.

"My mommy used to go on job hunts and always came home sad. Can I stay here instead?"

I looked at Rupert and asked, "Is she in the way?"

"No ma'am. The guests love her and they're giving us better tips."

"OK, but if the manager doesn't like it, Jo-Jo, you'll need to go up and stay in the room 'til I get back, understood?" She nodded, running along behind Rupert, carrying a guest's hat box to the elevator.

I decided to focus first on a photography studio close to Columbia Pictures, assuming actors always needed headshots. Columbia was located on Gower Street, a section of town called Skid Row on the map. Tinsel Town Photos was just around the corner from Columbia. It took me two buses and a few blocks of walking to locate the area. Trudging past

Columbia's studios, I wasn't impressed. Not nearly as glamorous as I'd imagined, just a few big ugly warehouses behind a fence.

Arriving at Tinsel Town Photos, I sat down on a torn chair in the small reception area, hoping someone would appear at the counter. The shop was deserted, and the back wall covered with dusty, haphazardly hung portraits.

Eventually, a stooped, older man with a mustard stain on his broad necktie, came from the back, wiping his mouth with a napkin and leaned against the counter, surprised to be looking out at me. I put on my broadest smile and approached.

"Hello there. Sorry to interrupt your day; I'm Nanette Jorgenson and I wanted to apply for an assistant's position. Is the owner in today?"

"That would be me, but does it look like I need an assistant? Business is slow. Nobody wants to get their portraits taken any more. Let my last employee go about three months past." Although no one was there but the two of us, he told me in a low voice, "Business been terrible. I may need to close the shop before too long."

"Oh, so sorry to hear that. You've been in business for a while?"

"Absolutely. I'm one of the first proprietors out this way. Been here twelve years, even before Columbia set up shop."

"Then I'm sure you're great at taking photographs and portraits, but maybe you need some help bringing in extra business. Am I right?"

He shook his head. "I've tried advertising, put out flyers; nothing seems to work. And I can't leave the shop to do more since I'm the only one here."

"I'm Nanette, by the way. What's your name?"

"Arnold Clemson."

"Arnold, I have a proposition for you. I can see you need help. I've worked for a photo studio back in Iowa, not as fine an establishment as you have here, but anyway, I'm willing to work free-of-charge for you strictly to bring in more business if you're willing to pay me forty percent of what I bring in."

"Forty percent? That's outrageous! I own this business."

"Yes, but I'm only asking you to pay me for business that you never would have had to begin with. After two months, as I bring in clients, if you don't like the monetary arrangement, we'll renegotiate. What do you say? You've got nothing to lose."

Still leaning on the counter, he was shaking his head at my assertive pose, with my hands on my hips and my most engaging smile. I could tell he was considering the proposition. "Hmmm, I don't know."

"Look, Arnold; you can go on like this, close in a month or two, or give me a shot at improving your business. I can go to six other studios I have listed here on this map and make the same offer. I guarantee you; *somebody's* going to give me a chance. Come on, what do you say? I'm actually anxious to get started. Time's ticking, Arnold." I could tell he was on the brink of giving in.

He looked me up and down. "In all my days, I've never seen anyone so persistent. You're right though. What do I have to lose? OK, let's try it out, but in *one* month I decide what happens."

I reached across the counter and shook his hand again. "Of course, it's your prerogative, and I have some immediate suggestions, but I'll run everything past you first. Oh, and there's one other requirement. You need to take some good shots of my daughter for her press kit and give me a list of some of the top agents and studios in this town."

"Now, how does that help my business, little lady?"

"For one thing, I'll let you hang a few photos of her in here. You need someone new, young and vibrant on this wall; that's for sure. And I need the agents' names because I'm going to be contacting each one and asking them to send all their new actors here for headshots."

"OK... I know a few off the top of my head and I've got a directory somewhere on my shelves in the back. Let me look around."

"While you're looking for that, I'll do a little cleaning for you out here. I guess you've let things go a bit since you're short-handed. You have a step ladder back there?"

"Sure, yeah, a little dusting won't hurt. Knock yourself out."

I immediately took down all the old and tired looking photos that were hanging chaotically behind the counter and noticed several other portraits stacked on shelves. I began arranging them in piles and yelled out to Arnold, "I'm going to need some nails and fabric, maybe some paint. What do you have back there?"

He walked out flipping through a directory. "Got a hammer, a few nails, some photo props, but the rest you need to get at the *Five and Dime* a few doors down. He looked around the front desk and asked, "Wait a minute. What are you doing with all this?"

"You'll see. Guarantee you'll love it. Arnold, could you wipe all these photos down, please? I've put them into separate piles so don't mix them up."

"I suppose... but we'll be discussing everything first, right?"

"Sure, I'll be back with the receipts shortly."

"Receipts for what?" he asked, as I banged the door behind me.

By the end of the day, the interior of Tinsel Town Photos was transformed. On one wall I'd created a bridal section, with white tulle fabric arched high above, then I draped it down both sides of the wall to the floor, with a portrait of a beautiful bride in a full-length gown in the center. Surrounding this were engagement photos and formal group shots. From the props in back, I pulled out an old fake bouquet and perked it up adding ribbons that trailed to the floor, then placed it in a vase on a white column prop.

I also created a family section, first pulling out an armchair from the back. As I dragged it to the lobby, Arnold objected. "Hey, that's my comfy desk chair. I use that for napping in the back."

"But it looks nice and homey. We need it up here for display. Why don't you use that torn chair from the lobby instead? Anyway, why are you napping? You should be either taking photos or at the counter, right?"

"Gosh-dang-it, Nanette, don't tell me my business."

"Now look how nice this side is." I purchased a small oval rug at the Five and Dime, then placed a table and lamp next to the armchair and surrounded the wall with a number of family portraits. In the center of the cluster, I hung a large photo of two adorable children.

Above the counter wall, I hung headshots of hopeful actors and actresses, but only the most attractive ones that Arnold had in his files. I asked him to cut out aluminum foil stars, which I hung from the ceiling surrounding these headshot hopefuls. This was to be our *Stars of the Future* section.

During the entire day, only one customer came in to pick up an order, while I rearranged Arnold's world. "Now Arnold, I suggest you paint this counter right away. I see chip marks and it looks dingy. Shouldn't take too long, right?"

"I can probably work on that in the morning. I only have one appointment scheduled in the afternoon."

"And one other thing; what is the lowest price you can shoot and print a dozen eight-by-eleven headshots and still make a profit?"

"Hmm, maybe five dollars."

"OK, good to know." Looking around at all of our work, I said. "I like what we've done with the place. Great job, Arnold!

Now tomorrow, I'm going to drum up some business. I'll drop off Jo-Jo with a few of her best costumes for her portraits and stop by late in the afternoon to pick her up."

"Hell, no. I'm not babysitting your kid all day. That's not part of the deal."

"You won't be babysitting. Jo-Jo will be your helper. She's very handy and will do anything you ask her. Very mature for her age."

"Well, I don't know… maybe, but *one* day only." We stood outside together as he locked up his lonely shop. He glanced inside one more time, chuckling to himself, impressed with the quick changes we'd made in only one afternoon.

"You know, Nanette, I been thinking about shuttering the whole operation lately, and suddenly, I feel better for the first time in two years. Guess I'll see you and your gal tomorrow."

"I feel better too, Arnold. Thanks for the opportunity. Oh, by the way, some of these sales calls may require a vehicle. I don't suppose you have a car I can borrow occasionally for those?"

"Let me think about that. See you tomorrow."

I walked to the bus station with a smile on my face. I didn't have a salary or even an hourly wage, but I liked the idea of earning my keep by commission. I could work with that.

# CHAPTER 37
# NANETTE

*T*hat evening, Jo-Jo and I celebrated with another round of chop-suey and egg rolls. I was excited to share my news. "I found myself a job today! Now, the pay might be sporadic for a while, but it'll come."

Jo-Jo nodded, popping the top of a crunchy egg roll into her mouth.

"And the best part is that you can stay at the photo studio, while I go out and solicit new business. You'll like Mr. Clemson and he'll need your help. Dusting, sweeping. That sort of thing."

"So, I have a real job?"

"Sort of. We'll work like a team for Mr. Clemson. But I'm also going to be on the hunt for your talent agent at the same time. So, either way, we'll both stay busy."

"Good. Rupert told me I'm an excellent worker. The bell-boys gave me these today." She pulled two silver dimes out of her dress pocket.

"Perfect. You save that. Keep it somewhere safe, Jo. We may need it one of these days."

The following morning, we dressed for work as I repeated

my Auntie's mantra. "Remember Jo-Jo, if we want to be successful..."

"We have to look successful!" Jo-Jo responded with enthusiasm.

"That's right; you remembered."

Entering the shop, I introduced her to Arnold, and explained what I thought Jo-Jo could do to keep the shop clean, and suggested she run any other errands he thought appropriate. "But remember Arnold, you promised to take Jo-Jo's new poses and headshots for her portfolio."

He rolled his eyes and said, "I don't believe I promised. I wanna say you commandeered me into doing it."

I ignored his comment and asked, "Where are your business cards, Arnold? I'll need several of those."

"Don't have any. What good would that do me?"

"Oh my stars! How can I promote your business without a card? I'm ordering you some today, and also some for me."

"Can't afford any so don't order them."

"We have to."

He stood behind his counter, arms across his chest, looking resolute. "I don't think this arrangement is going to work, Nanette. So far, you're spending *my* money, wanting me to use *my* equipment to photograph your daughter, *and* I have to babysit."

"You're going to have to trust me, Arnold. Remember just yesterday? You were optimistic."

"Well, my optimism is waning."

"Promise me you'll have a little patience. This is all going to work out. We just need some time. Now, can I get your car keys?"

"No! And be back by two o'clock. That's when I have my only appointment for the day and I don't want your kid blowing it."

Then Jo-Jo chimed in. "Mr. Clemson, don't be mad. We'll

have fun today." He looked down at her and I think she melted his heart a little bit.

I picked up the agent and studio list he had compiled for me and headed out. No matter what Arnold said, first on my to-do list was ordering business cards. For a professional look, it was a necessity. How could I call on potential clients and not have a card? I'd noticed a small print shop a few doors down from the Five and Dime. Much like Tinsel Town Studio, Hollywood Printers looked like it was down-and-out for the count. I waltzed in oozing enthusiasm.

"Hello miss. What can I do for you?" A smiling young man greeted me wearing a long black apron over a wrinkled white shirt.

"Hello, I'm Nanette Jorgenson. I assist Arnold Clemson, from Tinsel Town Photos. We were curious if we might strike a bargain with you, with business being so tight and all."

His face immediately looked less enthusiastic. "What kind of bargain?"

"We need a more modern look to our current business cards and heard you did great work. How about a little barter system? Hollywood Printers produces two-hundred cards for us in exchange for Tinsel Town offering discounted photo work included with your print jobs for six months.

"How would that work?"

"Let's say a customer needs a flier printed for a special sale. We could offer services of a photo of the shop or a photo of goods which could be incorporated with the flier. Not many printers are combining that service and you could offer it as a bonus feature at a great price."

He stood there rubbing his chin, nodding. "Interesting… you're right. Not many printers offer photo work with their jobs. How great a discount?"

"Forty-percent off, and let me tell you…our work quality is superb, top notch."

"So, old Arnold must be hurting pretty bad if he wants to tango with me."

"Oh, I didn't realize you two were friends." I panicked, thinking this might throw a fly into the ointment.

"We're not. We had a big argument over a parking spot two years ago...But maybe it's time to let it go. I can see how this idea might work out for us." The printer glanced up at the ceiling, thinking it through, and said, "OK. I accept. You get forty-percent off on the cards and I get forty-percent off the photography."

"That's not the deal I offered. I said you do the cards for us at *no* cost and you get forty-percent off photo work for six months. Surely you realize, one order of business cards would not be equal to six months of photo work."

"Hmm, let's say fifty-percent off your cards then."

I smiled, trying to remain calm and reasonable. "No. Absolute final offer, seventy-five-percent off the cost of the cards, with forty percent off photo work for six months." I shrugged my shoulders. "We can go elsewhere; I only came here because I heard you were the best."

Realizing the battle was over, he said. "OK. It's slow right now. Tell him I can have them for you in twenty-four hours."

"Fantastic."

"What does he want on the card?"

I went over the image I had in mind and ordered all of the cards with a Tinsel Town symbol and included Arnold's name on the bottom. So, I'd eliminated one issue. Of course, now I had the problem of explaining to Arnold why we were offering a forty-percent discount to his arch-enemy. I'd have to ponder that once the cards showed up.

Next was a visit to Columbia Pictures to see if I could find out who did their photo work and offer a more competitive price. I walked the few littered blocks to their gated entrance and noticed a crowd of people waiting outside. I hadn't anticipated an actual locked gate. I wiggled and side-stepped my way near the front of the crowd and asked a young woman what was going on.

She looked at me with a wary look in her eyes. "Extras, they got fifteen slots today." Then she pushed ahead of me, eager to be near the bars of the large gate. I wasn't interested in being an extra, but I also had no idea on how to gain admittance. I opened my bag, ran a comb through my hair and reapplied my brightest lipstick. An older gentleman was now standing next to me. Everyone was pressing forward, eager to be seen.

I asked him, "So, when do they decide?"

He shrugged his shoulders, and kept moving forward.

About five minutes later, a man in suspenders, carrying a megaphone, stood inside the fence and climbed up on a crate.

"OK, listen up… Only need fifteen of you guys today. Pay is one dollar. If I point and call you, come to the entrance immediately. When I finish, this crowd has to leave or I call the cops. Understood?" Mumbling, hand waving, and yells erupted from the crowd as everybody tried to stand out and be noticed. I was getting pushed and shoved as Suspenders began selecting the lucky fifteen.

"Pipe down! Here we go, uh… lady in the black hat." He pointed to the woman who had earlier inched her way in front of me. "Tall guy, check shirt. Blondie, blue coat. Old man, gray jacket. Mom and little boy, over here. Redhead, green dress, step in."

As he continued to point and call people out, I realized he'd said, 'Blondie, blue coat." I had on my blue coat; I was blonde. "Excuse me, passing through… thanks." I pushed my way through the rows and turned sideways through the small gate opening. Now what? I had no desire to be an extra, but had to find the casting department, or whoever ordered photo work. After Suspenders had his fifteen, he turned and barked at us.

"OK, eyes up here … Follow me in line. Do not get lost. Stay in the line. First, you're going to wardrobe and makeup. Second, you'll be going to the set, but only when called within an hour or two. Third, if the director decides he needs you past two o'clock, you will be served lunch. Fourth, you will be paid your dollar as you leave, *only* after returning your costumes to wardrobe. And no, I don't know what time that will be. Understood?" Everyone seemed in agreement and nodded at Captain Suspenders. "All right. Let's move out. Follow me."

All of the group, with the exception of myself, were a scruffy, unwashed bunch. We began following Suspenders through the lot, passing by workmen carrying scenery, actors dressed in western costumes, horses being led by trainers. I lingered, letting others in line pass me by. I was looking for the casting office and eventually noticed an exterior metal stairway leading up to a door with a sign on it which read: *Columbia Pictures--Home to the Stars*. This looked like a good place to start my hunt. As the line of extras continued walking, I hung back and took the stairs.

Inside was a harried looking woman wearing thick black glasses, sitting at an overflowing desk, speaking on the phone. I patiently sat down and waited in a chair next to her. I noticed a sign on her desk which read: *Anita Hunter—Central Casting*. I hoped I was in the right place.

After hanging up, she pulled out a sheet from a file piled on her desk, and began reading it. Continuing to look down, she asked. "What do you want?"

"Just some information please. I'm Nanette Jorgenson from Tinsel Town Photos. We're offering excellent prices on head-shots and promotional pics for your stable of actors. Who is currently handling that for you?"

"Who the hell let you in and sent you here?"

"Uh, a gentleman at the gate wearing suspenders, carries a megaphone."

"Sounds like Howie. He's an idiot." She was still reading from a file and hadn't looked at me. "Miss Tinsel Town, I don't order photos. I look at photos." Then she glanced up. "Hey, let me ask you a question. Woman to woman…what do you think of this guy?" She held up a professional photo of a young slender man with dark thick hair, large romantic eyes, dressed in a suit, definitely exuding an aura of charisma.

"Hmm, I'd say movie star material. There's something seductive but playful about him. Who is he?"

Anita read from a file. "Archibald Leach, actually. But recently changed the name to Cary Grant; thank God for that. At one point he was a stilts-walker. Ha! Imagine that. We're trying to decide whether to sign him. Looks good, but he's been in a few flops. Anyway…you need to be on your way… Shoo now." She was moving on to her next task and waved me away with her hand. "Try the promo department, downstairs, two trailers at the back. And don't get lost or security will throw you out."

Then she picked up her phone and was lost in another conversation, as I headed downstairs, still secretly clutching Mr. Grant's photo. I hunted briefly for the trailers she mentioned, eventually finding them. I poked my head in one and asked a younger woman if the promotions director was in.

"Guess I'll have to do for now. My boss is out of town."

"I'm Nanette. Work for Tinsel Town Photography; we're just around the corner from *Columbia*. Anyway, Anita Hunter from casting sent me here. She wanted you to know we're offering great prices on promotional shots, headshots, pack-ages. Whatever you need. Who are you currently using?"

"Uh, let's see." She walked her fingers through a thick

rolodex. "Looks like *Silverstein Studios* on Spring Street. Yes. Most of our work goes there."

"While he's away, would your boss like it if you saved his department *a lot* of money, and we delivered faster? Here's a sample of our work." I held up the photo of Mr. Grant.

"He looks good! Great angle and lighting on the face. I'm not sure...Tell you what. We just signed three starlets, put under contract for six months. Work up a package on all three: heads, full-body poses, pin-up. But you gotta beat Silverstein's price by twenty percent and have it all back to me within three days."

"Perfect, tell me his prices and send the ladies over tomorrow at noon. Let's write up a contract."

Yes! I had an order. Even if Silverstein remained their primary photographer, we might become a good back-up choice for rush orders. On my way out, I returned to Anita Hunter's office with the photo of Mr. Grant.

She looked up at me surprised at my return. "Lost again, Tinsel Town?"

"No. I found promotions, thanks. But I mistakenly walked off with that actor's photo. I wanted to return it."

"Oh, I decided to pass on him. Handsome, but probably not a bankable star. Thanks for returning it though."

"No problem. Miss Hunter, any chance of Columbia putting any child stars under contract?"

"Nah, not at this point. If we need a kid, we rent 'em out from another studio. I take it you got a wonderkid at home?" I nodded back. "Check out Alan Cummings. Big agent in town. He does kids. Hey, I gave you a lot of info today; time to hit the gate, Tinsel Town."

My allotted sixty seconds were over. "Much appreciated Miss Hunter."

I walked the short distance from Columbia Pictures to the photo studio and was surprised to see Jo-Jo outside in her top hat, tails, and tights, tap dancing across the broken sidewalk in front of the store.

"What are you doing out here in your recital outfit?"

"I dusted, swept, had my picture taken, then Mr. C told me to go out and play so I'm practicing dance steps. This sidewalk is perfect, and look." She held out her hand and showed me a quarter and a nickel.

"What's this for?"

"People gave it to me after they watched me dance. I made some more money."

"Soon you'll have a dollar if you keep this up. Can you beat that, kiddo! OK, you can keep dancing, but don't talk to any strangers except to say thank you. This isn't the best of neighborhoods."

I opened the shop door, calling out, "Arnold, I've got good news!"

## CHAPTER 38
## MARIAH

*F*or two months, every time I was close to Svenson's Drugs, I stopped to use their phone, continuing to badger Mr. Greenly to see if he'd heard anything. I also wrote to Clarice, reminding her to notify me if she received even a postcard from Nanette. Neither sent me any news and soon tired of my requests.

I also called police departments in Chicago, letting them know my dilemma. Some officials seemed concerned, writing down names and filing reports, while others seemed to think it was a domestic dispute between friends.

Sarah had her cousins, playmates from church, and Tommy Martin to play with. Although she missed her twin, she appeared to be moving on. When you're young, memory is short for kids and life is full of change. Perhaps she tucked her recollections of Jo away in the back of her mind, but hopefully her sister was never too far away. I would occasionally catch Sarah chatting to herself in private, and I believe she was talking to Jo.

It was different for me. I found myself easily agitated,

seldom smiling, clinging especially tight to Sarah, and always feeling guilty for my decisions regarding Jo.

During a Saturday afternoon visiting with my sisters, I broke down in front of them. They were prattling on about a winter party.

"How can you talk about this nonsense! None of it matters. My daughter is missing!" I sat back crying on my childhood bed and banged my head against the creaking headboard. "I should have tried harder to keep Jo here. I meant to visit more often."

"Mariah, you thought you were doing the right thing. We all did," Janeen said. "You had no way of knowing. I feel the same way about Jim sometimes. Like he's never coming back, but you must cling to hope."

"At least he sends you and the kids a little money. You know he's trying. *And* you know where he is. I should have convinced Elliott to let me bring Jo home sooner. Sam would be so disappointed. Some days, I swear Jo's absence is driving me crazy."

Arlene leaned over and grabbed me, "She'll be back, sweetie. I know it sounds easy for me to say, but you need to be focused on making the best life you can now for Sarah, and for Jo's return. Be patient. You've done what you can."

People in Green Tree gossiped about Jo and Nanette having gone missing, creating their own versions of the truth, many assuming there'd been a quarrel between Nanette and me. But eventually the chatter died down and people found other news to talk about. They forgot about the other little Anderson girl, the blonde one, the missing child. But it was hard for me; I was not so easily distracted.

Then right before Thanksgiving, I received a letter from Police Captain Leonard Olsen of Mankato:

*Dear Mrs. Anderson,*
*Forgive this delayed response to the report filed regarding your missing*

*daughter, Josephine. This report only recently crossed my desk and I'm not clear why it was not presented earlier. Be that as it may, I really have no encouraging news to report to you and only hope you have caught up with Miss Jorgenson and your daughter by now. I'm writing personally to you because I was acquainted with Miss Jorgenson. I actually met her the first night she arrived in Mankato and ran into her on other occasions.*

*As charming and persuasive as Miss Jorgenson can be, I can tell you, from my perspective as a police officer, her relationship with the truth was oftentimes stretched thin. I can also tell you, in strictest confidence, that she had an emergency female issue within three months of arriving in Mankato, which made her quite distraught and ended her possibility of having children in the future. I know this because she called me in distress to take her to the hospital that night. Pure conjecture on my part, but perhaps this is why she feels so attached to your daughter now.*

*Following up on your report, I did make inquiries with Mr. Phil Greenly, her former employer. He has not heard anything, but I did ask to check his files, which Miss Jorgenson managed for him. Checking earlier phone records, I did notice a few calls made to a Mr. James Diamond in Hollywood, California. These were the only unrelated business calls in their records. When I contacted Mr. Diamond, he said he met Nanette and her daughter sometime in September at the Le Grande Station in Hollywood, California, but after discussing business matters, she elected not to work with Mr. Diamond and he has not seen her since. Mr. Diamond is apparently some sort of talent agent. So, it does appear that she and your daughter traveled to Hollywood, not Chicago.*

*Hopefully, this may be of some comfort to you knowing they both appeared, at that time, to be safe and are possibly living in the Los Angeles area as of last September. If I hear any updates, I will contact you again.*

*Sincerely,*
*Captain Leonard Olsen*

I quickly sent him a letter back.

Dear Captain Olsen,

I appreciate your response. Your letter, indeed, gave me some sense of comfort. But I can't comprehend Nanette doing this to me. Most can't imagine the fear of the unknown that goes through a mother's head and heart when their child is missing. At least, we now have a place to begin a search. I can only hope that Nanette comes to her senses and returns Jo safely home. Thank you again for the information. I will update you if I have any address changes in the future.

Sincerely,
Mariah Anderson

# CHAPTER 39
# NANETTE

*I*t was my fourth day with Tinsel Town Photography. Jo and I walked through the unlocked door, as I looked briefly around the space. Two matching black chairs, no longer ripped, sat against the wall. Ten feet back, a freshly painted black counter contrasted with the white walls, which were covered with dust-free new photo groupings. The tiled floor was clean and the place smelled a little less like mustard and bologna sandwiches.

"Arnold, we're here! Jo-Jo, honey, grab the broom. Let's get busy."

Stepping out of the depths of his darkroom, Arnold looked at Jo and then shouted, "Not again, Nanette! I told you yesterday. I'm not your babysitter."

I continued looking down at the counter, organizing receipts, receivables and paid-outs from the day before. "Of course, you're not, Arnold. You're the proprietor of this lovely, organized, and now *clean* establishment. Did you get the Columbia Studios starlet prints done? Deadline is today. I'll drop them off."

"I got 'em. Hung 'em to dry last night. Wait a minute."

After handing me an envelope, I opened it, quickly glancing through the prints.

"Oh my, what a dish! These are aces, Arnold. That must have been a fun photo shoot for you. It's not every day you get to photograph three scantily-clad beauties."

"They were fine. I've seen better."

"Whatever you say, Arnold. Alright, I'm off to see six agents today to discuss client head-shot deals. Any chance I can use your car?"

"No. Do you even know how to drive?"

"Perhaps I don't have a license, but I did have some old boyfriends who gave me several lessons."

"I can only imagine. In that case, the answer is definitely no."

"Suit yourself. You two have fun today. I'll be back around four."

"Take your dang kid with you, Nanette."

As I headed to the door, Jo looked up at him with the broom already in her hands. "But Mr. Clemson, I wanted to clean your floor and counter today; we'll have fun." I quickly closed the door behind them.

Despite Arnold's reservations, Jo became a regular fixture at *Tinsel Town* while I went out and drummed up business. Permission or not, I kept dropping her off each morning and Arnold put up with it. Initially he threatened me, worried about what he was supposed to do with a little girl hanging about all day. But quickly, the two of them established a routine. Jo swept the floor and sidewalk each morning, cleaned the counter and front door, and dusted photographs she could reach with a step stool. The place stayed clean and Clemson appreciated the new business I hustled up. Eventually, I think Arnold was even happy having Jo for company.

Within a few weeks we became something of a Hollywood family of mutual accommodation, with Arnold serving as a new uncle. Soon he had Jo putting photo packages in envelopes, sitting on a stool behind the counter, while Arnold developed negatives in the dark room.

Arnold, prior to letting go of his former associates, had always eaten his noon meal at the lunch counter of the Rexall Drugstore down the block. Now, with Jo in place on her stool, he continued his lunch ritual. If a customer walked in, he trained her to say, "Please be seated. Mr. Clemson will be out of the dark room shortly." She would then go out the back door, run up the alley, enter through the lunch counter's back door, yelling to Arnold that he had a customer. Racing back down the alley, she'd walk into the reception area telling them, "Thanks for waiting. Mr. Clemson will be right with you."

After I'd made three weeks of talent agency rounds, a few new actors stumbled in with coupons I'd left with their agents. As word about our discounted prices got out, more extras, starlets and Hollywood hopefuls dropped in for their packet of headshots. If someone was especially good looking, Arnold offered to add their photo to our wall-of-fame for an extra dollar, explaining they might get discovered at TinselTown. Probably not a great investment.

One afternoon, after Arnold finally agreed to my use of his car, I came back early with a betrothed couple following behind. I'd recently visited most of the near-by churches in search of scheduled weddings and had located this couple's address, convincing them Mr. Clemson was the best wedding photographer in town. I brought them in to explain the array of wedding photo packages they could purchase and hopefully get them to sign on the dotted line. I loved selling wedding packages because the bride always wanted everything and family members often bought some also. Unfortunately, this young couple decided on the most basic package, so I tried to nudge them into buying the deluxe bundle which included the padded, satin-covered photo album.

"Now Bea and Thomas, I didn't mention this earlier, but I do allow the deluxe package to be sold on credit. It has the best value and is by far the most desirable. You can make small monthly payments and have it paid out in a year." Arnold heard me make this offer, which was news to him and he interrupted my pitch.

"Uh, Nanette, I think it's best to sell them the original package they first requested." Turning to the timid-looking couple, he said, "I guarantee you both will cherish your photos for a lifetime. The basic package will include your favorites."

They agreed, bought the basic and after they left, I raised my voice to him. "Arnold, I had them eating out of my hand. They would have gone for the deluxe. Don't undermine me when I'm selling."

He turned back around, before going into the darkroom. "Hey, I been doing this more years than you. Those youngsters are barely getting by. I can tell. They would have *never* finished those payments and you know it. Listen to me. Sell them what they can afford and you'll get them back in a year or two when they have that first baby, want a big family portrait with in-laws, and later on, for graduation pics. You gotta think further than the immediate sale, Nanette."

As much as I hated to say it, he made sense. But I still stomped off annoyed. "I'm getting a soda pop."

It was quiet that afternoon, and Jo-Jo was in the habit of going through stacks of old photos in Arnold's file cabinet. She would sit on the floor behind the counter picking out which photo could be her father, older brother, or a friendly aunt. She'd pick out a whole family of smiling headshots, name them, and introduce me to her photo family when I returned.

That afternoon, she was captivated by a little girl with blonde pipe curls wearing a pleated short dress and tap shoes. "Mr. C, who's this?"

"Oh, yeah... I remember her; a real natural, that one.

Heard she's been in a few picture shows lately and some of those Baby Burlesque shorts. Cute kid."

I took the photo from Jo-Jo and checked the back, "That's what I thought. It's Shirley Temple, the little actress I told you about before. I wonder who her agent is?"

"I think she'll be my sister," Jo said, adding it to the pile of her pretend family.

"Not sure she had an agent when she came in," Arnold said. "But she had one heck of a pushy stage mom. I remember Mrs. Temple. Always directing me, saying exactly how she wanted everything shot. Like I hadn't been doing this for years. She kept telling her little girl, 'Sparkle Shirley, give him the sparkle.' Actually, if Shirley's an up-and-comer, we need to add her picture to our wall of fame, don't you think, Nanette?"

"Absolutely not! We just put Jo's photo up there; they're too much alike."

Later, Arnold pulled me aside, away from Jo-Jo, and said, "Hey, I don't mind your kid here so much anymore, but I'm telling you, she needs to play with other kids, get outside more. It's sad; her only friends are these old photographs."

I sighed, shaking my head. "I'm working on it, Arnold."

# CHAPTER 40
# MARIAH

*T*he longer I stayed at the Martin's, the higher the tension ratcheted up between Elliot and myself. Perhaps I shouldn't have, but I blamed Elliott's stubbornness for playing a part in Jo's disappearance. If he had allowed Jo to stay with me earlier, Nanette might never have left Mankato with her. Meanwhile, Elliott was anxious about the future of his farm and declining crop prices and I was not being a sympathetic listener. Our conversations were short and clipped, each of us taking on a more hostile tone. We were two people locked in a house together, but neither had the key to leave. Elliott begrudgingly needed me to maintain the household, garden, laundry and kids. While I needed him for the roof over my head, the food I prepared, and my meager salary.

I clung to Arlene's advice, trying to focus on being a good mother for Sarah and creating a home base for Jo's eventual return.

One December morning, after the kids left for school and Elliott had retreated to his barn, I scanned the morning paper before tackling the sink full of breakfast dishes. A real estate notice caught my eye. Widow Doris Johnson had recently passed away and it looked like her niece and nephew were auctioning off her home, hoping for a quick sale. I knew the house; it sat on a corner off Oak Street, on the outskirts of town. It was way too large for my needs and looked as if it hadn't been repaired in decades. The front porch sagged in a spooky slant to the left, the white paint had faded to weathered-gray, with several window shutters missing or left to flap in the wind.

I worked the kitchen pump up and down, filling a sudsy pan and quickly washed the dishes, then prepared Elliott's lunch of cold chicken, bread, and cabbage salad. Popping into the barn, I called out to him, "I'm headed to town to pick up supplies. I'm taking the team. Buck and Shorty need a workout."

Elliott gave me his usual brusque nod. "Hey, pick me up a pouch of Red Man. I'm almost out." I nodded back as I led the horses out. With Elliott preferring his tractor, the horses were only occasionally put into agricultural service. I'd always enjoyed driving the team. It was a brisk morning, but the sun was out and I felt good bundled in a scarf and coat, sitting high on the bench, looking over the golden stubble of harvested stalks. Traveling the four miles into Green Tree, I crossed the Oak Street corner and stopped to give the Johnson house a closer look.

The auction sign was posted in the yard for the following Friday. Wanting to take a look inside, I tried the three exterior doors, all locked. I walked about the perimeter, and noticed some dry rot in the exposed wood near the roof. In addition, the support under the porch needed replacing. The windows looked secure, although two were broken. Peeking inside, the interior looked a little more promising than the exterior. An idea had germinated in my head on first reading the ad. Seeing the property again made that idea take root, and the potential reward had me excited.

I had to ask myself, was this house a big boondoggle or full of promise? I wasn't convinced either way.

I stopped at the newspaper office, where they often posted real estate notices. I knew Sheila, the young woman working at the front desk. We attended high school together and her parents owned the *Green Tree Sentinel*. She waved at me, while I started reading real estate notices. There were more homes for sale than usual.

I checked the prices of almost a dozen posted on the *Sentinel's* bulletin board. Most were with two or three bedrooms, a few with indoor plumbing, and priced between fifteen-hundred-dollars to three-thousand-dollars. These were newer, smaller homes, close to town and probably in far better condition than widow Johnson's house.

Looking up from her work, Sheila called out, "Hey Mariah, in the market for a new home?"

I sighed. "Not really. Just hoping and dreaming. Know of any really good bargains coming up?"

"Well, if you're in the market for a haunted house, widow Johnson's place is up for auction. Should be a real fire sale."

"Hmm, that old place? What do you think it'll go for?"

"Hard to say. It's run-down, but really big. Might be good for spare parts... Maybe as high as two-grand? You never know with auctions." Then her phone rang, as I turned to leave and waved goodbye.

I took the team down to Magee's and caught up with Arlene, as she was taking her break, going for coffee. I turned the horses around and she joined me on the bench. Although it was almost noon, the *Hot Cup* had only a few tables filled. I selected a table away from the ones with customers.

Once our mugs of coffee and kringlas arrived, I spoke in a low voice. "Arlene, I have a great idea and I want you to speak with Billy-boy about it as soon as possible." Warming her hands on her cup, she raised her eyes at me expectantly. "You know widow Johnson's property, just outside of town?"

"Yes, that dingy, gray clapboard monstrosity?"

Chuckling, I said, "That's the one, and keep your voice down. Now, hear me out... I think you, me, and Billy-boy should go into a partnership and buy it at auction, this Friday. What do you think?"

She whispered back at me, "I think you're crazy! That house is too big, too old, and too ugly. I wouldn't step foot in there. The floorboards would probably cave in."

"You're thinking about it as-is. But what if it was fixed up, divided into apartments, and used as rental units? Use your imagination... a lovely little apartment over the carriage house for you and Billy to start your new life together; no more living with Mom and Dad; no staying in a room over the barn at the Thomas farm."

She took another bite of her kringla and grinned. "OK, I'm listening."

"Do you or Billy have any money saved? I figure I can get a little over a thousand-dollars together from my salary and live-stock sale I've been hoarding, and *if* I can sell the team and wagon. I'm thinking you and Billy could pay for construction materials and handle the repairs. I was looking at the house today. If we gutted it, I think it could be divided into possibly eight apartments. The carriage house, four upstairs, two down-stairs, and perhaps one in the attic and basement... put a hot plate and sink in each. We'd keep the full bathroom as-is for communal use, maybe add a shower and toilet upstairs."

"I don't know? That's a lot of ifs and maybes. Seems like a long shot."

"Well, at least it's an idea that could generate income, and the first thing I've felt motivated about in months. If you and Billy took care of the construction and future maintenance, you both could live there rent-free. We should create a partnership. So many people are looking for apartments now, some-thing inexpensive. What do we have to lose?"

"Everything... our entire savings." Arlene looked at me like I was crazy again.

I rolled my eyes upward, exasperated at her reluctance. "Arlene, sometimes you have to take a chance on something. Look, everything's shaky right now, even the banks. I'd rather put my money in real estate. Something tangible that would provide revenue and a roof over our heads."

"I don't know. I guess it's not a terrible idea." She took a long drought of her coffee. "I'll talk to Billy about it tonight. He's picking me up after choir practice. You're right about one thing. Once we're married, we do want our own place. But how would you get enough money to buy the house? Even a run-down dump like widow Johnson's place is going to sell for more than a thousand dollars."

"Well, things usually sell for less at auction. I'd need to borrow from family, with an offer of repaying them with a higher interest rate than the bank offers. You should talk to Billy tonight and maybe the three of us can get together tomorrow." I lowered my voice again, saying, "And please keep quiet about this, Arlene. We don't want anybody getting the same idea."

She laughed. "Don't worry, I can't imagine anybody rushing out to grab that place. Oh golly, look at the time. I'm late. OK, Mariah, let's try to get together tomorrow night. Maybe I can borrow the Ford and come see you around seven?"

"Perfect."

Leaving the café, I still had a few more errands to run. At Whitmiller's Grocery, I turned in our eggs for store credit, and put staples on Elliott's tab, including his chewing tobacco. My last stop was at one of the town's two blacksmiths. Randal Gottlieb, a close friend to my father, had run his business for years and I knew he could be trusted for good advice. To supplement his business, Randal had added two shiny red and blue Standard Oil gasoline pumps in front and was supplementing the blacksmith business doing auto metal-work repair. Even though cars and tractors were quickly replacing horses and wagons throughout the community, there was still a demand for a pair of reliable plow horses.

As I pulled up in the wagon, he stood at the large wooden double doors of his shop with arms crossed. His longish silver hair was brushed back behind his ears and he still sported the largest mustache in town.

"Well, Miss Mariah, how are you today? It seems like yesterday you were knee-hi to a pony, always wanting to sit on the horses and buggy seats, pretending to be driving the carriages."

"Always loved coming here, Mr. Gottleib," I said as I climbed down. "How are you?"

"Can't complain. Got the best of both worlds. Seems like one foot is in the past and the other headed to the future."

"That's a great way to look at life. I like that. Actually, I'm considering selling the team and wagon. I live at the Martin farm now and we don't have much use for the horses, and frankly, I could use the money. I was wondering what you think I could get for them?"

He walked over and rubbed Buck's neck. "Old Buck and Shorty. Hate to see the team broken up, but someone might could use the two of them. Let's see… considering their age, the wagon's condition, leather harnessing, you might be able to squeeze out four-hundred-and-fifty to five-hundred dollars." He started examining the horses' flanks, hooves and teeth. Then pulled himself up on the wagon, checking the flat-bed and wheels. "Not bad Mariah. You and Sam maintained your team well. Getting a bit fat though. You're right; they probably need to work a little harder."

"I'm not positive yet, but would you be interested in buying them? If I decide, I will do it this week."

"Well, I don't need a team and wagon, but I might be able to resell a good pair and a wagon fairly quickly. I could swing four-hundred cash, making a bit of profit for my trouble."

"Make it an even five-hundred and I'll throw in their saddles. They're at the farm, but they're in really good shape."

"You drive a hard bargain, Mariah. Just like your daddy. I'll go as high as four-seventy-five, but the deal's good for this week only. That's horses, wagon, harnesses and saddles. Horses can be a risky business lately."

I shook his hand, thanked him, and asked him to keep our discussion to himself.

That evening, as I urged the boys into their long-johns and bed, Elliott told me Arlene and Billy-boy were at the front door. Surprised, I came downstairs and invited them up to my room.

I'd put Sarah to bed a half hour before and she had drifted off. I pulled out two chairs from my table and took the rocker for myself. "We'll have to whisper. Sarah's asleep. I thought you were coming over tomorrow."

Billy spoke first, pushing the fly-away brown bangs out of his boyish round face. "Mariah, I was excited about your plans. We think your Johnson-house idea sounds real promising. And you're right; people are looking for cheap housing. Mind you, the place needs a ton of work, but I think we could make a go of it."

I clapped my hands together silently. "I'm so glad you're interested, and Billy, you'd be the perfect person to do the remodeling, with our help, of course."

Billy nodded. "I actually worked in the Johnson place two years back, wiring some lights upstairs for the widow. If we update the rooms, rent apartments out for fifteen or twenty bucks a month, we could recoup our repair costs in a year, and then just collect rent. Of course, there's always maintenance required in an old place, but I been planning on going part-time with the Thomas family eventually. They're like family to me, but I need to get out on my own."

"I was asking Arlene earlier. Do you two have any money you could invest in construction materials? Everything I have and borrow would go towards buying the place."

Arlene rocked back and forth, now looking excited. "Billy and I talked about it. I've got close to two-hundred-dollars saved and he has six-hundred in the bank. We *were* going to spend some of it on our wedding and honeymoon, but decided, tonight, we'd rather invest in the Johnson house. Who needs a big fancy wedding? We'd rather have our own place."

I giggled at her enthusiasm. "I can't believe it was just this morning you were telling me the idea was crazy. What do you think, Billy? Would eight-hundred-dollars be enough for repairs and remodeling? You'll have to add wall partitions, sinks, paint inside and out, do some wood replacement, fix the foundation."

He was quiet for a moment, hopefully taking a count in his head. "It's a lot of work. Not sure, but eight-hundred would sure give us a good start. Until I get in there and start adding things up, I don't know for sure. But I think we're in range. I know a few places selling some really good deals on used materials. I might have to ask David or old-man Thomas for a little loan, but they know I'm good for it."

"All right then. Next up... let me see if I can find a few interested parties to loan me the balance of what I'll need to buy the place. With your repair work and eight-hundred-dollar investment, and my cash and loans for the cost of the home, I think we should be equal partners; the two of you owning fifty percent together, and me owning the other fifty percent. Agreed?"

"Agreed." They both replied in unison. We shook on it, all of us smiling ear to ear, as if our future was now secure.

The following morning, I decided to speak to Elliott before he started his milking. Because I would be selling my team and wagon, I needed to reveal my plans to him. I also wanted to ask about a possible loan, offering to pay him back with a good interest rate.

After I explained my idea about the house, Elliott whistled out, while he belted his work coat. "Well, you got gumption. All I've got in the world right now is this farm and about three-hundred bucks in the bank, but I feel like my three-hundred is safer in that bank than in that rotting old house. Big project for a little woman to take on. Best be careful."

"Who knows? It's an auction. It might all be a big pipedream."

"Probably." He slammed the door and left. I could have used his investment and encouragement, but on second thought, it was best that Elliott and his negative attitude were not involved.

For the next three days, I made the rounds to every family member in our area. The first door I went knocking on was my parents. I boldly laid out the plan to them, asked for five-hundred, promising to start repayment within six months at five percent above the current bank interest rate. Because two of their daughters and a future son-in-law were involved, they gave the project some thought. After a private discussion upstairs between Ma and Dad, they came down with an announcement.

Mom made the coffee, while Dad did the talking at the kitchen table. "You're asking for a big chunk of our savings, Mariah; no trifling ask here. But we got seed money secured, no major debts right now, so your Ma and I are gonna say *yes*. My thinking is banks are so unstable right now, trusting our money to my clever daughters might be the better bet. We know you've been through a real rough patch. It's our way of offering support."

I jumped up and threw my arms around each of their necks. "Your confidence means the world to me! Thanks so much."

I continued trying to rally extended family to the plan without success. A few cousins offered, "Sorry, no, and good luck," but eventually I convinced my favorite uncle to take a risk, and he kicked in another five-hundred. I hoped it would be enough.

The day before the auction, I tearfully sold Buck, Shorty and the wagon to Randal Gottlieb, hoping he would find a good home for my reliable team. Leaving the blacksmith shop, each time I looked back, the horses' eyes were following me. We'd been through a lot together.

I recalled Samuel walking behind the team, sun in his eyes, controlling the tiller, as he broke up thick clods of soil. I pictured leading the girls out on the horses for their first rides, and then packing up everything we owned in that wagon and driving the team out, down the road. My heart ached as I walked away, leaving the horses behind, knowing I'd divested myself from the last connection of my life with Sam and our farm. And with that sale, I'd also lost my only independent mode of transportation. Walking the four miles back to the Martin farm, I reminded myself to trust my gut and pray a lot.

# CHAPTER 41
# NANETTE

*A* month later we were still living at *The Palms Hotel*, but the novelty of elevator rides and life in a tiny room, climbing over piles of suitcases and clothing, was losing its allure. The Palms location was good, but the four-dollar-a-day price tag had exhausted my getting-settled-fund. I'd been checking the classifieds, looking for a larger rental unit cheaper than the hotel. Unfortunately, every rental in Hollywood asked for a hefty deposit and I was finding it difficult to save enough for a down payment *and* keep us at the hotel.

I scrambled each day to bring in enough business at Tinsel Town to keep The Palms general manager, Mr. John Bing, from throwing us out. By then, both Jo-Jo and I were well known to the staff. Every Friday, as we left for work, I tried to discreetly scurry past Mr. Bing as he loomed over the registration desk, hoping he'd miss me before waving our weekly bill in front of my face. But again today, he'd spotted us. Stopping at the desk, I attempted a different approach.

Bing looked to be in his mid-thirties, with slicked-back brown hair, wire rimmed glasses, and appeared to own two suits, a brown and a gray, which he rotated every other day. He was often on the desk in the mornings for check-out, spent afternoons walking throughout the property, and seemed to spend long evenings in his office.

"Mr. Bing, don't you look dapper today in heather-brown. New tie? Looks very smart."

He touched his Windsor knot and looked slightly embarrassed. "Why, thank you. Uh, just need to settle up on your weekly bill, Mrs. Jorgenson. Hope all is going well for you and your daughter."

I gently reached out and touched his arm. "Thanks so much for asking. I have to say, it feels like home here. Actually, Mr. Bing, I've been meaning to tell you… both you and your staff have been so kind to us. I wanted to show my appreciation. Any chance you have time for a coffee and roll this morning? My treat."

He nervously glanced down at his watch. "Uh, I don't see why not. For a few moments. Let me get my assistant to cover the desk."

The three of us went to the hotel coffee shop, located off to the side of the lobby entrance. It was a lovely little low-lit place with small round tables, thickly upholstered chairs, and the deep, rich scent of good coffee. I generally avoided the place because prices were triple those at the drugstore lunch counter. But on the plus side, I could charge the bill to our room.

We ordered two coffees and a juice for Jo. Looking around, I said, "It's so lovely here. Jo-Jo adores the juices. Do you have children, Mr. Bing?"

"No. Not married. Don't seem to have time for that sort of thing. I'm at the hotel so many hours a day."

"I've noticed. You're always on top of things and it shows. I so admire a well-run business."

Mr. Bing took off his glasses and wiped them with his handkerchief. "Well, thank you, Mrs. Jorgenson. Kind of you to say."

"Oh, call me Nanette. I wish my boss had more of your traits." I sighed and continued. "Some days I am single-handedly bringing in all the customers *while* trying to keep his accounts straight. And doing it all on a mere pittance. I'd love to have a boss like you. But things are getting a little better every day. I shouldn't complain."

We chatted a bit more about the challenges of running a big hotel and then I said, "Well, Jo-Jo and I must get going. We should do this again soon, maybe Friday mornings we could catch up? Please have the waiter put this on my account, Mr. Bing."

Again, he nervously touched his tie and straightened it. "I don't see why not, Nanette. And feel free to call me John."

Mr. Bing had forgotten about my hotel bill for today, allowing me another day of reprieve to earn a little more cash. But more importantly, I'd set the stage for a friendly alliance.

It wasn't long before John Bing and I escalated our Friday coffee meetings into wonderful dinner dates, his treat. Within the month, we became more intimate in the room he kept at the hotel. After revealing my rather dire financial situation, he mentioned he had a room with no view which he could let us have for only two-dollars-a-day. He also offered to store our luggage and trunk in the hotel basement. This was a big help, but the deal got even sweeter when I convinced him the extra space in the janitorial closet next to the room would hold our wardrobes perfectly.

On Sundays, Mr. Bing and I began enjoying our only days off together. We'd meet for a luxurious breakfast-in-bed in his room, while I let Jo spend the day with the bell-hops. They were the closest friends she had found. Although they certainly didn't need her assistance; they put up with her comradery. At the end of the day, she'd come to my room showing me her tips of nickels and dimes and stash them in her secret place.

AFTER RETURNING to *Tinsel Town* one afternoon, Arnold told me I'd received a letter. No one from my past knew I worked here, so receiving mail immediately made me suspicious. The return address was stamped: Wonder Toy Company. On my second day at Tinsel Town, I'd printed up the photos Willard Williams had taken of Jo-Jo and her doll, Millie, on the train. I'd kept his business card, and sent him a few of the best photos, hoping his company might use them for advertising. This had been two months ago and I'd forgotten all about it. Quickly opening the envelope, I found a letter and a check.

*Dear Miss Jorgenson,*

*I was happy to hear from you and pleased you and Jo-Jo made it safely to your destination. The results of the photos we took on the train were delightful. I was especially taken with the picture of your daughter sitting alone at the booth with her Curlie Cutie. I shared it with the company president who would like to use the image and have it hand-colored for commercial use. He has plans to print the photo on the box of each 2412 model. If you are in agreement with this, I have included a one-time payment of fifty-dollars for the rights in perpetuity to this image of your daughter. If in agreement, please sign the document included, and return it for our records; then you may cash the check. If you are not in agreement with this, please contact our president, Mr. Reynolds at Wonder Toy Company.*

*Sincerely yours,*
*Willard Williams*
*Territory Sales Manager*

After reading the letter, I waved the check in the air and called out to Arnold and Jo. "Fifty dollars! Oh my stars...this has come at such a pivotal time." I grabbed Jo-Jo, who was on

the floor buckling her tap shoes. "Darling, everything's beginning to turn for us. It's a sign!"

I immediately signed the agreement and popped it in the
mail. A few days later, once the excitement wore off, two
thoughts nagged at me. Perhaps I should have asked for more.
An image they could use in perpetuity for a mere fifty-dollars
was a trifle. My other thought was a bit more concerning. A lot
of people might end up seeing that photo.

"Look Mother, something's happening at the Paramount."

It was a pleasant, late-December Sunday afternoon, as Jo
and I were strolling down Sixth Street and saw a thick line of
people forming at the movie theater. Getting closer, we heard
musical numbers from the film, *42nd Street*, amplified on large
outdoor speakers. The theater marquee was lit up with the
stars' names: Ginger Rogers and Dick Powell. On both sides of
the entrance were large eight-foot posters of movie scenes,
enticing pedestrians to part with their quarters for tickets. Jo
looked up, entranced by the music and posters. "Pleeese
Mother. I want to see this. There's dancing and singing.
Please?"

"Jo-Jo, I'd love to, but I'm meeting Uncle Bing tonight.
Can't be late for that. We'll go another time. I promise."

Suddenly, Jo stomped her foot on the decorative tiled
entrance and pouted, looking up at me. "You always go places
with him. I want to see this movie." Then she stomped her foot
again, crossed her arms, and wouldn't budge. A few customers
in the crowded line looked back at me as I argued with her and
grabbed her arm. Jo jerked away from me, refusing to listen
and then stomped both feet. Abruptly, she tapped and then slid
both feet against the tile. Suddenly, she seemed entranced with

the echoing reverberation under the marque, and began tap dancing to the music blaring out around us.

Forgetting her tantrum, she fell into the tempo of the music, like a little tap-dancing machine, relying on the basic steps taught in her Mankato dance class: Ball-heel, ball-step, shuffle, shuffle, heel-step, repeat. Jo-Jo appeared to be lost in her own world, in love with the rhythmic sound of her shoes making contact with the tile. I stood back, letting her continue. She looked so happy.

Customers close to the lobby area turned around to watch and started clapping, which kept Jo energized, going through a few more intricate steps to the tune of *Shuffle Off to Buffalo*. Soon, the closest people in line made a circle around her, and began throwing pennies, nickels and dimes at her feet. She kept at it, showering her biggest smile at the change-throwers. After a few minutes, the manager walked out from the lobby and shouted at her.

"Hey you! Little girl. Get out of here or I'll call the cops."

Jo looked up, still smiling, then saluted him, saying, "Yes sir." She quickly scooped up all the spare change, as the crowd turned and booed the theater manager back to his post in the lobby. Showing me her hands full of coins, we easily had enough for the twenty-five-cent tickets. She grabbed my hand and said, "We'll go tomorrow, promise?"

# CHAPTER 42
# MARIAH

*I* was unable to sleep Thursday night, incredibly anxious about the auction. I wrestled with my sheets, listening to Sarah's wheezing breath across the room. Was she catching a cold? When would I see Jo again? Worry and doubt kept recycling through my mind. What if I was outbid immediately? Was the eight-hundred for renovations enough? Would anyone rent the apartments? I was twenty-three and a farmer's widow; what did I know about real estate?

I was in over my head, drowning in fear.

Then I recalled Sam. At sixteen with his own farm; at nineteen, with a wife and two kids. And he never looked back. Nobody could ever tell him he wouldn't succeed. I needed to harness that confidence; that inner strength which Samuel had always shown. Even with those memories bolstering me, I didn't sleep a wink.

I got up at four. It was a cold December morning but I wanted to get through chores well before the auction. I leaned over Sarah's bed, listening as she slept. Her breathing sounded better. I moved mechanically through the dark silent house as I prepared breakfast. Then going outside, I fed the hogs, pulled eggs and spread feed. Later I roused the boys and Sarah, and as the kids joined me, I sat down with everybody to eat.

"Seth, you have your map of Europe completed?" I asked while passing the toast.

Catching him with a mouth full of eggs, he nodded back at me. "Good. And Tommy, should we go over spelling words before the test today?"

"Maybe…just once more."

"We'll check your list after you finish eating."

Sarah jumped in saying, "I want to try the list too, Mommy."

"Sure, let's see how you do. And Eli…I don't want to hear about any fights today. If someone bothers you, just walk away."

"Miss Mariah. It wasn't a fight. We was only wrestling."

"Really Eli? That's not what I heard. And, mind your grammar; that's we *were* only wrestling." I shook my head at him and walked over to the stove. "Anybody want more eggs. There's a little left?"

This was my favorite time of the day. Although rushed, it was a time to check in with everyone. Almost like a real family. But this morning, I'd decided not to tell the kids about the auction, in case it all fell through and came to nothing.

Elliott had agreed earlier to let me use his Ford to drive into town. As I began the trip, my anxiety increased. My hands were shaking as I steered over the frost on the gravel road. I had Sarah bundled up next to me. I had taken her out of school today, so she could see what I was hoping to do. Billy was meeting me at the Johnson place and Arlene was at work, but was anxious to hear the outcome. My little idea had become a major family investment.

There were several cars parked alongside the Johnson property when I arrived. The house was now open and people were milling about checking the interior. I took a deep breath, convinced myself I was ready, and rushed over with Sarah, eager to take a look inside to see what could be salvaged. As I walked in, Billy came out, with the bill of his wool cap pulled down low.

"Follow me," he said quietly.

I laughed through my nerves, amused by his sleuthing. We followed him out to the back yard. "Mariah, when you go inside, don't look encouraged or excited 'bout anything. I been telling everybody how much money has to be sunk into this place to make it livable; shaking the loose banisters, and pointing out leakin' issues. We want the bidding to start real low."

"Will do, but how bad is it?"

"Nothin' I can't fix with a hammer, nail, wood and plaster. Actually, better than I thought. Definitely has potential. The staircase is solid. Plumbing seems workable."

"That's good news."

"I been scopin' everybody out. The Christian brothers from the lumber yard are looking to dismantle the place and resell the lumber, flooring, windows, and what-not. Their bids should be low. There are two guys in suits I don't recognize, a couple curious farmers, a few looky-loos, and the Johnson niece and nephew. We got a shot, Mariah."

Sarah and I walked quickly through the house as I tried to visualize the place as an apartment building and future investment. I could see it all so clearly: freshly painted, well maintained, updated lighting, a welcoming rug in the lobby, a blooming rose bush at the front door. I could almost hear the voices, full of life, coming from the apartments, and a front lobby active with tenants coming and going.

Then Sarah brought me back to reality. She tugged on my hand and whispered, "This house looks broken, Mommy."

The small group of interested parties and curious onlookers gathered in the front yard circling the auctioneer, who stood on the front porch. He introduced himself as Amos Goodnight, explaining that he was hired by the property owners. He was a tall, confident-looking man in a bowler hat, suit and vest, whose next step involved registering all interested parties, and reminding the bidders they had to have funds in place if their winning bid was accepted. After going over all rules and regulations, my anxiety was sky-high. Then Mr. Goodnight announced the auction would begin.

He started the bidding at five hundred dollars; this quickly jumped to seven with a bid from one of the two suited men. Who were those gentlemen? From the quality of the suits they were wearing, I was concerned about their obviously deeper pockets. The Christian brothers went to nine hundred, and then I heard a timid, mousey voice squeak out "one-thousand-dollars," and then realized it came from me.

A farmer in flannel and overalls, boldly claimed, "Make that twelve-hundred."

Although it was a cold day, nervous sweat drenched my armpits and waist underneath my jacket. The suited men quickly conferred, and one raised an arm for fifteen. The price was quickly escalating. At this point, the farmer seemed to lose interest, but the Christian brothers hung in there jumping to eighteen-hundred-dollars.

I raised my arm, this time calling out more confidently, "Nineteen."

There was a pause as the auctioneer looked around, then said, "Is that it, ladies and gentlemen? Anyone want to make it two-thousand? Going once, going twice…"

Perfect! Maybe I'd done it.

But the two suits looked at each other and one nodded to the auctioneer. Goodnight shouted out, "Very good, we have two-thousand."

With my two-family loans, my stash in the bank, and the recent sale of my horses and wagon, I had a total of two-thousand, two-hundred and fifty-eight dollars. I called out, "Twenty-two-hundred-dollars," praying the suits had met their limit at two-thousand. But no. They calmly came back at two-thousand, four-hundred. That was it. I had nothing left. My short-lived dream vaporized.

"Lots of potential here, folks. Any other bids? Let's hear two-thousand-five." Silence.

I felt a heavy hand on my shoulder and heard a deep, quiet voice behind me say, "She'll go to two-thousand, six-hundred." Eyes wide in shock, I turned around. It was David Thomas, my old neighbor and Billy's boss. He softly told me, "Just nod yes."

The auctioneer took my nod for affirmation. The suits shrugged their shoulders and shook their heads as the auctioneer asked, "Do we have twenty-eight-hundred...No? Twenty-seven?" He looked at the faces of the small group. "Going once, going twice, sold to Mrs. Anderson for twenty-six-hundred-dollars."

I turned and stared at David and a smiling Billy-boy. I was in shock. We'd done it! I turned and asked David, "Where did you come from? Oh, my God, I'm stunned. I thought we'd lost it." I shook my hands and fingertips in front of me. "I swear, my hands and legs are still shaking. Thank you so much." I offered a quick embrace to Sarah, then Billy, and the always uncomfortable David.

"Don't leave. I'll be right back." Then Sarah and I followed the auctioneer over to the current owners who looked relieved and pleased with the price. I explained I would meet them at the Green Tree bank in an hour with the cash to complete the transaction and title exchange.

I felt my face flushed with excitement, revealing an ear-to-ear grin, as I walked back to Billy and David. Sarah looked up at me asking, "You happy, Mommy?"

"So happy, Sarah. Mommy now owns a house and eventually our own business. It's a good day!"

"The broken house, Mommy?"

I placed my arm around Billy's shoulder. "Yes, but Billy's going to make it beautiful for us. I can see it already. Remember how the old barn was burned with a big hole in the roof? And then he made it better. Same thing."

Billy rubbed his hands together. "Yup. Can't wait to get started."

Sarah pondered this for a few seconds. "So, in this house we have room for Jo. She can move in again, Mommy?"

"Well, we will certainly make room for her." I rubbed my eyes for a second, thinking what Jo would have said about all this. She'd probably have broken into song, singing *Happy Days*, dancing across the battered porch.

David stood there with a pleased expression showing around his mouth and in his kind green eyes. Not a handsome man, but a good and reliable friend.

"So David, you're joining our little enterprise? I guess Billy told you our plans."

"Well, Billy told me that if all went well, he might be needing a little extra for house repairs. I think the idea has merit. To tell the truth, I wasn't going to get involved, but wanted to come out and see if you got the place."

"You certainly came through at the right time. I'm incredibly grateful."

Billy jabbed his friend and boss in the arm. "Gosh dang it, David, you really cut that close."

David stood there, looking down at the dirt. "I had a little money tucked away. I'm sure I'll get my share back eventually if you're in charge, Mariah."

"Yes, with interest, I promise. Your vote of confidence means so much. Let's all go over to Magee's and tell Arlene, and celebrate at the café. We deserve cake, even if it's only nine-thirty."

"Thanks, but I've got to get back." David pulled a small roll of bills from the bib pocket of his over-all's and handed it to me. "Here's my four-hundred. Billy, I'll see you later at the farm. You take care, Mariah."

We headed to Magee's, to share the news with Arlene as she prepared for opening. "I'm thrilled," she said, hugging me. "But now I'm realizing there's going to be *a lot* of work ahead for the three of us. A really busy six months."

Both she and Billy had their jobs to get to, so Sarah and I celebrated, splitting a big piece of chocolate cake. I felt a little guilty splurging at the café, knowing I now had a grand total of fifty-eight dollars to my name, in addition to owing fourteen-hundred to my investors. Instead of cash in the bank, I now owned a large crumbling house which would probably cost another thousand dollars, or more, to make profitable. But I was happy; no, I was thrilled! I'd organized this project, visualized a goal, and had finally accomplished something major. And today, no one could take that feeling from me. Let me eat cake!

## CHAPTER 43
## NANETTE

$\mathcal{I}$ had finally secured an appointment with Alan Cummings, the talent agent recommended by the head of casting at Columbia Pictures. I'd been trying to get in to see him for two months, and continued pestering his receptionist weekly. She eventually softened and granted us an appointment. I'd heard from several people that Cummings had essential contacts needed in the business. This could be a big day for us if Cummings agreed to sign Jo-Jo.

In the morning, I fretted about what Jo-Jo should wear to meet her potential agent. She had quickly outgrown clothes I'd purchased only a few months before leaving Mankato. Perhaps it was all the egg rolls and chop suey. I put her in a favorite dress but noticed the back buttons were straining.

"How does it feel, sweetie?

"Tight. Kinda hurts my arms."

"Yeah, it's a little short too." Checking my watch I said, "We're running late. Just put your blue coat over it and perhaps Mr. Cummings won't notice." She carefully put her coat on and we took the bus to his office while I coached Jo-Jo on what to say and do.

"Remember darling, look animated, smile, and laugh if he says something funny. Men like that. Speak up when he asks you a question and look him in the eye. Can you do all that?"

"Yes, I can do it. I promise. If Mr. Cummings puts me in the movies, will we move to a house?"

"We'll see, baby."

Cumming's office was located in a high-rise building. We took the elevator to the eighth floor and walked through heavy wooden double-doors and stepped out onto deep-pile red carpeting. The reception area was furnished with a black and white checked sofa and a table covered in movie magazines. Cumming's receptionist, an attractive lady with dark hair piled on top of her head, looked down from her desk and kindly smiled at Jo. "Mr. Cummings is ready for you both. Go right in."

I'm not generally the nervous type, but today I felt more anxious than Jo. I wanted this badly, but I believe Jo-Jo simply wanted to please me. Cummings' office walls were filled with photos of people he represented, many of whom I recognized from films. As we walked in, he stood at his desk, shouting on the phone.

"Hank, you better sober up fast and be there early tomorrow morning or you'll be kicked off the set! Don't let it happen again." He slammed down the black receiver and switched gears as he turned to me with a grin and said, "Well, aren't we adorable...the *both* of you. Have a seat."

Walking up to him, Jo-Jo stuck her hand out as I'd instructed her to do. "Thank you, Mr. Cummings. I'm Jo. It's a pleasure to meet you."

Glancing back at me, he said, "Oh, you were right to come in, Mrs. Jorgenson. She's got that spark and spunk. Both of you have a seat. What can I get you to drink... coffee, milk?"

Jo-Jo answered, "Milk please, and a cookie."

I said, "One milk, forget that cookie, and a black coffee for me would be great. Thank you, Mr. Cummings."

"Alan… please. No formalities here." He buzzed his secretary for refreshments. "Now, Jo-Jo, your mother says you want to get into the movie business. Is that correct?"

"Yes. Mother says it will be fun, but hard work too."

"She's right. Lots of work for a little girl. Now, I hear you can sing and dance. How about a sample?" Cummings came around from his desk and sat down on the sofa, closer than necessary, next to me.

She nodded and eagerly asked, "Shall I sing now?"

"Absolutely."

I'd been teaching Jo-Jo a new song; in case she had an audition. She got up in front of us, standing on the parquet floor, and belted out the popular Rudy Vallee song, *Brother, Can You Spare a Dime?* As she finished, Jo-Jo held her hand out in front of Mr. Cummings, probably in hopes of him handing her a coin. He didn't take the bait.

"Wow, never heard a child do that song. Good job!"

"I can dance too."

"Sure, show me a few steps, kiddo."

Jo-Jo did a few buck and wing steps, kicking her legs out on each side, and circling her arms around her head. With each step, change in her pockets began jangling and then bouncing out onto the wooden floor. Noticing the flying money, she wrapped up the dance quickly and slid down on one knee, raising her arms in a big finale. As she did this, I saw two buttons from the back of her dress falling to the floor with her coins. I was more than embarrassed.

But Mr. Cummings smiled and started laughing, gently patting his hand on my thigh, while I tried to smooth over the disaster and asked, "What's going on here, Jo-Jo? Why are you carrying all these coins around?"

She held out the sides of her blue coat. "These are the

biggest pockets I have. You said to put my tips somewhere safe." She looked up at Cummings and explained, "I get these coins when I carry bags at the hotel."

Cummings asked, "You're working at a hotel?"

"Yes sir, and also at Tinsel Town Studio."

I interjected quickly, "She most certainly *does not*. We live at The Palms and she's friends with a few of the bell-hops that let her tag along."

"And the studio?" He asked.

"Arnold Clemson at Tinsel Town watches her occasionally when I do outside work for him, but she's *not* working there, just runs a few errands. I can assure you."

Cummings knelt down and put himself at Jo-Jo's height. "Well little Miss Jo, I appreciate your young work ethic. Let's add one more job to the resume, shall we? Let's make you a sought-after Hollywood star. But maybe we'll change your name. A stage name…something more feminine and catchier. Jo Jorgenson just doesn't have any zing. How about Jamey, Jaqueline, no, I got it," he said, snapping his fingers. "What about…Jillian, Jillian Jordan? What do you think?"

Jo seemed perplexed, and looked up at me frowning.

I shrugged my shoulders, smiled at her and said, "Why not? I like it."

Jo, counting on her fingers, replied, "Josephine, Jo, Jo-Jo, Jillian…So like putting on new clothes? You try on a name and if it fits, you get to keep it?"

I nodded back, thinking a name change might provide additional security for us. "Sort of like that."

After signing an agent contract with Alan Cummings, Jo and I both decided to try on new names for size.

We were now Jillian and Nan Jordan.

MR. CUMMINGS HELD true to his word, and within a couple weeks got Jillian a few auditions for small parts at some major studios including Warner Brothers and Universal Studios. Initially, I was surprised at how dismal she was at auditions. Because Jillian couldn't read, she learned the lines by rote, memorizing a portion of the script word for word, as I read it aloud to her. But she concentrated too hard on getting every word correct, speaking without expression or emotion. After saying a few lines for auditions, casting directors offered up unenthusiastic smiles, followed by, "We'll call if interested. Thank you.... Next!" For some reason, they couldn't see the special essence that I knew was in her.

On a chilly evening in late January, Jillian made her film debut. It was a very minor role but she was on the big screen and we watched all sixty seconds of it, so proud and excited, as if she'd had a starring role. It all occurred because one of Cumming's child-actor clients contracted a bad cold while they were shooting an *Our Gang* episode. He called me at Tinsel Town that afternoon.

"Nan, one of my kids dropped out today... they've got a spot for your girl on the *Our Gang* set. How quickly can you get Jillian over to Hal Roach's studio?"

"That's fantastic! I'm with a client right now, but give me the address and I'll put Jillian in a cab."

I handed the address to a cabbie and told Jillian, "Ask for the assistant director and say that Mr. Cummings sent you. Do whatever they tell you and make me proud!" I was worried she'd be nervous going all alone, but when I met her later, she couldn't stop talking about the shoot during our entire bus ride home.

"Mother, it was so much fun. A man in a funny hat showed all of us our *marks*. That means where to stand. Then his friend, who smoked all the time, would clap two boards together and we'd do whatever he told us to do and say. But most of the time we played kick ball in the street until they called us for a scene. There are some swell kids there. When can I go back?"

Weeks later, Cummings, Jillian, and I attended our own little premier together at the Paramount when the *Our Gang* episode was screened as the opening short with *King Kong*. The three of us sat with our hands held tightly together as we caught a brief glimpse of Jillian jumping up and down. Then she clapped for a boy being hit in the face, as the teacher came in and broke up a playground fight.

That evening, in the dark grandness of the theater, I finally realized our dream and felt so proud of my little protégé. When Jillian was on screen my eyes teared up, while attentive Mr. Cummings handed me a handkerchief, placed his arm around my shoulder, and gave me a warm hug.

Soon, flower arrangements began arriving for me from Alan Cummings, arousing John Bing's suspicions. When Cummings arrived to take me to dinner in his long shiny Packard, John intercepted me coming off the elevator.

"What's going on, Nanette? So, the man in the big car… is that the guy who keeps sending you flowers? Are you *dating* him?"

"Don't be silly, John. He's Jillian's agent; we're only getting some dinner."

"Who's Jillian, and why would you be getting dinner with him?"

"Jillian…that's Jo-Jo's new stage name. I told you all about it. Don't fret John. I'll be back soon."

"I'm not fretting. I'm angry. It seems like he's courting you." He said this while banging his fist against the elevator door. "I thought we had something special, but obviously not."

I continued walking through the lobby without comment, not wanting a public argument. John would calm down. He was a reasonable man.

When I returned a few hours later with a box of left-overs for Jillian, there was an eviction notice plastered to our door, all clothing items from the supply closet were thrown in a pile in the hallway, and our suitcases and trunk from the basement were parked next to the pile.

Ready or not, it looked like our days at The Palms Hotel were over.

## CHAPTER 44
## MARIAH

*W*e were two months in on our renovations at the Johnson House, but the bitter cold and deep snow seemed to be slowing everything down. One Saturday, Sarah decided to tag along with me to the renovation. On an errand for Billy, we trudged through the snow, walking to the hardware store for nuts, bolts, and switch plates. Downtown was quiet for a Saturday, muffled in white, with a few tracks on the road and sidewalk. Inside, I inhaled the store's familiar scent of sawdust and paint. As usual, Sarah darted to the back of the store, enticed by the toy department. The toys were stacked on shelves, often featuring a few brightly colored Schwinn and Hawthorne bicycles with baskets, wooden scooters, roller skates, metal racing cars, dolls, and stuffed Mickey Mouses. Sarah loved to look and linger, knowing better than to ask for anything. New toys were an extremely rare treat.

"Mommy, come look." She stood staring upwards in front of a shelf.

I glanced down the aisle, waving her forward. "No time today, Sarah. We need to get back. Billy's waiting."

"Just come look. It's Jo."

Carrying my sack of hardware, I walked down the long, narrow store. "Don't be silly, Sarah." But then I reminded myself of the young blond girl in the Wonder Bread sign in Mankato, which had brought me to tears months ago. I stopped and stared at the doll she pointed at, which was in a tall box with clear cellophane revealing the doll's face and dress. "Oh, that's like the doll Nanette gave Jo."

Sarah nodded, still staring. "It's Millie, Jo's doll. But see the box. That picture is Jo with Millie."

On the outside of the box was a colorful painted portrait of a young fair-haired girl with ringlet curls, holding the same blonde doll on her lap. She did look surprisingly similar to our Jo, even wearing a blue coat like the one Nanette had bought her. "You're right. That painting looks a lot like her. But it's only a coincidence. We need to get back now."

"But it *is* Jo. It's Jo with Millie."

"Sarah, a lot of children look alike, especially in paintings. But you're right. Very similar. "Time's a-wastin, darling. Let's go."

Although I knew we had to leave, we both continued to stare at the picture silently for another moment and then moved on. Throughout the day, the more I thought about the box, the more I thought Sarah might be right. But who knew? It was probably what I'd called it earlier, a crazy coincidence. But there was something about the picture that kept nagging at me; the pixie-like face, her no-fear expression smiling straight ahead, the physical manner in which she confidently sat.

Arriving back at Johnson House, Billy was busy unloading supplies he had picked up during the week. "Billy, my goodness, where'd all this come from?"

"I told you I got my resources. Had word from a pal about an out-of-business hotel in Albert Lea. They're guttin' it. Picked up eight sinks and old piping. And they were practically giving away Murphy beds. I got eight stashed in the loft at the farm. Ten bucks a piece; so, I couldn't pass those up."

"Fantastic! What a turn of luck. And these?"

Billy walked over and picked up a wired bulb and glass shade from the floor. I snagged six of these from Willy Morris on Eighth Avenue. His family's house is all but abandoned now. Sold me the lights for half-dollar each, and said I could have all the doors for a buck-a-piece. Poor, desperate man. He was selling his house down to the foundation, piece by piece."

"Oh, that's terrible. So sad to hear about the Morris family. I knew Willy from school."

Arlene arrived after her shift at Magee's, and tied a canvas apron over her skirt and a scarf around her head. "Hello, sorry I couldn't get here sooner. Mariah, I already had three inquiries about apartment rentals while I was at work today. The word is spreading; hopefully, no need to advertise once we're ready to rent."

"Great to hear! Hey, what do you guys think about renaming this the Anderson Arms? I'm tired of referring to it as old widow Johnson's place."

Billy shouted out, "OK with me. Got a nice ring to it."

Arlene and Billy had postponed their wedding plans, putting in all their free time on the renovation. As my baby-sister, I'd always joked about Arlene rarely doing much strenuous labor back on the farm; but now, with her devotion to Billy, she worked side by side with him most evenings and days off. Her work ethic impressed me, as I saw her bringing Billy tools, sanding wood, hammering nails, and she had an amazing ability of keeping up his spirits. If Arlene was around, Billy was happy.

My Dad and brothers, Clem and Wilbur, even lent a hand some Sundays after church. Having four men working together was a huge help. My dad was curious about the project and also probably wanted to protect his investment.

Although the hole in my heart, created by Sam's death and Jo's disappearance, was still raw, my weekends spent together in that cold big house with Arlene and Billy were joyous times for me, despite the physical work. For hours, I immersed myself in the labor and it helped take my mind off my losses. For me, there was something special about working on a project that actually belonged to me; something I could later show my girls with pride. Billy, Arlene, and I became a tireless trio, slowly bringing the Anderson Arms to life.

On my next market day, I stopped at the drugstore. The painting on the doll box had been bothering me all week. I decided to make a call to Captain Olsen from the Mankato police department. As the call went through, I suddenly felt foolish telling him about a picture on a doll's box, but maybe it was a clue. I had to cling to any possible lead I found. We had never spoken to each other and only communicated the one time with our letter exchange. My anxiety grew as I waited for him to come on the line. He'd probably think the whole idea was silly. Feeling guilty for wasting his time, I reached up to disconnect.

Then I heard, "Olsen, here."

"Captain? This is Mariah Anderson…from Green Tree? You kindly wrote to me a few months back regarding my missing daughter, Jo, and Nanette Jorgenson."

"Oh yes…How are you? So, did Nanette finally show up in Green Tree with your child?"

"Unfortunately, no."

"Surprising. I thought sure she'd eventually bring her back. Nanette never struck me as the real mothering type."

"No, haven't had any news at all since your letter that I wanted to pass along, but I ran across something that's been on my mind. Do you have a minute?"

"Yeah, I got a few."

"I was in our local hardware store the other day, and Jo's

twin, Sarah, and I could swear we saw a picture of Jo printed on a doll's box. She was holding a Curlie Cutie doll. I know it sounds crazy but I thought you might want to know."

"Alright… Don't know what a Curlie Cutie is, or if there's much I can do with that information. You do understand that pictures of kids might look similar?"

"It's a popular doll, and yes, that's what I thought at first, too. But the more I looked at the box, the more convinced I became. Nanette actually gave Jo one of those dolls months ago. It's been on my mind all week, so I went back and looked at the box again today. I'm convinced; it's Jo. Knowing she's out there, maybe being used to sell products…well, it's disturbing."

"Uh-ha…Hmm. Let me think for a second. It was Los Angeles where we tracked Nanette and Jo to, correct?"

"Yes. You spoke with a talent agent, a Mr. Diamond, who confirmed meeting them in Hollywood. But then the trail went cold. I kept your letter and still read it from time to time, to keep hope. Also, keep in mind, Nanette was familiar with the workings of a photo studio."

"Interesting. Mrs. Anderson, I'm gonna go out on a limb here and ask a friend to do me a favor. You remember hearing about the Lindberg baby kidnapping, right?"

"Certainly. *Everybody* heard about that. Was in the paper for months. Just terrible."

"Well, about a year after that case, congress passed a law allowing the Bureau of Investigation to look into possible kidnappings when people are taken across state lines. Nowadays, because of the terrible economy, a lot of kids have been placed with others to be raised. There are so many more orphans now too. But because Nanette has never gotten in touch with you when she moved with Jo, this may qualify for the Bureau's jurisdiction, if you'll agree to press charges. I honestly have no idea if they'll look into your case. They're a busy bunch. I'll give my friend at the bureau the details we have, and *maybe* he'll put a bug in the ear of one of their investigators in Los Angeles. It's worth a try."

My voice broke and my eyes pushed back tears. "Certainly, please. Yes, I'll press charges! Whatever I can do. I want and *need* my daughter back. I'm sure you can relate. Do you have children, Captain Olsen?"

"No, no kids, still single. But I do understand what you and your daughter must be going through. Let me see if I can shine a little light on your missing child."

# CHAPTER 45
# NANETTE

Although the writing was literally on the door, I refused to believe that adoring John Bing could be so heartless. The following morning, after being cruelly thrown out with a very public eviction notice, I believed John would come to his senses and allow me to patch things up between us, hopefully at least long enough for me to rent a place and borrow his car for moving. In reality, what did I do that was so wrong? Received flowers? Eaten a delicious steak dinner? A working girl deserves a bit of charity.

I also had to consider whether or not Cummings was the better catch over Bing. Certainly, he held more sway in the movie business and obviously had more money, but my jury was still out on the whole debacle. John was a sweet and caring man and a good hotel manager.

Dressed in my most flattering suit, which featured a jacket with a fitted waist and fluttering peplum edge, I approached the desk, leaving Jillian on a lobby sofa with her doll, Millie. However, Bing chose to ignore me as I pleaded my case in front of him, while he manned the front desk.

"Mr. Bing...John, this is highly unprofessional. My

daughter and I have been excellent guests." I noticed a few people seated in the lobby, beginning to put their newspapers down to watch us. I lowered my voice, almost whispering, not wanting to create a scene. "Please be reasonable, John. It was just dinner, nothing more. You're the guy for me. Trust me."

That comment got him talking. Coming from behind the counter, he took my elbow with unnecessary pressure, and walked me out the door. "Trust you? That's a laugh. The veil has been lifted and you obviously seem taken by that, that... rake. Watching you get in his car last night was like a slap on the face. We are *done*, Nanette. I'm only grateful I realized who you really were before it was too late. Take that poor little girl, Jo-Jo... Jillian, or whatever her name may currently be, and remove yourselves from the premises by the end of the day. You have twenty-four hours from last night's notice."

I began to speak, but Bing lifted his palm, interrupted me and said, "Forget it, Nanette. I'm a busy man."

I stood on the steps, as two bellhops on either side of the sidewalk turned their backs, pretending they hadn't been eavesdropping. I pulled down my jacket, held my head high and walked back in, passing by Bing, and spoke to his assistant at the desk. "Mr. Samuels, please let the record reflect that Nan Jordan was forced to leave The Palms today under duress, after having *always* paid her bill in a somewhat timely fashion." The assistant looked back and forth between Bing and me. I snapped my fingers at Samuels and said, "Don't watch Mr. Bing. I'm the guest here. Now write that in your little book." My red polished nail tapped impatiently on the black leather registration book. "That's *Nan Jordan.*" He began scribbling away in the ledger. "Thank you, sir, and good day."

After making my dramatic and effective exit, I had to backtrack and approach the desk, yet again. "Oh, I also need to use your courtesy phone for a local call please."

I'd made a mistake and miscalculated Bing's feelings. I had

obviously broken his heart and wounded his pride. Now, I would have to scramble to find a place by the end of the day and hire an expensive cab to get our stuff moved. Highly inconvenient. I'd been careless. I should have hidden Cumming's attentiveness more effectively. I called Arnold and told him Jillian and I wouldn't be in because of an unexpected eviction.

"How'd you screw that up, Nanette? I thought you had your hotel manager wrapped around your pinky."

"Oh Arnold, mind your own beeswax. I was calling to see if I could borrow your car?"

"No. It's for business purposes only, and as you said, you're obviously not working today. Be here tomorrow, nine o'clock sharp."

I stood in the lobby, taking deep breaths, gathering my thoughts. I grabbed an abandoned newspaper left on a sofa, took Jillian's hand, and returned to our room."

"Looks like it's time for a house hunt, sweetie. You wanted that, right?" While Jillian began packing our bags, I started my search for potential apartments.

BY LATE AFTERNOON, we located two rooms in a small Spanish-style bungalow duplex, featuring beige stucco walls, and a red-tiled roof. Although dated, the look of the area was a real departure for me and felt quite exotic. It was the first address we looked at, and it took a streetcar and two bus transfers to get there from the Palms on Spring Street. Although dingy, and in need of interior paint, there was a decent-sized living room with a kitchenette, bedroom, and a bathroom located at the back, shared with duplex neighbors. It was on a hilly avenue, with a few tall, thirsty-looking palms, and conveniently located on the bus line. Jillian loved the tiny backyard with a chain-link fence and was already mentioning pets. We were surrounded by similar rental duplexes, barking dogs, and lots of ragged-looking kids playing in the street.

I wasn't that concerned with the lowly outward appearance. I was sure that we'd be moving up and out soon. I waved my fifty-dollar bill from Wonder Toy Company in front of the landlord and said, "We'll take it."

# CHAPTER 46
# MARIAH

$O$n a beautiful early spring morning, I was in front of the oven, pulling out a fresh loaf, when Elliott walked in, white as the flour I'd just baked. He slammed down his mug on the table, pouring himself a cup of this morning's reheated coffee.

"My God, what's wrong Elliott?

"It's gone, Mariah. Every last dollar."

"What are you talking about?"

"You read about the banking holiday the feds put into place? All the banks closed for a few days so people would stop pulling their money out. Sort of a temporary calming of the waters."

"Yes, read that in the paper. Seemed like a good idea."

"Well, I went to town this morning and the Green Tree bank didn't reopen like they were supposed to. Farmers at the seed store say the bank's gone; shut down for good." He pounded his fist on the table in anger. "Damned if I'm not wiped out, Mariah. All the money in my account is gone. I can't believe it."

In a daze, he held his chipped coffee mug with both hands,

staring out the back door. I set the bread on the stove top and sat down across from him.

"I'm so sorry, Elliott. I never thought it would come to this in Green Tree. Maybe it'll reopen."

Elliott continued staring. "I trusted the Smith family at the bank. Known them for years. I could have pulled my money out months ago, but didn't. I'm a damn fool. Wanted to help keep the bank solvent… and what do I get for my support? Nothing. It wasn't much, but it was all I had, Mariah. That was my spring crop."

"There's cash from my last two pay-days, in case I needed it for the renovation. Thank God, I never took the time to deposit it. I'm happy to share if you need some cash."

"Don't gloat. I'm not asking to borrow."

"I'm not gloating. Just offering to help. Look, I've read the government is coming up with low interest loans for farmers. Roosevelt isn't going to turn his back on us. Everybody needs crops in the ground."

He shook his head and leaned his head on his arms on top of the table and mumbled, "I'm not one to take handouts. It's not my way."

"Well, it's that or let your farm blow away. You didn't cause this banking turmoil. Fight for what you have, Elliott. A special low-rate loan isn't a handout.

"I don't know… some days aren't worth getting up for."

"You'll find a way out. You've got your health, three strong boys, and a good farm here. You can't give up."

"Damn it, Mariah. You're always like a Little Miss Sunshine. Can't you ever keep your mouth shut?" He pushed up from the table, walked out, slamming the door behind him.

His anger and tone shocked me. I knew Sarah and I would be leaving the farm eventually, but his last comment made me want to move immediately. I felt terrible for his dilemma, but I hated being around someone so negative. Unfortunately, it would be at least two to three months before our rooms in the Anderson Arms would be ready.

From that point on, I kept to myself, tending to the boys and Sarah, and let Elliott solve his own problems.

∾

WITHIN A FEW WEEKS, I received another letter from Captain Olsen.

> *Dear Mrs. Anderson,*
>
> *I'm happy to report that a bureau agent in L.A. has agreed to look into the case to see if they could dig up any more details on Jo's where-abouts. I've given them the information we had to start their investigation, regarding the talent agent, James Diamond and the doll box. It may take them several weeks to get the case rolling. My colleague mentioned that thousands of newcomers have flooded into the Hollywood area hoping to find jobs in the movie business. Seems it's a pretty unscrupulous industry. Lots of graft going on there, but the bureau might uncover something.*
>
> *Best Regards,*
>
> *Captain Olsen*

This simple letter lightened my heavy heart. It was a start. Although Jo was still missing, at least I had hope that the best detectives in the country were looking for her. I sensed that Nanette would at least attempt to keep Jo safe. She struck me as a survivor, always landing on her feet, much like a scrappy nine-lives cat. I truly hated Nanette and her deceitful nature but perhaps a bit of luck was finally turning my way.

# CHAPTER 47
# NANETTE

*W*ithin days of moving in, Jillian developed a friendship with two brothers living on the other side of the duplex with their single mother. Tink and Taylor, ages six and eight, let Jillian tag along on their neighborhood escapades which involved a red Radio Flyer wagon and the hunt for frogs, lizards, and any bug they could catch in a jar. On weekends, she climbed trees, played hopscotch on the street, and hide-and-go-seek throughout the neighborhood.

Jillian quickly noticed during weekday mornings all the kids left on a big yellow school bus. Although we had not celebrated her birthday, I knew Jillian was now six. When we originally met, Mariah had mentioned that the twins had recently turned five. Now that she was six, she could attend school, but I had no idea what type of identification papers would be required. I decided to put her education off until next fall.

Standing at the bus stop one Monday morning while headed to Tinsel Town, Jillian refused to get on the city bus. As I stepped up the stairs, she remained on the sidewalk. With arms crossed, she announced, "I want to go to school. All the other kids go. I'm tired of cleaning at Tinsel Town."

I turned and roughly yanked her up the bus steps, sat her down on the seat, and explained, "Jillian, going to school right now will interfere with your film career. You're just getting started. We need you ready to audition at any opportunity. You'll go next fall."

"But what about reading," she whined. "Everyone knows their alphabet, but me. Even Tink, and he's not so smart."

"I don't think you're ready, sweetie. You'll learn soon enough. How about this... I'll get you signed up for singing lessons and advanced tap classes to take in the evenings. That's kind of like school. You'd enjoy that, wouldn't you?"

Wiping her eyes, she said, "Yes, please."

I stared out the window and patted her hand. "Good. No more talk of school, Jillian. We'll be at work soon."

It wasn't long before Alan Cummings became a regular guest. Over a few weeks, I'd learned more about him. The down side of the relationship was that he appeared happily married with a wife of fifteen years and they had two children several years older than Jillian. The upside was that he was generous and often came bearing gifts. He tended to come by on Tuesday and Thursday evenings. I had no idea what he told his wife regarding his where-abouts on those nights, but she seemed quite accommodating.

I had just put Jillian to bed when he pulled up to the house in his Packard, bringing wine and chocolate, my favorites. While I sat on the sofa, with his head in my lap, I stared down at his moderately attractive face. He had dark, shiny bril-liantined hair, with a slightly off-center part, a small mustache, and large brown eyes. If you squinted and stood back a distance, he looked quite similar to the handsome actor, Clark Gable.

"Relax Alan, let me rub your temples. Close your eyes. This is going to feel so good. You're looking especially handsome tonight."

Alan sighed in contentment, as his tension melted. Eventually, our conversation turned to Jillian, when I asked if he'd heard of any new auditions on the horizon.

Still lying in my lap, he looked up and said, "I gotta say, Nan, recently every time I put Jillian up for a role and send over her headshots, most casting directors tell me the same thing. 'There's already one Shirley Temple, we don't need another.'

I cringed when he said that. "Oh, that name... Shirley Temple, Shirley Temple! That's all I hear from people. When Jillian and I walk down the street, people always stop us and say, 'Do you know who she reminds me of?' It makes me so angry. We aren't *copying* her. And anyway, other mothers at auditions have told me Shirley is just a little scene-stealer."

"I don't know about that, but they're the same size, close in age, same hair, and they both dance and sing. We need a new look. Something that makes Jillian stand out; makes her more unique. Every studio is afraid to touch her, thinking if they use Jillian, they're trying to copy Fox's success with the Shirley kid. Everyone wants an original."

"I hadn't really thought about it like that. Honestly, I'm too tired to worry about it now. Let's do something a little more fun."

"That's why I came over, darling."

I considered Alan's advice and the next evening covered Jillian's hair in a medium-brown hair dye, and restyled her curls into a straight side-part bob with a big bow. Jillian looked in the mirror, pouting. "I feel different. It's not me. Mr. Cummings asked me to do this? For what role?"

"Oh, not really sure. Something he's putting you up for.

You'll hear about it soon. We'll have to ask Arnold to take new headshots for you."

"Well, I don't have to like it," she said, while squinting at her reflection.

Soon, I had her posing in front of Arnold's camera wearing a miniature sailor's outfit that I *borrowed* from the Universal Studios' wardrobe department while waiting on Jillian during an audition. In Tinsel Town, we took down curly, blond Jo-Jo from the stars-of-the-future wall and hung the new and improved bow-headed brunette, Jillian Jordan.

Alan's suggestions seemed to help. After using the new promotional photos, Jillian received an audition playing the child of a con-man being taken to jail. She had to grab his leg as he walked out the door and plead for her daddy not to go away. Because her lines were limited, she gave a very credible, tear-stained audition. After a second audition two weeks later, we got the call for the part. I felt sure this might be the big breakthrough we needed.

A MONTH LATER, after dropping Jillian at the makeup department at Warner Brothers, I walked down the street past Universal Studios, noticing the early spring buds on the crepe myrtle trees. I felt lucky to be living in this bustling modern town, with blue skies over my head and the scent of opportunity on the wind. I had an appointment for a photo contract with a big client, the public relations director from RCA, and was happy about Jillian's blossoming career. Life felt pretty darn good right now for a little nobody from Green Tree, Iowa.

Pushing open the door to Tinsel Town, I saw Arnold behind the counter looking like all the color had drained from his face.

"Hey Arnold, what's got you spooked? You look terrible."

Arnold's voice was low and angry. "Some man from the Bureau of Investigation was just here; said they were looking for a little kidnapped girl named Josephine Anderson. Nanette, what kind of crap have you got me mixed up in?"

# CHAPTER 48
# MARIAH

"*H*ate to be the one to tell 'ya, Mariah, but I got some bad news." Billy-boy opened the door of Thomas' old truck, as Sarah and I slid across the cracked leather seat, headed for a Saturday afternoon of renovation work.

"Well, that's a lovely greeting, Billy. Can't you wait until I get into the truck before you hit me with the latest tragedy. It was March and the Anderson Arms repairs were chugging along, and we were beginning to visualize the end of our project.

"Sorry," Billy said, "but I knew you were lookin' to get into one of the downstairs apartments early, but termites might have slowed down the plans."

"What are termites, Mommy?"

"Sweetie, they're horrid wood-chomping creatures that love to eat up homes. But, Billy, they're actually pretty rare in Iowa, right? Maybe it's not so serious. How bad is it?"

"Bad. You're right though. I haven't run into near as many problems with 'em here as there were in the south. But it's probably 'cause the place was vacant so long and we had a warmer winter. We gotta replace a couple weight-bearing supports they've already tunneled through… they're close to crumbling. But the biggest problem is money. I've already budgeted everything down to the last nickel."

I slapped my hand on the seat cushion. "Does it ever get easier?" I let out an exasperated sigh. "Go ahead and start work on it Monday, and we'll have to cut some other items until we start collecting rent. I've got a little cash to get your replacement wood."

"Okey-dokey. It'll set us back a few weeks and then we'll need to treat the whole place for infestation, and that ain't cheap."

"Any good news?" I asked.

Sarah turned to me and placed her head on my shoulder. "It's a nice sunny day, Mommy."

I smiled and hugged her. "It is indeed."

This weekend we were sanding and staining the oak floors on the first level. I'd convinced my oldest sister, Janeen, to join us there, offering her a promise of hot coffee, conversation, and apple pie in exchange for her labor. Getting right to it, Janeen and I sanded, as Sarah followed behind us sweeping up sawdust.

Later Arlene arrived, kicking off the buckled pumps she'd been wearing all day at Magee's. She grabbed a slice of pie and sat down on the stairs. "Finally…What a day! So glad to be sitting down. We had a lot of people in the store, and some were actually buying."

I looked up from my sanding for a second and asked, "So what are you selling that I can't afford?"

"Oh, let's see…swing coats, gorgeous little feathered hats, some new longer-length flared dresses. You'd love them."

Janeen chimed in, "Not much call for feathered hats at the farm; I'd probably scare the chickens half to death. Anybody come in that we know?"

"Yes… Catherine Anderson, for one. Looking at new dresses for the VFW spring dance."

"How's she doing?" I asked. "I've only seen her a few times since my terrible trip to Mankato. Maybe she avoids me now, knowing Nanette was her close friend. Probably feels guilty for introducing us."

Refilling her coffee from the thermos, Janeene said, "Certainly wasn't Catherine's fault. I guess that witch, Nanette, had her fooled too. I wonder if Catherine has a date for the dance? Hope so; she needs to get out from under her mother's thumb."

"Isn't that the truth?" Then out of Sarah's earshot, I whispered, "My mother-in-law is *so* controlling."

Arlene added, with a knowing look, "I got the sense that Catherine wanted to look really nice for somebody."

Billy, shoring up the loose banister, stopped hammering. "Are you ladies gonna gossip all afternoon about Catherine Anderson, or are we gonna get these floors done? If you three hung out at the right spot, like the Farm and Implement Store, you'd know for a fact that Elliott Martin asked Catherine to the dance."

I looked up stunned. "Are you sure?"

"Sure as snow is gonna fall next winter. Overheard it myself from her older brother, talking to Eldo, as he sharpened my saw. Leave it to me to have all the facts, ladies. Mystery solved. Now let's get them dinged-up floors shining again."

Sweeping up behind us, Sarah asked, "So, Mr. Martin will be dancing with Aunt Catherine?"

"Sarah, it's not our business. We don't know for sure," I said. "We don't want to start rumors at the house."

"Well, I definitely know for sure," Billy yelled from the top of the stairs.

Arlene looked excited. "Ohhh, this *is* interesting. You know, I think we should all go to that dance next week. Why not?"

Pointing at me and Janeen, she said, "*You two* haven't done anything social, except go to church, in ages. Let's all go, please, Billy?"

"Already got the dang tickets. Knew you'd want to go. I agree. We should *all* go. And get those bachelor brothers of yours to show up too. Tell Clem and Wilbur."

I stopped sanding again and announced, "Sorry, not in the mood for dancing, and *if* Elliott is going with Catherine, I'll need to watch the kids."

"Mommy, you should go," Sarah said. "Seth can be in charge."

Janeen added, "I don't know about me either... I honestly would love to go but I am *still* a married woman."

"Oh, for heaven's sake, you two," Arlene said. "Mariah, Elliott's oldest boy is capable of babysitting for one night and Janeen, you're just *dancing*. A married woman can certainly attend a dance, and you'll probably only be dancing with our brothers. They're too shy and awkward to ask anyone else."

On Wednesday evening, as Sarah and I were shelling peas at the Martin's kitchen table, she brought up the dance. "So, did you decide on Saturday night?"

"I just don't feel like dancing, Sarah. I have no reason to be celebrating and nothing to wear."

"Wear the dress you made for Mankato. You never wear that and it's beautiful."

"I never wear it because it brings back bad memories. I don't know...Maybe I could do with a night out."

"I want you to be happy, Mommy."

"Oh, sweetie, I try. I really do. I'm sure I don't smile enough these days. For you, Sarah, I'm going to try harder. Is it difficult living with someone that's an old grump all the time?"

"Well... you're not too old, and look really pretty when you smile."

"I'll keep that in mind. You're so wise, Sarah. I do love you; sorry if I don't say it often enough."

The screen door in the mudroom slammed as Seth and his dad walked in from the barn. Elliott nodded to us as they both washed their hands in the kitchen sink, then looked around expectantly for their dinner.

"Ten minutes and everything should be on the table. Sarah, let's set up in the dining room. Elliott, I may be planning on staying with my parents Saturday night. OK, with you?"

"Well, I'm going out myself Saturday, but I suppose Seth can watch the others, right son?"

"Sure. Just make sure Eli knows I'm in charge."

Once decided, I began to feel enthusiastic about going. A little break in the monotony of work would be welcome. Saturday evening, Sarah decided to stay at the Martins to play with Tommy. Janeen picked me up in Pa's car and on the way to my parents, we stopped at the drugstore. We both splurged on silk stockings and lipstick, which I hadn't put on since Sam's death. As we shopped, we both giggled like school girls instead of young mothers weighted down with problems.

While getting ready downstairs at my parents' house, Janeen, Arlene and I, dressed in robes with our hair rolled up in rags, took turns ironing our dresses. While waiting, Arlene dialed into *Your Hit Parade* and began showing brother, Clem, a few basic dance steps. He desperately needed lessons, moving gracelessly, his legs stiff as boards. As I finished ironing, I helped my older brother, Wilbur, with his necktie. My brothers were pleasant, quiet men, who continued to live at home. I think they were reluctant to date many women knowing their prospects were limited with this economy. Both planned on taking over a portion of Dad's farm eventually, but they also knew they'd have to take on additional acreage to be profitable; all these steps were required before starting families of their own.

Ma walked in on us and laughed. "Now you boys better not let those clean clothes go to waste. I don't wanna hear how you two stood against the wall all night and let those poor town-girls dance with each other. Just go right up and ask them all to dance. Trust me; they don't care if you don't know all the steps. Isn't that right Mariah?"

"Well, yes. But do try to avoid stepping on their feet."

They both nodded, looking nervous. Then Clem said, "Not to worry, we'll be fine. I'm bringing a little liquid courage to get my feet moving."

Later, as the five of us walked into the lively VFW hall, I reminded myself it was OK to laugh tonight; I'd spent a year-and-a-half feeling sad and guilty. If I had one night of fun, it didn't mean I was forgetting Sam and giving up on finding Jo. It's surprising how grief works in debilitating ways, holding you back.

The hall was a simple, large wooden building a block off Main Street. Primarily a bar, it was often used for community meetings, special dinners, and occasional dances. Tonight, it was decorated inside and out with strings of lights. Long tables were set to one side of the room, covered with white table cloths and vases of early spring flowers. On the small stage, there was a live band featuring two vocalists that were warming up as we walked in.

"Oh good, punch!" Janeen guided us across the floor to grab a glass. While at the punch table, Elliott and Catherine turned around with freshly filled glasses, looking surprised to see me.

"Mariah? I didn't know you were coming to the dance," Catherine said. "How *are* you? It's been what, four, five months? Too long. We've *got* to talk."

"I only decided to come a few days ago. Great to see you too."

Catherine was all smiles and guided me away from

everyone else. "I suppose Elliott has told you, but I'm so excited."

"About what?"

"We're engaged! It's happened so quickly my head is spinning. I'm deliriously happy."

"Well… then I'm happy too." As I gave her a quick congratulatory hug, it felt like my face was paralyzed as I attempted a grin. I couldn't believe he would not have told me. "So, when did all this transpire? Elliott hasn't said a word."

"Oh, I thought for sure he'd say something. Gosh, maybe a month ago? He came to speak to my dad about some business, selling off some of his land, and before I knew it, he'd asked me out a few times and then he and my dad formed a business partnership. It's been a whirlwind of a romance. The wedding is in a few weeks. I'm nervous but excited."

"A wedding? Oh my. That is *quite* the whirlwind."

"I know… imagine me, with an instant family to boot! But Mariah, I have you to thank for taking over the Martin household for all these months. I know you've done a great job with Elliott's boys."

I looked up seeing Elliott watching us from the table where all the Andersons were sitting. "Thanks Catherine. I'm truly happy for you. Couldn't happen to a nicer lady. Actually, Elliott looks like he's missing you already. We'll speak soon. OK?"

I honestly was glad for Catherine. She'd been wanting to move out of the Anderson compound for a while. I only hoped Elliott would treat her as well as she deserved. Hearing her news also had me realizing my days at the Martin's would be ending sooner than I anticipated. Looks like I was being replaced with a better-dispositioned, salary-free model, and one with the added benefit of her father's loans. But for me, it meant no more paychecks and immediate scrounging about for short-term housing.

Holding my glass of punch, I looked around in a daze for

my family. Arlene waved me over to a table, yelling, "We saved a place for you."

Walking up to the table, I was surprised to see David Thomas next to Billy. Although I rarely went out anywhere lately, David was known as the ultimate homebody, rarely making public appearances except at church, or occasionally picking up provisions for his parents. I'd had no contact with him since his kind windfall loan to me, offered at the auction.

I leaned over the table and shook his hand, "David, so good to see you. How have you been?"

He nodded his head and may have whispered out a response, but I couldn't hear it with the noise of the hall. Billy stood up and pulled out the chair next to David. "Here Mariah, have a seat."

I was feeling slightly set-up, but David was a true friend who'd come to my aid several times. As I sat down next to him, Wilbur pulled out his flask of gin and offered to top off our glasses. I was glad he and Clem brought a little alcohol. It might help loosen up my brothers' tongues and maybe coax a conversation from David.

Taking my seat, I asked, "So David, do you enjoy these dances?" I leaned in, knowing his voice would be a soft mumble.

"Don't know; this is my first. I'm sure I have two left feet."

I smiled, looking under the table. "Nope, a left and a right. Looks normal to me. So, what brings you here?"

"Billy dragged me. Said you were coming so I knew I'd have at least two friends here." He chuckled and added, "Mother almost lost her false teeth when I asked to borrow one of Dad's ties for the dance. I'm sure she'll ask me all about it later, like I was a little kid."

Then the band began playing in earnest, starting with *Begin the Beguine*. I had to speak up over the music. "These vocalists sound amazing. Let's give you and your mother something to talk about. Care to dance, Mr. Thomas? It's a beautiful song."

David picked up his glass of spiked punch, downed it in one gulp, looked at me with fear in his eyes and said, "Now?"

"That's what we came for. Don't worry. I'm not much of a dancer either."

My family looked on with awe as normally tongue-tied David Thomas led me out on the dance floor and Billy shouted after him, "Remember what I taught you."

Clem and Wilbur must have been encouraged by solitary David's dancing attempt and quickly got up, looking around for possible female wallflowers. The dance floor quickly filled up which made me feel more at ease for both David's and my sake. I hadn't danced in a few years and was pretty sure David was making his debut.

He was a tall, full shouldered man, with a more filled-out build than Sam's. I didn't want to compare, but I couldn't stop myself. Sam was the only man I'd ever really danced with. I could tell David was nervous. His hand shook as he took mine and then put his other arm around my waist. He looked down and apologized, saying, "I can only do the slow dances. That's all Billy taught me so far."

I had to laugh as I visualized Billy and David practicing dance steps, probably in the Thomas barn after their afternoon milking chores. I would have paid money for that show. "You're actually doing great, Mr. Thomas." As he swayed back and forth on rigid legs, I initiated a minor twirl under his arm, and we kept moving around the floor. "You're dancing David; you're dancing!"

# CHAPTER 49
# NANETTE

*I* looked around the empty lobby of Tinsel Town, all my senses suddenly on alert. The two chairs were empty; Arnold was behind the counter, apparently by himself. I took a quick breath and then slowly let it out. I'd never seen Arnold so angry. And I'd seen him angry a lot.

Cautiously, I asked, "Arnold, you're alone?" He nodded back. "Look, it's not what it sounds like. Calm down. Tell me exactly what the federal agent asked you."

"I am calm; just mad as hell. At you. It was pretty cut and dried. He asked me if a Nanette Jorgenson worked here and if I'd ever seen her with a little blond girl by the name of Jo Anderson, six-years-old. Either of them people ring a bell with you Miss *Nan Jordan?*"

A deep chill raced through my body. "What did you tell him?"

"I lied through my teeth praying you wouldn't come waltzing through that door with Jillian while he was here. But I will tell you this. I ain't gonna continue to lie if they come back and keep asking questions. For all I know, they're outside watching the place right now. By the way, your old boyfriend from The Palms was the one telling them where you worked."

I shook my head, wishing John Bing would simply disappear. "Thanks, Arnold, for covering for me. I owe you."

"I want you to clear outta here permanently… right now."

I panicked hearing his ultimatum. "I'm sure these questions will all die down. And I've got a big RCA client due any minute, and then there's Jillian. Where would she stay while I'm working?"

"You need a big slice of reality, lady. I'll take care of the client. All the rest is up to you." Arnold leaned forward on the counter, gripping it tightly. "Look, I don't know what kind of relationship you have with that little girl, but if you're *not* her real mother, you need to make things right. I want you to leave out the back door and don't come back. I mean it. I can't be involved with any of this. As far as I'm concerned, we never officially worked together. I always paid you in cash and you told me your names were Nan and Jillan Jordan. Leave now and don't mention me or my business name to anyone."

I sat down on the lobby chair, not wanting to budge. "After all I've done for Tinsel Town? You're throwing me out? That's rich. At least have the courtesy to pay me for the time I worked last week and perhaps my monthly bonus."

"I've got last week's wages in an envelope right here, but don't come back for nothin' more. Go now. You and Jillian take care and get that little girl back to her mother. *Her real mother.*"

I cried, producing actual God-given wet tears, while stepping up to the counter to grab the envelope of cash. "But, Arnold, you don't understand. I can explain all this. Her mother gave me custody; she couldn't take care of Jillian. It was pitiful. And she could never have offered her the opportunities I've given her."

"All I know is that the Federal Bureau is involved. Those G-men don't mess around and I want no part in any investigation. And I sure as heck won't be going to the big house over this." Arnold then pulled the ladder out of the back and took Jillian's latest photo off the *Stars of the Future* wall and also handed me the old photo featuring little blonde Jo-Jo. He put them in a bag and said, "Here, best take these with you."

Then he unlocked the back door and held it open, watching me skulk down the alley for a block, as if I was some kind of criminal. My heart began pounding as I detoured through the back door of the drugstore, across their kitchen, and then up to the lunch counter. I ordered a cherry-flavored cola, attempting to calm down and blend in.

One of the regular soda jerks was working the counter. "Hey Stew, I was meeting someone here. Anybody come in recently and ask for me? Probably a serious looking guy in a suit?"

"Nope. Nobody I noticed." He stopped in front of me, cleaning the counter with a dirty rag. "Hey Nan, when are we going on that stroll down the beach you promised me?"

"Next full moon, Stewart. It'll be more romantic that way. What do I owe you?"

"On the house, doll. I'll be checking that lunar calendar."

I nodded and laughed. "OK, if I use your restroom?"

"Sure. Here's the key."

I went inside, deciding to pull all my hair up inside my hat, in case the agent was on the corner looking for blondes. I also stopped in the hair products aisle and bought a bottle of brown hair dye. If Jillian could go brunette, why couldn't I? I left, walking quickly away in the opposite direction of Tinsel Town Photography, and never looked back. I loved Jillian and our life here together, but obviously our work at Tinsel Town was now over. I had to plan my next steps with an enhanced awareness.

Jillian was at Warner Brothers, filming her scenes. That was probably a safe place for me to stay for the day, hidden in a waiting room with other parents. I turned the corner, walked two blocks over and caught a street car to Sunset Boulevard. Climbing the landing to the car, I glanced around looking for any men on the street that appeared to be following me, but saw nobody suspicious. Hopefully nothing would come of all this hubbub.

Going home later with Jillian, she was bubbling over with excitement about her day. The film, a top project for Warner Brothers, was titled *Trouble in Sing-Sing*. "Mother, everybody was really nice to me. I got ice cream after lunch; as much as I wanted. And the man playing my father is so handsome. I wish I had more scenes. It was fun."

"Well, I'm thrilled things went so well. We'll have to see if Uncle Alan has any other good parts for you. He should be stopping by tonight."

I was anxious to ask Cummings his opinion about Arnold's disturbing visit by the Feds. Maybe he'd have some sound advice for us and Jillian's career. After seven, it began to get dark and Alan still had not arrived. I'd have to reheat the spaghetti dinner I'd made. I eventually put Jillian to bed and waited by the open window. It wasn't like him to be late. We had a standing date, every Tuesday and Thursday. Around 9:30, I finally heard a car pull up. It was very dark and his car was black, but I was pretty sure it was his.

I came down the sidewalk calling out, "Hey there, you're late. I missed you."

Someone reached out and grabbed my arm, hustling me back up the sidewalk. In a whispered voice Alan said, "Go in immediately. We've gotta talk." Once inside, he closed the window and curtains, and checked the bedroom door. "I had a visitor today. Feds looking for you, babe. Not good for you and *definitely* not good for me. You need to leave town immediately."

I sat innocently on the couch and patted the space next to me, but Alan began pacing across the small room while I asked innocently, "What are you talking about?"

"Why didn't you ever tell me Jillian's not your daughter? Do you realize what liability you put me in? How could you be so stupid? You're being charged with kidnapping, a federal offense if you take a child across state lines." His tone became more agitated and his volume grew louder. "Thank God, I put her contract under another name. But you need to clear out. They're on your trail and someone is gonna talk. Nan, you've rubbed shoulders with a lot of people in the industry. It won't take them long to find you if you stick around."

"I can explain everything, but how did they know to contact *you*?"

"Somebody at The Palms gave 'em my name; said you were a resident. Hell if I know."

I made a mental note. Never underestimate the anger and jealousy of a scorned lover. And John Bing had seemed so promising at one time. Now I was the one getting agitated. "So, what did you tell the feds?"

Gary's voice level went low again. "Nan, I was an actor before I was a talent agent. I bluffed my way through it. Told them I had no Jo Anderson on my roster. I even had my assistant bring out my client book, and compared the bureau's old photo of Jo to Jillian's latest publicity photo, saying, 'Here's the only little girl I have as a client that's even close to that age; name is Jillian and obviously not who you're looking for. She has longer dark hair, no curls, looks a lot taller than the kid in your photo. You're barking up the wrong tree here, gentlemen.'"

"And they went for that?"

"Yes! Climbed down that tree and high tailed it out of the office."

Fear and confusion started my tears rolling again. "But how can I leave? What about you and me, and Jillian's career?"

"You should have thought that through before you left Minnesota with someone else's kid."

"There's so much more to it than you realize. You don't understand... and I love you, Alan. We have something special here. I know you feel it too."

He finally took a seat next to me on the couch, handing me his handkerchief. "Look... I had a thought driving over here. Maybe a temporary fix. I do business in New York from time to time. I know a guy; he'll get you set up in a little apartment but you gotta leave the kid behind. Send her back to the real mother. It's your only chance. Maybe, once she's back home, things will cool down and they'll stop looking for you."

"But Jillian is *like* my real daughter. I have a custody paper. This feels like a nightmare. I can't lose her."

He hugged me and held me tight and then pushed away, shaking his head. "It's too dangerous right now. We can't be together. Maybe later—in New York. We'll see." He scribbled a name and phone number on the back of a business card and thrust it in my hand. "In Chinatown, there's a guy. He'll get you set up. He owes me."

"How will I get there? I don't have the funds."

He pulled out his wallet from the breast pocket of his suit jacket. "Here's two hundred bucks. It's all the cash I could get my hands on. Pack tonight. Go to Le Grande Station early tomorrow. I know the Santa Fe line has a seven-AM to Chicago. Send the kid home and from there you can transfer to New York. Be on that train and do *not* call me again. My career and reputation could be ruined if the rumor gets out that I had a hand in any of this." He got up quickly and headed to the door.

"That's it? You're leaving me?"

"I'm afraid so. Goodbye, Nan." Alan firmly closed the door on me and our relationship.

# CHAPTER 50
# MARIAH

"*E*nough?" I asked, looking up into David's perspiring face. He offered me a relieved nod and we headed back to our table. "That was fun. What do you think of your first official dance?"

"I admit, it was a little uncomfortable. Maybe it'll grow on me." David pulled out a handkerchief and wiped his forehead.

"David, you're just a late bloomer. I think you're doing great." As we sat down, a livelier tune took Billy and Arlene onto the dance floor for a swing dance and Janeen convinced brother Wilbur to attempt the quicker steps with her. "You look a little warm. Want to get another punch and step outside a minute?"

David nodded. Outside, the chilly air felt good after the closeness of the poorly ventilated hall. Under the front awning, several young people congregated, smoking and drinking as we side-stepped the boisterous group.

We took a turn down a neighborhood sidewalk and I suggested, "Let's take a spin around Town Park; we're so close."

"Just like on the dance floor, you're still leading, Mariah."

I laughed. "Sorry, can't help myself. So, how is life on the Thomas farm; everything good?"

"Making a go of it. Seems like our numbers will be better than last year. We may even get out of the red, as if that was something to cheer about."

"Well, it *is* something to be proud of. These past few years, think of how many farmers had to leave it all behind after banks called in their loans. It sounds like your family will weather the storm. I have full faith in you. Speaking of, how are your parents?"

"Well… that's another story. Mother broke her leg a few weeks back. Didn't even realize it was broken for a couple days. I thought she had just twisted an ankle. I taped it and sent her to bed, but Doc eventually showed up, felt the break, and created a cast. He says she'll slowly recover, but it's so surprising to see your parents aging right before your eyes."

"Yeah, we think they're going to be our rock forever and before you know it, we're the ones taking care of them. Please tell your mother I'd like to come by for a visit soon."

"She'd like that. We don't get much company."

"And your father?"

"A little slower, tires more easily, but that's why I'm there. And, of course, with your remodel, Billy's been gone a lot. He's like a kid brother to me and he's gonna be hard to replace when he decides to leave. I'm hoping to pick up another sixty acres at a land auction next month. So, we'll probably need to hire another part-time hand soon.

"Really...Expansion right now?" I looked up at him surprised.

"Now's the time to do it. Land and real estate will *never* be this cheap again. You should think about it too."

"Me? I haven't even opened my first apartment building."

"But now you have good collateral. Borrow on that. Start

shopping for another rental investment within the county. You're a smart woman, Mariah."

I blushed in the dark, shaking my head. "I'm flattered, but honestly, there's days I have no idea what I'm doing."

"You'll figure it out. So, you're still at the Martin's place?"

"Funny you should ask. I only found out this evening… Elliott is marrying my sister-in-law, Catherine Anderson. In two weeks! I had no idea they were even courting. I'm sure Sarah and I will need to move out soon. Elliott and I have developed what I would describe as a *prickly* relationship.

"Ah, sorry to hear that."

We walked in silence for a while and then opted for a park bench to rest a minute. The square green park was dark and empty. I could hear distant laughter and music from the dance occasionally floating by, and a bit of moonlight broke through the trees overhead.

After a minute, David spoke up. "Billy mentioned Jo's still not back. I'm surprised Elliott hasn't agreed to have her stay with you."

"Well, that was the first problem, but then her caretaker, Nanette Jorgenson, has apparently kidnapped Jo and fled to, of all places, Hollywood." I pulled out my handkerchief and dabbed my emerging tears.

"What?" David stared at me with his mouth hanging open.

"I know…this all sounds crazy. I'm sorry. Talking about it gets me so upset." I looked down at my lap, twisting my handkerchief.

"Are you talking about the same Nanette that used to live in Green Tree? I think she was three or four years my junior."

Nodding vehemently, I said. "The very one. The whole story is bizarre. I can't imagine what is going through Nanette's mind. I honestly don't bring it up to people in town. It only seems to foment gossip. But I remembered Jo was always so enamored of you after Sam's passing. Thought you'd want to know."

"Yes, a really special child. Remember her singing to us at your dinner? Never one to hold back, is she? I have no words. Sorry certainly doesn't cover it. So are the police checking?"

"Actually, the Federal Bureau, *finally*. They haven't located Nanette, but at least they're going to investigate." I rubbed my eyes with my jacket sleeve. I was ready to change topics. "Hey, I'm getting chilly out here. Ready to go back in?"

"I appreciate you telling me." David stood up and offered his hand. "So, you're really going to make me dance again?"

"I didn't buy these stockings for nothing. I need to show them off."

"You are truly a glutton for punishment, dragging me around."

Once back inside the hall, I danced with David a few more times, but also ran into some old school friends, danced with a few men from my church and caught up on town activities with friends living in the village. Around midnight, we all said our goodbyes and headed back to my parent's. The five of us tip-toed rather clumsily up the stairs, giggling softly as Clem and Wilbur kept banging into the walls. Perhaps a little too much gin-infused punch had been consumed, but it had been a fun night. My sisters and I collapsed together on our old childhood double-bed, but attempting to sleep with two other adult women certainly didn't feel the same as when we were kids.

I desperately looked forward to a restful night, but instead, laid on my side with eyes wide open, worrying where Sarah and I would stay for the next few months. It seemed there was always something to worry about.

# CHAPTER 51
# NANETTE

*A*fter Alan left, the dreams I'd felt so confident about seemed to be disappearing; romance, Hollywood stardom, endless blue skies, and all the oranges we could eat. And it was only this morning that everything seemed to be turning aces for us. Life was so unfair.

I went down the hall to the bathroom. There was silence on the other side of the wall. We shared the bathroom with my duplex neighbors, and it seemed they'd gone to bed. I applied the dark hair dye, rinsed carefully, cleaned the sink, and brought the empty bottle back for my final load of trash. I selected our two medium-sized suitcases. We'd have to travel light and leave everything else behind. Jillian had outgrown half of her clothing anyway, and I hurriedly packed essentials needed for a cooler climate. After packing, I dumped the cold spaghetti I'd made on top of the rest of the trash and put the bag in another neighbor's can across the alley.

I spent the rest of night sitting on our tattered sofa with a single light on, contemplating how my life could possibly go on without Jillian. She had become essential to me. Alan's comments all made sense but I didn't think I could send Jillian back to Mariah. Everything had already changed so much for her. Perhaps, the two of us could find a place and easily get lost among the masses in New York City. Surely, nobody would be looking for us there. Jillian was my lucky charm; things always had a way of working out for me when she was around. We were happy together. And, of course, in New York there were vaudeville and Broadway productions. I could see success for Jillian as a child star on stage, with audiences applauding her singing and dancing. It could still all come together for us. New York might be just the ticket we needed.

At four o'clock, I shook Jillian awake and told her she needed to get dressed. I'd already selected her dress and light coat for the trip. She was drowsy and hard to rouse; in contrast, I was wound up tight as a spring, dressed and ready to walk out the door.

"Come on Jillian, we're taking a surprise train trip. Won't that be fun?"

She rolled over and looked up at me. "No. I don't want to go."

I pulled the blanket off her. "Well, we have to. Uncle Alan suggests we go to New York. It'll be good for your career."

"But what about everything here?" She started to cry, shaking her head on the pillow. "I have friends now. Tink and Tayler, and I like this house."

"Get up Jillian. We're wasting time."

Then she tried to reasoning with me. "But Mother, we can get new furniture and make it look really pretty. Fancy, the way you like it. I'm tired of moving. Let's please stay here." Jillian suddenly sat up in bed with her eyes wide open. "Why is your hair brown?"

"Get-up-immediately. We don't have time for this." I yanked her up, pulling her legs over the side of the bed, while I tried to put socks and shoes on her uncooperative feet, with her legs and feet dangling like wet noodles. "And keep your voice down. We can't wake the neighbors."

"I don't want to go to New York."

"Stand up now and raise your arms." She sighed and reluctantly stood as I pulled a print dress over her head and buttoned it in the back. "Here's your coat. Certainly, you're capable of putting that on. I've packed a bag for you already."

"Where's my blue coat? Did you pack it? I need that."

"No, it's in the closet and too small for you now, Jillian. Forget about it."

She immediately went to the closet and pulled the little blue coat off the hanger. Jillian opened her case and stuffed it inside, forcing it to fit. "It's special and I'm not leaving it and I have to take Millie. I won't go without her." She stomped her foot, which I now recognized as her most defiant pose.

"You can take Millie but *you'll* have to carry her and your case. We need to go now. We have two transfers to make on the bus before getting to the train station."

"What about my tap shoes? And I'm hungry." She sat down again at our small table, clutching her blonde doll, which had recently taken on a bedraggled look.

I was getting anxious as the minutes ticked away. "I already packed your tap shoes." Then I pulled open the refrigerator, staring at the meager contents. I grabbed a bruised apple and a couple crusts of stale bread. I sliced the apple up quickly, spread peanut butter over the crusts, slammed the bread slices together with the apples, and wrapped it all in an old tea towel. "Here, put this in your coat pocket and eat it on the bus."

She stood up and took it, looking dejected, and glanced around the little duplex. "So, we're leaving everything? What about my movie?"

"Don't worry Jillian. We'll catch it at a theater. I've got

bigger plans for us." I locked the door behind her and walked quickly down the cracked sidewalk, glancing at the dark shadows of the low-rent bungalows and rough-looking street. As I pulled her along, I whispered, "Sweetie, cheer up. Hollywood just wasn't what I thought it was going to be. We can do better."

## CHAPTER 52
## MARIAH

*T*he morning after the dance, I got up early, borrowed Dad's car, and drove to the Martin's to pick up Sarah for church. It had been a while since I'd attended my family's country church. On the way over, Sarah asked all about the dance, wanting me to describe every detail. Later, sitting in our family pew, we joined hands with heads bowed and gave thanks for the spring rains. As we sang along to Agnes Turnball's slightly out-of-tune voice and organ, I looked down the bench, grateful to be surrounded by family.

My parents were in the center, smiling proudly. As I'd said to David last night, my parents were our rock; from heartfelt advice, to a simple pat on the back, or the occasional stern lecture, they had always been there for us. I dreaded asking them if Sarah and I could move in for a while. My poor parents could never seem to get rid of their adult brood, and now they had their hired couple's baby to contend with.

After the service, I ran into David. He was with his father, speaking with Billy and a few other men on the outside steps. He followed me down the walk, cleared his throat, and asked, "Mariah, if you were interested in visiting Mother, I could take you over there now and drive you back later to the Martin farm."

"Oh... today, David? I was planning on working at the Anderson Arms..."

"It's just that this morning I mentioned to Mother that you wanted to visit and she seemed really happy about it. She suggested you and Sarah should come by for lunch, but if you're busy she'll understand."

"Actually, today will be fine." I thought about all the kindness Eleanor and her family had extended to us after Sam's death. I could certainly give her some of my time. "I haven't seen your mother in months. We'd be happy to come for an hour or two. But is she mobile enough to have lunch guests? We don't want to be any trouble."

"She's not cooking or even standing much right now, but I know she would enjoy the company. Father hired a lady temporarily that comes in to do the day's cooking for us each morning. We're useless in the kitchen."

"All right then, if you're sure we'll be no trouble."

Once Billy heard Sarah and I were coming over, he invited Arlene. After arriving at the Thomas farm, Arlene and I set the table and heated up the prepared lunch. The Thomas' home had a spacious dining room with a polished oak table, matching ladder-back chairs, and a buffet cabinet. We added the center leaf to their dining table, covered it with a fine white damask tablecloth we found in the buffet drawer and added their silver cutlery and bone-China plates. Arlene made a mixed green salad and I quickly baked biscuits, adding to the chicken and roast potatoes prepared earlier. When David carried his mother downstairs and seated her at the table, she was beaming seeing the room set up properly for company.

"So good of you girls to come. Mariah, you were always my favorite neighbor, you know." Just then, Sarah walked in bringing me a handful of wildflowers for the table. Eleanor said, "My, look how she's grown. Little Sarah is getting tall. And where's your sister today?"

I jumped in and said, "Unfortunately, Jo isn't with us now."

Sarah turned to Mrs. Thomas and added, "Jo's missing, but they're looking for her."

"Sarah, we don't need to burden our friends with that."

"What do you mean, missing?" Eleanor asked. "How can we help?"

"Oh, I assure you, we have the Federal Bureau checking into a kidnapping." I told David's parents a brief summary of what I knew of Nanette and Jo's disappearance. "It's been several months. But let's leave it at that. It is the most awful feeling, just not knowing."

"I'm so sorry. I had no idea. Well, let's say grace and put in an extra prayer for little Josephine." Looking at David, Eleanor said, "Son, give us a good prayer today." She touched her eyes with her napkin as he said a short, simple prayer.

We did our best to steer the conversation to happier subjects. Of course, we discussed rainfall, per-acre-yields, the price of milk, and improvements in the latest John Deere tractor. Arlene shared store gossip and talked to Eleanor about the newest styles in shoes, and Sarah talked about the books she was reading for school.

We had cookies and coffee in the front parlor, while listening to a music program on the Thomas' tall Philco radio. Three hours had passed and I knew Elliott and his boys would be expecting their Sunday dinner.

David drove Sarah and me back through the rough farm roads in silence. Sometimes, no conversation was fine, a time for reflection. I noticed Sarah had fallen asleep in the back seat. As we neared the Martin farm, David finally spoke up. Going down the long driveway, he seemed to struggle for words, as if he practiced several sentences in his head before anything ever came out.

"You know, Mariah, I admire you. I know you're a good mother, but also not afraid to try new things."

I glanced at the back seat. Sarah was now awake and probably listening.

He took a breath and then kept going. "You've literally held two households together here. That's impressive. I'm pleased to call you a friend." He was looking down at his hands on the steering wheel, clearly nervous.

"Well, thank you, David. I'm honored to call you a friend as well." I smiled thinking that was as romantic as David Thomas was ever going to get.

As Sarah and I got out of the car, I thanked him again for lunch. Walking in through the Martin's back door, I was surprised by the delicious aroma of ham, tangled up with warm bread and baked potatoes. I peeked into the dining room and saw Elliott, the boys, and Catherine sitting at the table enjoying a late lunch. I felt oddly out of place, like I'd just stepped into the wrong house.

"Hello. Smells great in here. I was just about to start dinner, but it looks like you've done it for me, Catherine. How is everyone?"

Catherine looked over at us and smiled, "Hello! We're great. Join us."

Sarah asked, "Mommie, can I eat? I'm hungry."

"All ready? Sarah, it wasn't two hours ago that you had a big lunch. Maybe later." I looked over to Elliott and said, "I'll be down in a while to clean the kitchen."

As Sarah and I turned to go upstairs, Elliott said, "Oh, Mariah...a letter came for you yesterday from Mankato. I put it on the mantle. And, when you have time, Catherine and I want to have a little talk with you."

"Certainly, let me know when you're finished."

I picked up a letter from Captain Olsen and tore it open eagerly, as I climbed the stairs to the sky room.

*Dear Mrs. Anderson,*

*I'm writing to give you an update on what the bureau agents have found so far. The talent agent, James Diamond, was visited and the feds pressed him a bit more into remembering that he had dropped Nanette and Jo off at The Palms Hotel, a place he frequently took clients to. Surprisingly, the manager there was quite forthcoming about Nanette and Jo, remembering them well, and even knew where he thought Nanette worked. Highly fortuitous and unusual for a hotel manager to be so helpful! Unfortunately, the trail went cold when the bureau agent visited the photo shop she supposedly worked at. The owner seemed to know nothing about her. They are also working the doll lead you gave me. No news on that yet. But the case is officially open now, so hopefully they'll come across something soon. I'll certainly keep you informed.*

*Best Regards,*
*Captain Olsen*

# CHAPTER 53
# NANETTE

*T*he train was scheduled to pull out in minutes. I quickly bought two tickets on the Santa Fe Line to Chicago. We ran down the boarding platform of Le Grande Station, suitcases banging against our legs, only catching our breath after we climbed up the stairs panting, handing our tickets to the conductor.

This trip, I'd decided against sleeping berths to save money, and we would not be frequenting the dining or club cars. Our budget was minimal and I now had a more realistic view of the cost and difficulties when starting a new life in a big city. I wanted to travel unnoticed. I'd purposely worn my frumpiest old dress, had not curled my darkened hair, nor put on any makeup. I passed myself in the restroom mirror and hardly recognized the reflection staring back. It was an embarrassment to look so poorly, but I thought of it as almost a disguise. And if anybody asked, we were now traveling under new names, as Fran and Jessica Jordan.

As the train fell into its swaying rhythm, Jillian's eyes closed and I pulled her head into my lap so she could curl her legs up in the seat and sleep. I ran my fingers through her baby-fine hair, rubbing her temples. I knew she was feeling confused and upset with this unexpected move. But I remembered my life as a child had been difficult too, and I had survived.

My mother I never knew; having died giving birth to me, and my father passed away when I was twelve, after farming me out to Auntie Edwina in Green Tree. Although I didn't always show it, I was grateful to have lived with her, knowing she had saved me from a childhood in an orphanage. Thinking back, Green Tree hadn't been the worst place to grow up. I'd had friends, a comfortable home, all my basic needs taken care of, and being a town-girl had its benefits. But all that seemed so long ago. I massaged Jillian's perfect, soft skin in a circular motion. Realizing I was exhausted, I closed my eyes as well.

We both woke up hungry several hours later. I knew Alan Cumming's two-hundred dollars would be stretched thin getting us to New York, and I needed to set aside a small fund for settling into our new space. We would have to be content with eating once a day on this trip. Checking the time, we had three days before making the Chicago transfer. Luckily, the train provided a sandwich car where less expensive meals could be purchased. Leaving Jillian's doll, Millie, to hold our seats, we passed through several cars to visit the restroom and stretch our stiff legs.

Walking through, I glanced out the windows as the train pulled into a small depot after passing another sprawling Hooverville. It was a brief stop in a dusty desert town called Las Vegas. At the station, I noticed a sign for The Hitching Post, a business advertising that couples could get married or divorced in a heartbeat. What a ridiculous premise for a business. Glancing at the drab, rustic surroundings, I wondered why they had bothered building a depot. Why would anyone ever stop here?

As we walked into the sandwich car, there was a line forming. While waiting, we perused the shelves next to the counter selling newspapers, magazines, and children's books. Jillian picked up a picture book and looked my way. "Please Mother. Buy me this. The only thing to look at outside is dirt. It's boring."

Not wanting another tap-dancing-tirade, I relented and also purchased a cheap coloring book and crayons for her. It was going to be a very long trip. For my amusement, I picked up a new *Silver Screen*, and a copy of *The Hollywood Reporter*.

We decided on chicken-salad-sandwiches and Baby Ruth candy bars, then reclaimed our seats. After eating, I leaned back, starting to finally feel relaxed for the first time in over thirty hours. Picking up my copy of the *Reporter,* that calm feeling quickly evaporated. I was suddenly unable to tear my eyes away from the back-page classifieds. In the upper right-hand corner was a two-by-two, black and white photo of little blonde Jo-Jo holding her Curlie Cutie doll, with a bold heading placed below:

### Missing—Darling Doll Model

*Josephine Anderson, the model gracing the box of the popular Curlie Cutie doll, is missing. She was last seen living with her caretaker, Nanette Jorgenson, at The Palms Hotel in Hollywood. If you have seen this child or Miss Jorgenson, contact the Los Angeles Federal Bureau.* This was followed by a phone number.

My heart skipped a beat and then went cold. Oh my God, this was getting out of control.

# CHAPTER 54
# MARIAH

*S*arah, Billy, and I had just arrived at the Anderson Arms to do some late afternoon work. I'd been hoping, by some miracle, our rooms there would be ready soon, but plumbing issues had been pushed back because of the termites, and there were still walls to construct downstairs dividing the apartments. I'd been agitated and quiet on the way over.

As Billy buckled his tool belt he asked, "What's eating you today, Mariah? All quiet and everything."

"Just worried. Sarah, honey, why don't you carry the paint and drop-cloths upstairs?" After she left, I explained. "We need to move out of the Martin's this Friday, but I still haven't said a word to my parents about moving back home. Do you suppose we could just bring some blankets and pillows here and make do for a while?"

Billy shook his head. "Sure, if you like living in chaos, while sleeping on the floor with no heat. Right now, it'd be downright inconvenient. Look, why are you making things so dang diffi-cult for yourself? The solution is simple."

"What solution?"

"Good lord! Why do I have to spell everything out for everybody? And here I thought you were so smart."

I looked at Billy, exasperated, waiting for his explanation. "Tell me, Mr. Know-It-All."

"Mariah, you saw it all yourself last Sunday. You know Mrs. Thomas has a broken leg, right?"

"Right," I responded.

"None of us fellas at the Thomas farm can cook. Right?... You catching on yet?"

"Oooh...I see."

"Mrs. Thomas thinks highly of you and I think David does too—although the man will never admit it. You just gotta offer your services to David and his dad to run the house for a few months in exchange for room and board. I bet they'll throw in a little salary too. Mrs. Thomas can't walk. She needs help cooking, cleaning, gardening; all things you're good at. They got a nice guest room. You and Sarah should be comfortable. And that way, we could drive in together to work on this place."

"You think so? It *is* a rather brilliant idea. They wouldn't mind?"

"Hell no; we'd all welcome it. We need a little organization around the place, and the cook they hired— let's just say her biscuits taste like bricks of you-know-what." Billy slapped his hands together. "OK. Problem solved. Let's get to painting."

"Can you ask the Thomas family for me tonight, Billy?"

"I guess. Seems like I do everything else around here. Why not that too?"

"You know, you are quite amazing. I appreciate you."

I gave him a friendly hug, excited about the idea. Billy was right. It would probably be a perfect fit. Excitedly, I ran upstairs and asked Sarah, "How would you like to move in with the Thomas family until our rooms are finished here? Wouldn't that be fun?"

She turned to me, not looking happy. "Is it because David Thomas likes you?"

"No silly. What makes you say that?"

"I have ears. I heard him when he took us home last Sunday. He likes you."

"Not sure about that… but Sarah, remember his mother? She needs help. Maybe they'll let us stay at their farm while she recuperates."

Spreading the floor coverings, she turned her back to me. "I'm not moving. I'm staying in the sky room."

"But you know my job at the Martin's is ending. I explained it all to you last Sunday. Aunt Catherine is marrying Mr. Martin."

"I know. But Aunt Catherine likes me and Tommy is my best friend. I'm *not* moving. He and I decided."

"Huh. I'm sorry to tell you… you'll need to undecide. For one, Seth already announced he's moving into the sky room soon. *And* Mr. Martin is expecting you to leave with me. But how about this? I'll take you over there to play every Saturday."

"No! I never get to keep a friend. You made Jo leave, now you're making me leave Tommy. It's not fair. You only get what *you* want."

I rolled my eyes, thinking there was never a simple solution. "Let's talk about this later. We have painting to do right now. I understand your feelings though and I'm sorry your life feels so disrupted. Please know I'm doing the best I can and I know your daddy wants us to stay together."

She refused to look at me and was quiet for two hours while she kept paint loaded on the brushes as I painted. We eventually stopped for a dinner break and went downstairs where Billy was working. I'd brought ham sandwiches and potato salad for the three of us. Billy and I sat on the stairs, but even while eating, Sarah refused to talk and sat on the floor, turned away from me.

"So, what's got sweet Sarah's tongue tied up in knots this afternoon?" Billy asked loudly. Sarah ignored his comment, pouted, and continued eating. "Hey Mariah, I got a good idea. What about the two of us running up to the pool hall after dinner and gettin' ice cream cones?" Billy winked at me.

"I'd love that, Billy." Hearing that, Sarah swiveled around and looked at us.

"Oh, so you wanna go now too?" Still silent, Sarah nodded. Then Billy said, "OK, but you gotta say please and smile for me."

She did as requested, with a wisp of a smile coming out, and the three of us got in the truck with Sarah next to the window. We drove up Main Street, as Billy and I discussed a Blue Earth property which looked like a promising rental project we might undertake next. Looking out the window, Sarah finally broke her silence and laughed. "Look Mommy, there's a girl dancing by Gottlieb's gas pumps. She looks so funny."

# CHAPTER 55
# NANETTE

$\mathcal{I}$ stared at Jillian's doll, Millie, sitting across from us, her glass blue eyes staring back accusingly at me, as Jillian colored away, humming. I sprang up and said, "I'm putting Millie overhead with the luggage to create space. You can sleep with her when it gets dark." Why had I agreed to do that Curlie Cutie ad? So stupid on my part. At least, there was no photo of me on the box. And had the bureau bothered to go through Arnold's files, they would have found a couple of very flattering headshots of me.

I had half a mind to go back to the sandwich car and buy up all their copies of *Hollywood Reporter*, but that might look suspicious. I ripped the back page off, crumpled it up and flipped the paper over to the front page. On the cover, I stared at the big half-page headline announcing Cary Grant as the hottest new actor in the country. I normally would have taken great pride in predicting that months ago, but all I could think about now was the deep shit I was suddenly drowning in.

On the very narrow edge of the bright side, I had to assume the Feds were still searching for Jillian and me in the Hollywood area or they wouldn't have run a classified ad in a local paper catering to the acting trade. But, then again, I knew a lot of people that read the *Reporter.* I'm sure Alan Cummings was blowing a gasket right now.

Trying to calm my nerves, I reminded myself we were already one state away. The Feds had no idea we had left California. I had six more states to travel through before reaching Chicago, and three more after that before arriving in New York; plenty of time for me to contemplate my next steps.

I looked down at Jillian, who was busy coloring a little girl walking her puppy. "You're doing a good job, sweetie. Hey, if anyone should ask, during this trip your name is *Jessica,* your character's name from *Trouble in Sing-Sing.* So, just play your part. Won't that be fun?"

"I guess."

"But no singing and dancing on this train. No matter how bored you get. We don't need any attention right now. Somebody bad may be looking for us."

"Bad? Who's bad?" She whispered, her eyes opening wide.

"Some people that don't want us to be together. I can't explain it right now, but don't talk to any strangers, no matter what. Not even the friendly train porters, OK?"

"But why?"

"Just do it, Jillian," I said with an exasperated sigh.

"Don't you mean *Jessica?*"

"Yes, my smart girl!"

She nodded, smiled, and continued to color her dog.

THE MONOTONY of the three days wore us down. Neither of us spoke to anyone else, keeping contact with train personnel to a minimum. Each night we quickly scurried to the restroom as it got dark. We'd get out and stretch our legs for a few minutes at the depots of smaller towns, where I'd check the local papers, but saw nothing about us. The train was no longer selling copies of *The Hollywood Reporter;* probably unable to get them once away from the west coast. The highlight of each day was selecting what type of sandwich we'd eat.

On the morning of our third day, Jillian woke up hungry and insisted on pancakes. I firmly told her, "Forget it. It's not in the budget."

Jillian clammed up, angry at my quick response. She then stood up on the train seat on tip-toe and grasped at her case in the rack above, pulling out her blue coat. She grabbed a large handful of coins from the pockets and asked, "Will this get us pancakes?"

Amazed, I counted out over three dollars in her hand, surprised she was still hoarding coins from her tips. "More than enough. I guess we're getting pancakes and juice in the dining car. But no talking to strangers." We headed down the aisle, thrilled about an early meal and something other than a sandwich.

We were still three hours outside of Chicago, seated at our table, and busy inhaling the sweet scent of buttermilk pancakes, smothered in butter and maple syrup. Then I heard, "Well, my goodness gracious! Fancy meeting you two again." I looked up, pretending not to recognize the outgoing man in a plaid suit and gray hat tilted back on his head. Damn it! Our first time in the dining car and this happens.

But Jillian immediately said, "I remember you. The doll man! Hello."

He quickly took the chair opposite me. "Yes, Willard Williams, Wonder Toy Company. Headed back to home base, Chicago. Mind if I join you for a minute, Mrs. Jorgenson? I never forget a face or a name. It's the salesman in me, I guess."

"Actually, we were just about to enjoy a *quiet* breakfast, Mr. Williams," I said.

"Oh, I think we should talk for a minute or two. Funny

thing I'm running into you. My boss tracked me down in Topeka two days ago by telephone. Imagine this… He received a call from the Federal Bureau. Seems they had a question about who was authorized to represent Jo-Jo on our doll boxes?"

Then Jillian spoke up and proudly told Williams, "I'm called Jessica now. That's my new movie name."

I put pressure on her arm and said, "That's enough Jo; Mr. Williams doesn't want to hear about our silly games." Then I leaned over to him and whispered, "I have no idea what you're talking about."

"Oh, I think you do. Seems there's a question about proper custody and my boss bandied about the word, 'kidnapping.' But… I might be willing to forget this mix up and not mention I ran into you *if* you could do something for me." Williams' confident, smiling face was now upsetting my stomach.

"And what would that be?"

"I'd love to see you later, alone. Why don't you plan on meeting up with me at my apartment, downtown? Just the two of us; I have a wonderful view you should see."

I stared at him for a second, calculating my options. "Hmm. Perhaps I could make that happen. I've got business to take care of on State Street first, and I'll need to drop Jo-Jo off with friends, but give me your address. That might be fun."

He wrote an address on the back of his card. "Now put this somewhere safe. Let's say eight o'clock?"

"Actually, looking forward to it, Willard."

"Good. I'll be in the club car, if you still enjoy gambling. I remember you got pretty lucky with pinochle. I think you and I may have a lot in common." He stood up, tipped his fedora, and sauntered through the car.

Jillian said, "I like Mr. Williams. He always seems happy."

"Sweetie, stay clear of him. People are not always who they seem to be."

Then she whispered in my ear, "Is he one of the bad ones?"

"Most definitely."

After breakfast, my stomach began twisting and it wasn't just from the overly sweet pancakes. I had a dilemma and decision to make. I hated the thought, but had to consider sending Jillian back to Mariah. Doing that would help take the heat off me. Should I really meet up with Williams tonight? Would he keep his word and not report seeing me and Jillian? Would any of that matter anyway? I had to think things through. My head began throbbing and then I felt the urge to vomit, making a dash to the restroom.

Back in my seat, feeling green around the gills, but with my head and stomach clearer, I stopped a porter, tipped him, and asked for a few sheets of stationary and an envelope. As Jillian sat staring out the window, I wrote Mariah Anderson a letter. My heart broke a little more with each sentence I wrote. Pulling into Chicago's Grand Central, I grabbed our bags and the doll, and hustled through the enormous station, heading to the ticket offices. Then I took Jillian to one of the station's many cafés and told her to choose whatever she wanted on the menu.

The place was crowded and noisy, forcing us to sit very closely together at a lunch counter. As her catsup coated meatloaf was placed in front of her, I said, "Jillian, I have something very important to tell you. Listen carefully. Your mother, *your real mother*, wants you to move back home to Green Tree." Jillian's blue eyes widened and stared back at me. "She can take care of you now. I don't think she wants my help any more. I thought maybe we could start a new adventure in New York, but I don't think that's going to work out. You're going to travel the rest of the way back to Green Tree by yourself."

Panic flooded Jillian's face, as she dropped a fork on her plate and grabbed my shoulders. "No, Mother, no! Don't go.

You said you would never leave me. We would always be together. My mother doesn't want me anymore. I remember... You told me. She only wanted Sarah." Her tears were flowing as we began receiving concerned glances from people sitting around us.

I patted her back and hugged her, calming her down, then leaned away and said "Sweetie, things have changed. She wants you back. She really does. Your sister wants to see you too. Remember also, in Green Tree, you have a big family; grandparents, aunts and uncles wanting to see you."

Jillian was frightened and suddenly looked so small. "But what about you? I'm your family. Uncle Alan, Uncle Bing, Arnold...they're gone now. I thought you said we'd always be a family? Who'll take care of you?"

Now my eyes were tearing up. "I'm not sure, Jillian. My little princess. I'll miss you so much, but I'll be fine. Just keep our dreams about New York to yourself; it'll be our special secret. OK?" Jillian nodded and I wiped her eyes with a napkin. "I'm going to walk you to your train soon and tell a very nice conductor to watch out for you until you get home. You need to be quite brave and remember some important things." I took out my letter to Mariah and while putting it in Jillian's suitcase, I said, "Give this letter to your mother when you see her." Then I safety-pinned Jillian's train ticket to her coat lapel, writing *Green Tree Iowa* in bold letters across the top. "These are your tickets, and it says where you get off."

I checked the departure boards for the platform number for Davenport Iowa, and walked briskly to the loading train. I was tugging on Jillian's hand as she dragged her feet behind me. It was a five-hour ride that would get her home by late afternoon. Then I located the conductor and explained that Jillian was traveling alone to see her mother. I offered him a four-dollar tip to watch out for her. The conductor agreed and allowed me to walk Jillian to her seat.

I selected a window seat for her and sat Milly next to her. "Remember, darling. It's OK to ask questions, but only ask the people working on the train. Mariah doesn't know you're coming, but she'll be so happy to see you." I held her face and looked directly in her eyes. "Pay attention now. When you get to Green Tree, walk from the depot into any store downtown, and ask them to contact Mariah Anderson; she's your mommy. Can you repeat what I just said?"

She nodded. Her eyes were big and wet, dropping tears across her fair cheeks as she spoke. "You said only talk to train people, get off at Green Tree, and ask for Mariah Anderson."

"You're so smart. I love you so much." I gave her a big hug and kiss. "I need to leave." I took out my damp handkerchief and wiped her running nose and wet face.

Jillian held up Millie, placing the doll in my arms. "Take her. You need Millie now." Panic returned to her voice as I began to walk down the aisle. "Mother, I don't want you to go! Please don't leave. What's my name now?"

I turned around, barely able to get the words out. "You're Jo Anderson; that's the role you were born to play. Goodbye, sweetie. I'll stay by the window outside until the train pulls out."

Her little face was pressed up against the window, staring at me as tears rolled down my face and hers. I had never cried this much in my life. As the train pulled out, I waved frantically and continued staring at the back of the caboose until it disappeared.

Hustling back to the ticket office, I dropped Millie in a trash receptacle and bought a one-way for a train headed to New York City in thirty minutes, hoping to simply disappear. As I boarded the train's stairs, I glanced nervously around, worrying about Williams and his threat. But then I laughed, remembering how easily I'd beat him at pinochle and thought, Willard Williams could go fuck himself.

# CHAPTER 56

# MARIAH

*O*n the way to get ice cream, Sarah had interrupted my conversation with Billy. "What were you saying, Sarah?"

"A little girl back there, tap dancing by the gas pumps, all by herself."

"Odd. How old did she look?"

"About my age."

I looked back but couldn't see anyone. "Billy, turn the truck around. Go to Gottlieb's."

"I thought we was getting ice cream. We're already here." He pulled up in front of the pool hall and parked.

"OK, you and Sarah go in. I'm going to check on something. Be back in a minute."

Randal Gottlieb was the blacksmith and family friend who'd bought my horses and wagon. His place was across the street and a few stores down. I walked briskly across, and just like Sarah said, I saw a little girl still tap dancing on a wooden platform next to Randal's pumps. Even from a distance though, I could see she had longish straight dark hair with a big bright bow on her head. I'd had a glimmer of hope, dreaming it might be Jo. But I was being foolish.

As I started to turn back, I noticed Randal driving up in my old wagon, being pulled by Buck and Shorty. I was surprised he'd never sold them. I walked closer, happy to see the horses and Randal, and waved to him as I approached.

He smiled back and jumped down from the bench seat and called out to me, "Well, good news travels fast. You got yourself a surprise visitor." He put his arm around the little brunette girl.

I blinked. Could it be? No. She looked over and waved, while I squinted my eyes. Oh my God, I could never forget that face. It was Sam's grin smiling back at me. It *was* Jo. I was dumbstruck; Jo was here, standing fifty feet away! I ran full out and then fell to my knees in front of her, hugging and holding on tight while her body remained rigid, without a word coming from her. "It's Mommy, baby. It's your Mommy. I've missed you so much." I looked up at Randal and asked, "How did she get here; who brought her?"

Jo pulled back, looked at me, and proudly said, "I asked for Mariah Anderson when I saw someone in a store."

"You found me, baby. I'm Mariah. I'm Mommy. Sarah's here too. Seeing you is going to make your sister so happy."

Randal stepped over and said, "Yeah, this little doll came trudging in carrying her own big suitcase, with railroad tickets pinned to her coat, announcing she needed to see you. I could tell she was yours and Sam's immediately. I went and got the horses and wagon to take her over to the Martin's. Thought she'd enjoy seeing your old team again, Buck and Shorty."

"I told him I'd take care of the store," Jo said confidently. "Nobody was stopping in, so I thought people might come if they saw me dancing."

"Miss Jo, about the only thing that attracts customers here

is lame horses and empty gas tanks," Gottlieb said. "But I thank you for trying."

My voice was shaking with emotion that I couldn't control. I'd dreamed of this day for so many months. "I can't believe this. I have so many questions, but let me take a look at you." Her hair had obviously been colored a dark brown. It was straight and longer. She'd grown taller too, by at least two inches, appeared heavier, and already missing a front tooth, but she was my Jo.

I grabbed her again for a hug. Then stood up and kissed Randal on the cheek, getting tickled by his long silver mustache. "Hey, could we take the wagon to the pool hall? This calls for ice cream! There's someone there, Jo, who would like to see you very much."

Gottlieb said, "Sure, let's take a ride." He picked up Jo, putting her on the bench and said, "You're a big girl now, want to take the reins and help me drive the team?"

"Sure. You betcha. Kind of like being in a western movie?"

"Yup, kind of like that. 'Cept the cowboys don't usually get ice cream."

I climbed on board and they drove the team together up the street for a few minutes, and then made a wide circle turning around, upsetting a few honking cars. We pulled up next to the Thomas' truck, just as Billy and Sarah stepped out, licking their cones.

I yelled from the wagon, "Sarah, look who I found! Our Jo was the girl you saw tap dancing!"

In her black-patent tap shoes, Jo scurried down from the bench of the wagon as the twins hopped up and down together, reunited again. I watched with joy as they skipped down the sidewalk, sharing Sarah's ice cream and their secrets. I eventually went in and got cones for Randal, Jo, and myself and sat on the outside bench with the two men, just grinning, not taking my eyes off the twins.

After a minute, Billy said, "You know, Mariah, watching those two, I was just reminiscing. I remember when the Thomas family took me under their wing. After my parents passed, I was all on my lonesome, on the road for months, and it took me a while to trust anybody, even the Thomas family. I didn't believe people could be so kind. Thought there must be some kind of angle that made me wary. I shouldn't be the one to tell you, but I'd give Jo some time. She's been through a lot. She'll open up eventually, but Jo's gonna probably have *a lot* of mixed-up loyalties. Who knows what that woman told her... know what I mean?"

"I think so. It's been a strange situation, but you're probably right. Gosh Billy... farm hand, carpenter, and head-doctor. You do it all."

Gottlieb added, "Well, somebody's gotta be in everybody's business. Might as well be Billy-boy."

I turned still grinning and asked, "By the way, Randal, why do you still have my old horses and wagon?"

"Oh, had a few offers for each horse, but you know, there's some things that just don't need splitting up."

I nodded, looking at the twins. "You're certainly right about that."

Later that evening, I brought both girls to the Martin farm, and told a surprised Elliott that Jo had suddenly returned, and announced we'd all three be sleeping upstairs for the next few nights, until I moved out. Elliott simply smiled, nodded and said, "Welcome girls." It appeared his upcoming marriage to Catherine had definitely improved his disposition.

First, I took the girls to the basement and dunked them both in the small tin tub for a much-needed hot bath. That night together felt so special. The sky room was cozy and the twins put on night gowns and cuddled together in Sarah's twin bed, with rag-dolls between them.

Once settled, Jo suddenly hopped out of bed and opened

her suitcase. "I forgot; Mother told me to give you this." Jo saying, *Mother*, referring to Nanette, made my blood run cold, but I remembered Billy's cautionary words. I decided not to press the matter. She handed me a letter in an envelope written in Nanette's flowery script, which I quickly scanned. Jo sat next to me on my bed and looked up.

"Do they make movies here too?"

"No sweetie, no movies; there's not even a movie theater here."

She nodded looking disappointed. "In Hollywood, I made some movies. It was fun."

"My goodness! That sounds exciting. You'll have to tell me all about that tomorrow. What else did you enjoy doing?"

"Hmm, I had a friend, Tink; we played games in the street. And I helped Mr. Arnold in the shop. But then we had to leave."

"That's too bad. Friends are important. How about school?"

She shook her head, looking down. "Couldn't go, 'cause of auditions. But I had singing and dance lessons. Mother said those were kind of like school."

"Yes, kind of. Maybe we can find a way to continue that if you enjoyed it. But I think you'll love school here in Green Tree. And you'll meet so many new friends. But it's getting late. I bet you're tired."

Jo sighed. "I guess. I'm worried about Mother. Does the letter say where she is?"

"No, darling, it doesn't. But you must understand, I'm your Mommy. I want you *here* with us. We're a family again and I won't let you go."

She walked back to Sarah's bed. "Yeah, Mother told me that a few times too."

With that comment, I realized Jo's trust would not be automatic. She was in a fragile state, feeling abandoned. Her trust in me would have to be rebuilt and earned overtime, carefully. I prayed I could do that. Then I reread the letter, studying the words of the woman who had caused this rift.

*Dear Mariah,*

> *If you are reading this now, then I can only hope Jo is safely in your care. I know you must hate me, having left the area without your knowledge, but please understand I meant no harm. I recognized Jo's many talents and thought they would be wasted living on a farm. Now I realize, that was not my decision to make, and I'm so sorry. But at the time, it felt like Jo and I were meant to be together. There was such a bond between us. It's difficult to explain. I always only wanted the best for her and I hope someday you will find it in your heart to forgive me. She will be greatly missed.*
>
> *I understand the Federal Bureau is searching for Jo's whereabouts. Please contact them to make sure they are aware she has safely returned to Green Tree.*
>
> *My deepest wishes for a happy reunion,*
> *Nanette Jorgenson*

After reading, I quickly folded the letter back up, barely wanting to touch something she had a hand in creating. And no, I could never forgive her. She was selfish, cruel and seemed to have written this only to get the heat of the bureau off her back. My hatred ran deep.

But thankfully, Jo did appear healthy. For that I was grateful. And tonight, I wanted to fall asleep with my heart happy, not dwelling on the mixed-up mind of Nanette Jorgenson. Tomorrow, I would begin rebuilding Jo's trust, one step at a time. I put the letter away in a safe box, kissed my pair-of-ones, and lay down to do some talking to Sam. We had so much to discuss.

# EPILOGUE
JO ANDERSON

## MARCH 1946, TWELVE YEARS LATER

*I* was with my family at the Green Tree depot, anxiously awaiting the train that would whisk me away to the wonders of New York City, the entertainment center of the world; only two-and-a-half days and a world away.

"Honey, are you absolutely sure about this? You verified hotel reservations; what about packing that pretty dress Grandma made for you? Oh, your extra cash—did you remember to hide it in your shoe?"

"Yes, yes, yes and no. And if I forgot something, Mom, it's too late now."

As usual, Sarah, Miss Responsibility, jumped in attempting to make our mother feel calmer. "Mom, I double-checked Jo's reservation. It's the Dixie Hotel, and everything's sorted in her luggage. But we decided to put the shoe money inside the secret pocket of her trousers. And, don't forget, it's only two months until we're coming for a visit." My twin threw her arm around my shoulder. "Jo, I'm so excited for you."

We heard the train whistle in the distance. I hugged Mom, Sarah, my step dad, David Thomas, and little brother, Sammie, promising to write them all soon. I'd been so eager, so ready to leave. But now a sudden surge of fear and tears welled up in my throat.

The train pulled up. The screeching wheels, the whistle, a uniformed conductor, the waving hands, tear-stained faces... a load of repressed memories flooded into my head. They'd found me years ago near the train station; I guess I still had fears of traveling on my own again.

I took a deep breath. I was eighteen; not a kid anymore. I could do this. I handed the man my one-way ticket to Manhattan. Then turned to tell everyone goodbye once again, wiping my tearing eyes. "I'm going to be fine. Everybody gets a postcard by next week. Love all of you!" I climbed aboard and found my seat.

As the train pulled out, I leaned my head back against the upholstered seat, thinking about all I hoped to achieve. I loved my family dearly, but I'd been dreaming about this move for years. The big war had officially ended last September and Manhattan's entertainment district was back in full swing. It was time.

I'd been training as a big frog in my tiny pond from the age of six. Always the lead in every school play and musical, the president of the school choir, with my mom scraping funds together and doggedly taking me to dance and voice lessons in the larger town of Albert Lea. I was ready for the Big White Way to embrace me or spit me out, but I had to go there and try. It was all I could ever remember wanting to do.

My sister, Sarah, was the excellent student, already attending college at the University of Iowa. I'd limped through high school and graduated with her help, never feeling the tug to take the regular curriculum seriously. My plan was to audition for chorus lines, Broadway shows, radio programs, perhaps become a jingle-singer, a band vocalist, a recording artist. I was open to any and all opportunities and ready to fall on my face, fail, and then try again. Hopefully, persistence and talent would win out in the end. That's what Mom kept telling me.

She had admitted her early dreams to me. A younger Mariah had always wanted to move to New York and find a 'modern job' but things had never quite worked out. And now Mom was knee-deep in her successful rental businesses, and committed to my ever-patient stepdad, David, and little Sammy. But I knew if I succeeded, my parents would be incredibly proud of me.

Sarah had done the research and reserved a hotel for me near Times Square. The Dixie Hotel advertised that every room had a bed, radio, window and its own bath, for twenty-dollars a week. Sarah believed it had the best value because it also had two lounges and a cabaret theater, where she assumed I would quickly find a job on site. My sister was kind, naive, and overly confident of my abilities.

I'd tucked away two-hundred-dollars in my secret pocket, a culmination of years of birthday gifts, part-time jobs, and graduation donations. All of this hopefully would allow me to survive, while I hunted down possible jobs.

Finally arriving in Manhattan, I was awed by the enormity of Penn Station. But even more so as I stepped outside, hearing the bustling cacophony of the streets, craning my neck, looking up at a small swath of sky while surrounded by so many skyscrapers that I soon felt dizzy. I now only vaguely remembered my days in bustling Hollywood, but in comparison to this, Hollywood seemed like a very small town.

At Penn Station, I found a kiosk selling tourist maps and newspapers. I bought one of each and asked the man behind the counter to point out directions to Times Square, where the Dixie Hotel was located.

Looking down at my suitcase, he snapped his fingers and said, "Let me guess. A looker like you, legs like a racehorse … gotta be a dancer or a singer, right?"

"You got me there, straight off the farm from Iowa."

"So, you ready to make your mark? Miss, be careful out there; it's a rough business. Take my advice. Go see a few shows, take a ferry around the island, see the Statue of Liberty, and then go back home. Save yourself the heartbreak."

I was shocked at this frank advice from a stranger. "Well, that's quite discouraging. I *can't* go home. This is my destiny. It's all I've ever wanted to do."

"Yeah, been there myself. Good luck, Iowa."

The wide sidewalks were thick with pedestrians, busy-looking women in bright printed shirt-waist dresses, and a lot of young men in suits or still sporting military uniforms. I felt an energy on the streets I'd never felt before. People passed by with an urgency in their step. Approaching the massive seven-hundred-room Dixie Hotel, I was awed and felt a little like a fraud. Did I belong here?

My room was small and simple. I hung up my few garments and began studying the classified sections in the paper. I was encouraged to see a large section of listings under the heading *Entertainers*. I began circling job possibilities: clubs seeking exotic dancers, bands needing torch singers, night clubs seeking shapely cigarette girls, Times Square shops hiring ener-getic dancers for sandwich-boards. I was willing to give anything a try. Although I wondered what type of dancing was required of someone considered exotic, and why were people singing with torches?

Then I noticed a classified sub-section for *Actors*. Tomorrow morning there was a casting call for dancers and singers for a new musical. The play was called *Annie Get Your Gun* and they were holding auditions at the Imperial Theater. At the bottom, the ad stated: *Equity membership and agency representation preferred.* I wasn't sure what that meant but *preferred* did not mean *must have*, so I thought I'd try out first thing tomorrow. The call was for nine. I'd decided to go early and arrive by eight-thirty. I studied my map, located the theater, and took a bath.

The following morning, I was excited and nervous, but in a good way. I walked to the Imperial Theater on Forty-Fifth Street. My excitement dropped to discouragement as I saw a long line of hopefuls, starting at the theater's back door, up the alleyway, and then pressed against storefronts for a block down Forty-Fifth. I joined the end of the line, checking out my competition, dressed in various forms of rehearsal wear, many carrying their dance shoes.

A handsome young man joined in behind me. "Guess we're last to the party. I overslept; worked until three last night."

I turned around nodding. "Yeah, I'm new to all this. The ad said nine. It's not even eight-thirty yet and look at this line."

"I can assure you, newbie, most of these hoofers were here by six or seven this morning. My agent is gonna kill me."

"Oh...so do most of those trying out have agents?"

He shrugged his shoulders, "Not all, but a lot of us do. I take it you don't?"

"No." I laughed and said, "I did when I was five or six, but that won't help me now."

I turned and tried counting the line of hopefuls ahead of me and noticed a more mature woman right at the turn into the alley. Longish red hair, styled similar to Kate Hepburn's, wearing a fitted, fashionable bright blue suit. She was talking to a girl in line, handed her a photograph, patted her back and seemed to offer encouragement. Her mannerisms seemed vaguely familiar. Perhaps she was the girl's mother?

Then I heard the guy behind me say, "Oh shit. Not this morning!" He tapped my shoulder. "Hey, mind if I duck in behind you." He turned his face slightly to the wall, standing in my shadow. The lady in the blue suit looked up and down the line and moved over to chat with another person, and handed him some paperwork.

As she walked closer, a cold dread enveloped me. I knew that face. Could it be? Charming, smiling, chic, critically appraising the people in the line, tall and intimidating with her stylishly sharp shoulder pads.

But she looked past me and said, "Damien... end of the line? What are you thinking? This is Irving Berlin. This could be the season's biggest hit on Broadway. Turn around, damn it! I know you hear me."

The guy hiding behind me turned towards her, and stepped forward. "Oh, hey there, Fran. Sorry, late night. Won't happen again."

"It better not. At this spot in line, you'll be lucky if they even have time to look at you. One more mistake like this and you're out."

I knew that voice; that confident strident tone, the beautiful face. Older, thinner, but it was her.

By now, several in line had turned and were staring back at poor Damien while Nanette Jorgenson stood directly next to me, lambasting this guy who appeared to be her client. Although he called her Fran, I knew it was Nanette. I began shaking, nervous she'd recognize me.

Through the years, Mom had slowly revealed to me all the lies Nanette had told, all the letters Mom had mailed, but Nanette had never read to me. This was the lady who had told me Mariah was the one who chose Sarah over me. And that my mom didn't want me back. All lies.

Now, this attractive redhead was right next to me. The old Nanette was gone, but she'd reinvented herself. Perhaps though, Nanette might be the solution; the person who could navigate me through this entertainment business I was so naive about. If anyone could, Nanette would smooth the way for me, get me in front of the important people, push me to get ahead. And I bet she'd do it for me in a heartbeat.

But I was determined to do this on my own.

She looked right past me, patted Damien's shoulder, then gave him a hug. "OK, screw-up; knock 'em dead today. You'll be fine, and don't fuck it up." He nodded, looking relieved.

I kept my mouth shut, turned my face forward, and held my breath. I continued to remain invisible to Nanette, as she turned and quickly walked down the street in her formidable heels. Then she turned abruptly, squinting at me for a brief second. Shaking her head, she continued walking the opposite direction with her back straight, head held high, as if she was queen of Broadway.

## ABOUT THIS NOVEL

The backdrop of this story came to me from stories shared by my mother, ElDora Criswell. Growing up during the tumultuous decade of the 1930's, she and her younger sister spent their early years moving often with their parents, from Iowa to Chicago, and then back again to southern Minnesota, living on leased farms, or those owned by extended family. Although times were difficult and jobs scarce, most of her childhood memories were of play, camaraderie, and celebrations shared with her large extended farming family of numerous cousins, aunts, uncles, and grandparents. My mother also had stories of attending a one-room rural school house, with a harried young teacher attempting to corral and instruct grades one through eight. Eventually, ElDora became a town-girl, leaving the farm with her family and moving into the small town of Kiester, Minnesota. Spending her teen years here, again, held special recollections for her as an eager student involved with school activities and part of the high school marching band. For summer jobs she often hired on as extra help on some of her relatives' farms.

Although ElDora's memories provided background mate-

BOBBIE CANDAS

rial for me, all primary characters and their stories in this novel are entirely fiction, as is the fabricated town of Green Tree, which is a compilation of several of the small rural towns of the farming area skirting the Minnesota-Iowa border. In addition to Kiester, I researched other neighboring towns during this time period which included: Blue Earth, Clear Lake, Albert Lea, and Mankato. Many of these towns were at their population peak in the thirties, forties, and fifties. I wanted to capture the difficulties, joys, comradery, and sense of family prevalent in this fertile, productive area of the American Midwest during this challenging economic period.

Although the political, economic, and entertainment related details mentioned throughout the novel are historically correct and fall appropriately into the timeline of the story, there is one detail regarding a bank closing event which actually took place in February and March of 1933. For this story's purposes, I have changed the date to February, 1934.

The popular song, *Happy Days Are Here Again,* sung by Jo and Sarah Anderson in this novel, was written in 1929 by Milton Ager and Jack Yellen. It appeared in the 1930 film, Chasing Rainbows and was the campaign song for Franklin D. Roosevelt's 1932 presidential campaign.

The following books were insightful in preparation of this novel: *Child Star,* by Shirley Temple Black, and *The Little Rascals: The Life and Time of Our Gang* by Leonard Maltin and Richard W Bann. In addition, information provided by *Iowa PBS* offered a wealth of information on the plight and economics of farmers during the great depression. To read more, follow this link: https://www.iowapbs.org/iowapathways/my-path/2591/great-depression-hits-farms-and-cities-1930s

# ACKNOWLEDGMENTS

I wish to thank my earliest readers on the first draft of this novel. I always appreciated the feedback offered by Jeanne McCaffrey, Susie Criswell, Jaci Grisham, Arlis Linder and ElDora Criswell. Thank you for your patience and encouragement as the story wound its way into its current and final draft.

Also, I'm so appreciative of comments and critiques from my brave group of Beta readers. It's not easy taking on a rough version of a novel of this length. I am indebted to Liz Brammer, Vicki Brumby, Susie Criswell, Katie Clayton, Julie Flo, Bird Thomas, and Jeanne McCaffrey. Your encouragement pushed me forward through several more revisions.

In addition, most chapters of this novel were workshopped by my intrepid writers at Dallas Creative Writers Group. Your weekly feedback forced some beneficial changes that always made the writing better. Special thanks to John Archer, Hal Branson, Melanie Wittrig, and Ian Sykes, who all provided helpful insight from both a creative and technical standpoint.

One cannot discount the emergency aid and patience of tech-savvy husbands. A massive thanks to Mehmet Candas for his help when files would occasionally just disappear or power surges fried my laptop.

And a big shout out to Betty Martinez with Reedsy, who designed this amazing cover. I gave her a bit of insight about my primary characters and she ran with it and captured my protagonists perfectly.

## ABOUT BOBBIE CANDAS:

I'm a Texas girl: grew up in San Antonio, went to school at UT in Austin where I earned my degree in journalism, and settled in Dallas where I raised a husband, two kids and a few cats. My husband, Mehmet, and the cats will probably disagree on who raised who, but I'm a sucker for a robust discussion.

For years I was involved in retail management, but have more recently focused on my writing, taking deep dives into the lives of my characters. When you can pry my fingers off the keyboard, I enjoy entertaining, sharing food and drink with friends and family. I enjoy shopping, usually on the hunt for apparel, with a special weakness for shoes, and will frequently jump at the opportunity of an unexpected trip to a far-away place.

And I always make time for reading. I keep a stack of novels ready and waiting on my night stand, with a few tapping their toe in my Kindle. I bounce around genres, and I'm always ready for a good recommendation.

## ALSO BY BOBBIE CANDAS

*Welcome to Wonderland: A Dramedy*

*Imperfect Timing*

*Luck, Love and a Lifeline*

## FOLLOW BOBBIE ON

Facebook: Author Bobbie Candas: https://www.facebook.
com/bobbiecandasauthor

Good Reads author link: https://www.goodreads.com/author/
show/8292457.Bobbie.Candas

Amazon Author Central: https://www.amazon.com/stores/
Bobbie-Candas/author/B00MNS6KV0?ref=ap_rdr&isDram
Integrated=true&shoppingPortalEnabled=true

Instagram: Author Bobbie Candas

For author updates add your email at: bobbiecandas@
gmail.com

Continue reading for an excerpt from
Bobbie Candas' novel
**WELCOME TO WONDERLAND: A DRAMEDY**

# WELCOME TO WONDERLAND: A DRAMEDY

## AN EXCERPT

## BY BOBBIE CANDAS

# CHAPTER 1
# VIOLET IS BLUE
VIOLET HILL

*M*other considers me awkward, graceless, and socially challenged, but always has hope for improvement. I disagree and think of myself as critically shy. Is there such a diagnosis? I've learned I do best when I can control limited social encounters. That's why I'm better working alone, in a world I'm comfortable and familiar with, the study of soil, seeds, and grasses.

I've been working as a research assistant with Dr. William Hirshfield. After finishing my masters at UT in Austin, I gratefully found my hidey-hole at the UT School of Environmental Sciences. After being hired, I realized it was the perfect job for me. For a year, we've been running experiments and collecting data on soil absorption, attempting to come up with a microbial substance that will turn arid lands into potential blooming fields of agriculture. All well and good for keeping me in my cozy, solitary research lab, but with the added bonus of working toward saving a warm and crowded planet.

Then yesterday happened.

Dr. Hirshfield called me unexpectedly to meet in his office. We normally only met every two weeks for consultations on experiments. I sat down across from his desk, with my sweating palms gripping the arm rests of the chair. The meeting opened with congenial small-talk. I said, "Hello."

As with most people I conversed with, I found it difficult looking at Hirshfield when he spoke. Today I found his floor-boards especially interesting. Wide wood panels which had me wondering, were they deliberately distressed or actually marred from age? As he shuffled papers on his desk I reached down and touched the floor. Definitely faux distressed.

He nervously coughed and then continued, "Violet, I must say, your work has been exemplary, but…"

Oh shit… The proverbial *but.* I shuddered slightly.

As I pretended to be intrigued with the floor, Hirshfield said, "I'm afraid I have some bad news to share." He coughed again. "I'll just get right to it. I hate to tell you this, but our next year of NIH funding has been cut. They haven't renewed the terms of our project at the previous level and claim our results are not going as quickly as we initially projected."

He seemed to be talking to himself now, explaining his problems to the ceiling as my eyes nervously flitted up occa-sionally to watch. "Seems our study is on the low end of their priority scale regarding research grant money. But our idea has so much merit! It dovetails perfectly with climate change issues and food production for overpopulated areas. Anyway…it's probably all politics. Therefore—" He coughed a third time. *Nervous tick or avoidance? Either way, not a good sign.* "I'm having to cut most of my research staff, including your position."

Please no. Had I heard correctly? I was praying he'd single me out as too good to let go. But of course not. My eyes became moist and my body went cold. I had finally found my place in this chaotic world, my comfy, musty den. Where I could reach my fingers deep into sandy soil and disappear into another world within my microscope. I'd clock in for hours of uninterrupted work, eat a sandwich over my work station by myself, needing to only interact with others regarding information I was knowledgeable about.

Now apparently all that was gone.

And what remained? Going home to Mother? I was devastated. I felt like laying down on those faux floorboards and curling up in a ball.

"Dr. Hirshfield, p-perhaps p-part-time. Tw-Twenty-five hours a week?"

In case you missed that, I have a noticeable stutter, which seems to come into full bloom during times of stress.

"I only wish that were possible, Violet. The grant has been downgraded to include lab equipment, supplies, and compensation for only a few key personnel. I'm so sorry. This has all come as quite a surprise. So, we're making adjustments immediately; I can keep you for another two weeks. I wanted you to hear it from me, personally."

I mumbled, "Th-Thank you," then stood up, wrapped my arms across my chest, and meekly asked about a possible reference letter. He went back to shuffling papers and nodded, agreeing to my simple request. I quickly walked out with my head down, making my exit before he had the chance to shake my perspiring palm.

I spent the next few weeks desperately attempting to find a position with another research team within the department. There were several available for volunteer and credit work, but all paid positions were fully staffed. Although my educational credentials were excellent, my interviewing skills were a little shaky. I considered customer service positions, but they never seemed a good match, and I truly wanted to continue within my field of study.

At the end of the two-week period, I decided to call in for financial reinforcement. Via email, I sent my mother news of the change in job status, then requested funds to keep me in

Austin while I continued to look for work, but instead of an electronic deposit, she offered this:

> *Dear Violet,*
>
> *So sorry to hear about your job loss. I know you've been happy with your little research position. Sometimes these minor hiccups work out for the best. I think you need more stimulation and interaction in your work. When I visited, your lab job seemed so sterile and lonely. I'm sure I can line something up for you through my contacts in Dallas. Come home, darling. The guest house was recently redone and you're welcome to use it. It'll be fun hanging out together again. I believe I'll call Lexy and see if she can revise her schedule and set aside sessions for you. What day should I expect you? Can't wait to catch up! --Mother*

She was not going to be sympathetic to my cause. I made a second stab at job hunting, knowing it was only a delay tactic. Was I being an ungrateful little bitch? Sort of. But I knew I'd have to deal with my mother's incessant smiling face, popping in without warning, spewing false cheer, urging me to conform to her standards, and always sending out subliminal messages regarding her underlying sense of disappointment in me.

It had been five years since I'd lived at home. My first year in the dorms had been a disaster. I was happier on my own, renting an apartment for three years while earning my bachelor's and another two for my masters, comfortably surviving in my small, quiet efficiency.

In contrast, Mother's home was palatial, but for me it was a luxurious prison sitting on a green oak-studded hill overlooking White Rock Lake in Dallas.

I dragged out my move. I felt no incentive to rush home knowing what lay ahead; struggling through painful interviews, going through clothing issues and social events with Mother.

Yes, still a tender issue at age twenty-four. Then, once again, I'd start sessions with my speech therapist, Lexy.

Unfortunately, research assistant's pay was low, Austin rents were high, and the guest house at Mother's was free. Economically, it made sense. Emotionally, I was an unhappy wreck.

And who could I complain to? *Call 911* -- My mother is inviting me to move into her newly renovated guest quarters. *Put her on trial?* -- She insists on buying me new clothing suggested by her personal shopper at Neiman's. *Lock her up?* -- She's offering me therapy for an affliction which admittedly has recently become worse.

I was a pathetic whiner. Time to get up, pack it in, and get moving.

# CHAPTER 2
# THE GLADIATOR
TURNER COOPER

*T*he landline was ringing again but I didn't bother to pick up. Letting it go to voicemail, I listened to my wife's warm Texas accent roll softly through the office over the speaker of an antiquated answering machine.

*Hi, there. It's Allie. Turner and I aren't here. You know what to do; bye now.*

Sighing, I ruffled the soft shiny fur of our Irish Setter, Blaze. Leaning back on my leather sectional, I stretched my legs out over the ottoman, closed my eyes, and wondered how many more hours it would be before I could go back to bed without seeming too pitiful. Perhaps a half-tumbler of Dewar's Scotch and a movie would help pass the time. I silenced my cell and closed the office door so there would be no interruptions. Amazing how many solicitations there were after you signed up for the no-solicitation list. I never realized before... because I rarely was home to hear them. I smiled, recalling a recent conversation with Allie.

'I swear, Turner, we need to get rid of that phone. Unless you're in the market for a time share or extended car warranty, it's useless. No one we know has a landline anymore.'

'But Allie, what about missing out on the all-expense-paid cruise of our dreams, or lending my social security number to a Nigerian prince?'

'Uh, those guys don't call much anymore.'

'I promise, babe… I'll get around to it.' But there it was, still ringing.

Petting Blaze's head again, I said, "Yeah bud, you get what they say about old dogs and new tricks, don't you Blaze?"

Hearing his name, my dog looked over at me expectantly, and then laid his head down on the thick rug. Back to a movie choice. I could punch up something on Netflix, but lately, most of those movies were lame. Either stupid rom-coms or crazy fantasy. How about an old favorite instead?

I got up and perused our shelves of old DVDs on either side of the six-foot screen. "Here's a good one, Blaze. Haven't watched this in years. You'll love it." I popped in *Gladiator*, starring Russell Crowe, sat back down, put my feet up and took a deep sip of Scotch. It was a long film; maybe it would require a full tumbler. Or two.

Three hours later, I'd surprised myself, managing to remain awake through the entire film, and on this viewing I saw the story so differently. That happens sometimes when rewatching a film. My previous memory of it was all about warring strategies, power struggles, and grisly scenes of bodies being torn apart. But this afternoon, I realized the gladiator's greatest desire was to leave all power and politics behind him and return home to his wife and farm. Somehow before I'd totally missed that aspect.

I got up and stretched, checking my watch. "Well, boy… time for that walk now, right? Let's go." Blaze was ready. Hearing the word *walk*, he began looking anxiously about. "Come on, downstairs. She's not here today." I walked through the utility room, switched from bare feet to slip-on tennis shoes, attached his leash, and left through the garage.

The sun was still thirty minutes away from sizzling into the lake, with the air feeling less humid than usual. Even in September, Dallas weather could be brutal. "So, what are you up for? Long one or short one?" I looked at the dog's inquisitive golden-brown eyes. "That's what I thought too."

We headed down our street, turned at the corner and walked down to the bike trail. Under the shade of trees, wearing a loose tee-shirt and shorts, it actually felt good to be out. We walked the half-mile to the large dog park by the lake. I unleashed Blaze, sat down on a bench, and watched him run, dodge, and scamper with joy among the wide range of large breeds released for play by their work-a-day parents.

Eventually, another guy came and sat down next to me and, like a proud papa, pointed. "Mine's the Goldendoodle. Which one's yours?"

"The Irish Setter with all the pent-up energy. He's used to getting out more."

"Oh, yeah. He's a beauty. Wait…is that Blaze? Man, I'm so sorry. I didn't realize…your Allie's husband, right? She was up here with Blaze all the time. Great lady. I'm so sorry, dude. I'm Kevin. Kevin Wells. My wife and I live nearby."

I nodded, smiled stiffly, and stood up. "Good to meet you, Kevin. Thanks. I'm heading out now."

I walked toward my dog, knowing he'd hate being pulled out so soon, but it was time for us to leave. Kevin got up and called out after me, "Hey, if you ever need to talk or anything, I'm here most evenings. Allie, she was awesome. Really gonna miss her around here."

I nodded, putting the leash back on the setter. "Sure, thanks man." We weren't ready for those conversations yet. Blaze and I were damaged goods.

# CHAPTER 3
# THE WINNING TICKET
ROSARIO GUZMAN

*T*he alarm went off with news blaring through the radio, jolting me awake from a deep sleep. It was ten PM. I'd showered before bed and rarely bothered with makeup anymore. When your job was washing and folding laundry at a twenty-four-hour *lavanderia*, what was the point? I put on my favorite fitted jeans, a clean white tee shirt, and pulled my shoulder length brown hair into a tidy bun. I forced a smile in the bathroom mirror before brushing my teeth and then repeated my mantra, "It's going to be a great day!" I tried to keep the sound of my voice upbeat, but lately, maintaining positivity was becoming more challenging each day.

My second cousin, Miguel, owned Bright White Laundry, where I'd worked the eleven PM to six AM shift for a year. I was grateful for the work but knew I was capable of so much more. It was boring, repetitious, and surprisingly busy. At eleven PM, Diaz Avenue in East Dallas was dark, but Bright White Laundry sat on the corner of the sketchy business block like a shiny fluorescent-lit beacon for the unwashed.

I walked in waving to co-worker, Enrique, another distant cousin. I hated following Enrique's shift. He was lazy and usually left a string of unfinished tasks in his wake after clocking out.

"¿*Qué pasa*, Enrique? How 's business tonight?"

Seeing me, he'd already grabbed his backpack and was walking to the office to clock out. He stopped and nodded towards the bathroom. "Welcome to Wonderland, Rosario. I just locked the bathroom. Man…you do *not* wanna go in there. That place is nasty. Tonight, if I was you, I'd keep the street people outta there."

I shook my head, once again surprised at his lack of work ethic. "Enrique, you know the person on each shift has to clean the bathroom. That's your job. You expect me to work 'till six tomorrow morning and not use it?"

"Well, I'm not doing it. It's up to you, chica. Gotta fly. Things to do tonight."

"OK, but I'm telling Miguel."

"Do what you have to do, man," he said with a little laugh. "Do you think I give a flying fuck about this job?"

Apparently not. I watched him walk out, while shaking my head. What a jerk! Sad to think I was loosely related to him. Very loosely.

I checked out the place. One lady and two guys were doing laundry after carving out their own personal space amongst the machines. Pretty slow for a Thursday night. I gingerly unlocked the bathroom, needing to see what I was dealing with. Yeah, it was bad. I took a picture to show our boss, pulled up my mask. put on rubber gloves, and got to work.

At six AM, I clocked out and went next door to Daylight Donuts, also owned by Miguel. As usual, I grabbed a chair in the back, craving my morning cup of hot fresh coffee with lots of milk, and then bit into a soft and sweet pineapple empanada. Heaven! The front doorbell began to jingle as I tied on my white apron, ready to face the early risers and day laborers needing their morning sugar rush. I put on my smile and joined the team of two others already manning the front counter.

By eleven AM there were a few late donut-seeking stragglers, but two could easily run the front while I finished cleanup in the back. After clocking out, I walked down the street and boarded DART, eating my lunch from a paper bag as the yellow city bus carried me to the outskirts of Dallas. From there, I walked the remaining few blocks to *Construction Connection.* From noon until four, I worked the final leg of my day in a warehouse cleaning *porta orinales*, or what everyone here calls Port-A-Potties. A place filled with tall, nasty smelling blue boxes that needed a thorough scrubbing and sanitizing before they were sent out for another day of duty at construction sites.

A co-worker, Yolanda, and I punched in at the same time. From our assigned lockers we donned knee-high black, lug-soled rubber boots, elbow length rubber gloves, and tied on long black canvas aprons.

Trudging out to the warehouse, we crossed a road where two guys driving forklifts were moving sanitized port-a-potties onto trucks. As I walked by, they both hooted, whistled, and called out, "Looking good today, Rosario! Your ass, in those jeans… so hot."

I blushed and tried to ignore them, amazed anybody would think me sexy in my rubber encased work clothes.

Yolanda tapped my shoulder. "Hey, don't mind them; they're harmless. Enjoy it while you can. Trust me, nobody's whistled at me in ages."

"How long you worked here, Yolanda?"

"Ten years, girl. Can you believe it?"

"Shit!"

"That's right. Ten years of shit."

I pulled the mask up over my mouth and nose, grabbed a power hose and yelled, "If we're both working here ten years from now, just shoot me. Promise, OK?"

Yolanda laughed and nodded, "Sure, but then who's gonna shoot me?"

At four my shift ended and once home, I had five hours before the whole crazy cycle started again. I knew the schedule was extreme but it was the only way I could maintain an apartment and manage to send a bit of money to my mother in Mexico.

Standing outside my apartment, I pulled a white envelope out of the dented tin mailbox. A thrill momentarily pulsed through me. Carefully opening the white envelope from the U.S. government, I pulled out an unimpressive looking, but oh-so-important, printed paper card qualifying me for legal work in the United States. The coveted *Green Card*. My ticket out of the shadows, away from working lousy jobs that nobody else wanted to do for less than minimum wage.

I'd applied a year ago--scrimping and saving, paying all the filing fees, going to interviews, paying an immigration attorney. And now, here it was; but suddenly my excitement fizzled. Receiving it felt so bittersweet because I had no one here to share my news or happiness with.

I'd purposely tried not to befriend people since coming to Dallas. And I didn't want the people I worked with to know I'd be looking for other work. I wasn't sure who I could trust. Most of my family, the few I cared about, were in Ciudad Juarez in Mexico or dead. That evening, I felt so alone.

I placed the card in a hidden compartment in my wallet, set my alarm for ten PM, removed my clothes, took a shower, and then smiled to myself in the mirror.

# CHAPTER 4
# QUEEN OF DIAMONDS
VIOLET

$\mathcal{T}$aking a deep breath and then releasing, I pulled my Subaru into Mother's long circular drive, trailed by a small U-Haul. The four-hour drive from Austin to Dallas, up busy I-35, was stressful. Checking myself in the rear-view mirror, I pulled my long dark mane out of a hair-tie, brushed it, and pushed it off my face with a headband. When I stepped out of the car I shook my hands while attempting to release nervous energy, and told myself all would go smoothly.

Unlocking the front door, I called out into the echoing foyer, "I'm home." No response. I followed chattering voices down a long hallway to the sunroom, calling out again, "M-Mother, I'm here."

"Out here, darling. Come say hi to the girls."

By 'girls' she meant her bridge playing pals of the fifty-and-up club. I stopped near the entrance and saw Mother and her gaggle of girlfriends sitting on cushioned white wicker, amongst the dwarf palms, ferns, and birds-of-paradise. I vaguely recalled these women while I stood there slightly frozen.

Waving me over, she said, "Oh, for heaven's sake, Violet,

come over and say hi. You know the girls. Viv, Jan, Chris." She pointed to each one with a playing card in her hand, exposing the queen of diamonds. "Violet's come home for a while, ladies. We're gonna see if she can crack the job market here in Dallas. Give your mom a hug, baby."

I walked over and leaned in, giving her an air pass across her cheek and an awkward pat on the shoulder. "H-hello, ladies. G-Good to see you again."

Mother shook off my attempted embrace, tossing her thick tawny-streaked hair back across her shoulders. "Violet, Maria made a batch of pina coladas if you want one."

"No thanks. I sh-sh-should unload."

"In that case, the key to the guest house is on the bar. Go ahead and get yourself settled in. We'll go out for a nice dinner tonight. There's a new place I want to take you to."

"Thanks M-Mother; s-s-see you later."

Of course, I felt their whispers as I exited, sure they were patting Mom's arm in sympathy for her cross-to-bear, the awkward stuttering adult daughter. Screw them. A few sessions with my speech therapist, Lexi, and I would be back in the saddle, speaking with a lighter spraying of word bullets. *M's, P's, S's*--all trouble spots for me. Too bad *Mother* started with that tricky *M*.

I circled the drive and pulled around to the back. On the opposite side of the pool, up the hill from the main house, stood my new home, for now. Both the lower and upper levels of the front walls were glass, offering a perfect vista to the expansive green lawn, a long rectangular turquoise pool, and the lake in the distance.

I unlocked the French doors and was immediately impressed with the update. The walls were painted a clean white and on the left side was a low-slung off-white sofa covered with numerous throw pillows. Above the couch, a large abstract painting pulled out the same soft colors as those of the accent pillows, and a sleek white leather chair and ottoman perched opposite a large bookcase with a flat screen. Note to self: Keep ballpoint pens and markers on the table only.

On the right side of the room was a stone kitchen countertop lining the entire wall with updated appliances and across from the counter was a rough-hewn farm table and chairs. Mom must have given her decorator carte blanche on this one.

I pulled the sheer draperies back and then went to the U-Haul to begin unloading. Within a few hours I had all clothing hung upstairs, bathroom accessories in place, and a small selection of kitchen utensils put away. To hold my vast collection of textbooks and novels on the shelves, I pushed Mother's art objects off to the sides.

As I was emptying my final box, Mother opened the door. "All settled in, darling?"

"Getting there."

She looked quickly around, suddenly appearing agitated. "The shelves. Violet, shouldn't these sculptures stand out more?" She walked over and held a tall swirling hunk of something. "This piece…hand blown glass, by the way, is a beauty. It's a Hughes Lamont. You're totally hiding it like this, Violet."

"J-J-Just had to find a place for everything." I was immediately reminded of the white quilted comforter and canopy bed I had as a child—the bed I could never sit or play on.

She went across the shelves, shaking her head, pulling out her collected art pieces, adjusting their positions, showing them off to their advantage. Sighing with relief, she said, "Much better now, see?"

"Sure. Looks good." I had no energy for an argument within her perfect world.

"So, dinner tonight. Let's try Turkish--Cafe Izmir? She looked at the jeans and faded tee I was wearing. "The place is casual but not *that* casual. I think a change of clothes is required. Six o'clock? So glad you're home, Violet."

I robotically nodded yes to all comments and finished with, "Yeah, m-me too."

I braced myself and thought, take the bad with the good. Dinner with Mom--pros and cons: good food filled with a minefield of conversation. I breathed in and out slowly, calming myself. I'd eaten little in the last few weeks. I needed to have a healthy appetite or she'd think I was having eating disorders again. Checking my watch, I decided there was time for a short nap before hunting down an outfit that wouldn't have me put under house arrest for a fashion faux pas.

At six sharp, she swung her Range Rover in front of my door, just as I tied a scarf around my neck that would hopefully help disguise the black *Target* t-shirt and basic black trousers I'd put on.

I stepped out and told her, "P-Prompt as always." I had to laugh. "Th-thanks for the lift."

"Well, I know that driveway is so steep. So, in the mood for Turkish?"

I stepped up into the seat. "I g-g-guess…don't know if I've had it before, but I'm game. I'm actually r-really hungry."

"I'm so glad you mentioned that. You're looking unnaturally thin. You've got to try the *Iskender*. I'll order for you. It's to die for, with lots of butter. Perfect if you're needing to gain weight."

I shook my head. *Here we go*. "I'm f-fine. Just a few pounds under. The move has kept me b-b-busy." *Just drive, Mother*.

Soon we were seated at a small round table, lit by candle light, drinking a deep red Cabernet. It perfectly complemented my enormous plate of grilled beef and lamb, served over soft pita bread, topped with a tomato sauce and searing liquid butter. Exquisite and packed with calories. Chalk one up for Mother.

As we finished dinner and contemplated dessert, she jumped into it. "Now, baby, let's talk jobs. By the way, that scarf looks good on you. The blue plays up your eyes. You should do that more often, play up the eyes. They're beautiful, you know. You favor me in that regard."

"Thanks."

"Back to jobs."

I was about to take a gulp of wine, but stopped. "Actually, if you don't m-mind, I'd like to do m-my own job search first."

"Well, a little headstart and a push certainly never hurt. Remember, in job hunts it's *who* you know, not necessarily *what* you know."

"That's unfortunate. I appreciate it, but g-give me some time to check around." *Good job, Violet…Assertive but not ungrateful.*

Later that evening, I plugged in my laptop and did some searches at UT-Dallas, UT Health Science Center, Southern Methodist University, and some local commercial labs. There were a few promising openings, so I excitedly filled in online applications, attached my CV and personal statement, and pressed send. This was all followed by a bout of stomach cramps. Nerves or rich food? I was never sure.

After giving my new spotless bathroom a full workout, I stood in front of the mirror practicing casual interview banter. But I sounded worse than usual. Who could listen to that voice? I was seeing eye rolls and embarrassment looking right back at me.

Perhaps Mother was right. A friendly reference with a personal introduction would make everything go smoother. Reconsidering her offer, I typed out an email request to Mother for her help. But wasn't I taking the easy way out? Was my stutter and anxiety *that* bad? I had strong academic credentials and a great ability at retention. Didn't that count for something?

With determination, I went back to the mirror and practiced additional interview conversations. But I sounded even worse. "M-M-Mrs. Jones, happy to m-meet you." I watched my contorted face struggling over numerous consonants. I returned to my laptop, read through my email to Mother and pressed send.

# CHAPTER 5
# DEAD WIFE, MESSY LIFE
TURNER

*T*he first thing I spotted was the empty Dewars bottle on the nightstand. Not surprising, considering my head felt like oddly shaped Legos rattling around when I attempted movement. Crap, eleven AM. Way late for work. Then I remembered; I was in mourning. Sleeping late was perfectly acceptable behavior. I rolled back over, my arm reaching out to pat the space next to me. Still empty. I closed my eyes again.

Now someone was knocking. On my upstairs bedroom door? Weird. I squinted toward the clock on my nightstand. High noon. I sat up, shook my head, knocked the cobwebs and Legos around, followed by yelling out a raspy, "Hello?"

Through the door I heard a muffled voice. "Mr. Turner, it's Sally. Your maid. Allie always had me come Wednesdays. You want me to clean up here?"

"Sally?" *Our maid was named Sally?* "Uh, hold on, please." I stretched out my shaking legs on the side of the bed, threw on yesterday's t-shirt and shorts, finger combed through my mess of bed-head, and opened the door. Sally looked like she was ready for business. Hands on her hips, a stout, fortyish-looking woman with short graying hair, khaki shorts, and a tucked-in Izod polo. "Hey, Sally…we ever met before? Seems like we should have, since you obviously have a key to my house."

"Briefly…maybe once in passing? So sorry about Allie and your recent loss, sir; she was one of my favorite clients. I've been cleaning your home for--wow, three years now? I guess it's time we officially met. I put off coming by for over two weeks." She held out her hand, and offered an engaging smile.

"Good to meet you. Call me Turner." I coughed, clearing the rust from my voice. "So…what's the procedure here?" I stepped out into the hallway, looking at her armory of cleaning tools next to my bedroom door.

"Well sir, first I should ask if you want to continue Allie's arrangement. Once-a-week cleaning, bottom to top, full day service, off two-weeks a year with dates to be decided by me. I come nine-to-five every Wednesday. She gave me the house keys a while back; with all those meetings she had on Wednesdays."

"Meetings, huh? Glancing at my watch, I said, "So, you've already been here over three hours? You're either a very quiet cleaner or I'm a heavy sleeper."

"I'd say the latter, sir." She patted the top of her vacuum. "Little Betsy here is effective but makes a racket. Actually, I tried your door earlier. Thought I'd let you sleep it off."

"Alright, heavy sleeper, obviously. Uh, considering it's only me living here now, maybe once every two weeks would do it?"

Sally squinted and shook her head. "Turner, I hate to say it, but this week has to be the worst condition I've ever seen this house. I think you may actually need me twice a week. Unfortunately, I have no openings in my schedule, so it'll have to be once a week, every Wednesday. Lots of dog hair, man hair, rings on the tables, crumbs in the kitchen, garbage and laundry piling up. Hate to say it, but you *really* need me, sir."

"Damn, Sally, sounds like I do. OK, for now, *mi casa es tu casa*. Go forth and vacuum. I'll be downstairs if you need me."

"Thank you, sir. Just keep it clean down there."

"Yes, Captain." I saluted and smiled thinking I *did* need a Sally in this new solo life. I turned toward the stairs as she spoke up again.

"Oh, sir. Blaze was fed and walked this morning."

"Bless you, Sally."

Coffee. I followed the scent of freshly brewed aroma to the kitchen and poured myself a cup. Blaze got up from his bed in the utility room and padded over for a head rub. "Sorry I'm so late today, buddy. Rough night."

Deep in the recesses of my cargo shorts pocket, I heard my cell buzzing. My company, *Rapid Logistics*, flashed across the screen as I picked up. "Hey Fern."

"Hi, Mr. Cooper. So very sorry to bother you. We miss you. Your father's on the other line. Hold please."

I knew I needed to take a seat to get through this call. I grabbed a stool next to the kitchen island.

"Turner...we need you, boy. When you coming in? It's over two weeks now."

I sat at the counter, sipping from my cup, with my banging forehead resting in my hand. "Not sure, Dad."

"You need to come in, son. Everyone has questions and it seems you're the only one that has answers. It's time to get your head back in the game."

"Sorry Dad, can't say I feel quite right in the head or the heart right now. Like someone siphoned all the gas in my tank and let the air outta the tires."

"Maybe the work will get your mind off Allie."

"It's not just Allie, Dad. It's everything I've been doing. I need time to think."

"Well, *think* up here at the office, and get yourself a shrink to talk about the rest. I've got all the department managers meeting me here at three today. We need your leadership, son."

Every bit of my body ached, from hair to toe nails. I had no desire to hear about all the multiplying supply chain problems. I paid managers a lot of money to figure all this shit out. Surely, I wasn't the only person with solutions. Business was a mess, I felt like a mess, my life was a mess. But glancing around the kitchen, I had to admit, my house was now quite ship-shape. It was a start.

I sighed, pounding my fist on the counter. *Fuck it*. "OK, Dad. See you at three."

Down the hall from the kitchen, I headed to a guest room to shower, knowing when I tried, I could clean up pretty good. But there were some messes a hot shower just couldn't solve.

# CHAPTER 6
# NIGHTMARES AND DAYDREAMS

ROSARIO

*I*'d crawled beneath my iron bed, but even with a pillow pulled over my ears, I could hear the rumbling of yells and threats outside. I couldn't make out the words but I knew *La Linea* was doing the threatening. Along with voices, I heard the pop of gunshots, or was it the backfire of a car? Neither were uncommon in our Juarez neighborhood. And then...a chilling thump against the door, followed by two heavy whacks.

I waited under the bed for silence to surround our small house. The quiet came over like a slow dark fog, only interrupted by the barking of a few backyard dogs. I finally scooted myself out across the linoleum floor and stood up. I didn't want to open the door. Those final noises had set my teeth on edge. I peeked out the windows. All neighbors' lights were off.

I turned on the phone's light and slowly undid the latch and pulled. The rough-planked door felt heavy and weighted. The hinges squeaked in a slow eerie pitch as I yanked harder, watching it swing in. Then I gasped and fell to my knees, keening over in agony and terror, vomiting at the threshold. I forced myself to look up again, letting out a howl like a crazed animal as I wiped my mouth with a pajama sleeve.

Hanging from the door, by the serrated blades of two large knives slicing through each hand, was the body of my twin brother, Roberto. Blood was everywhere, now coagulating on his body, clothing, and the door. I recognized the splattered white Puma jacket he was so proud of and a silver belt buckle my father had given him. A scribbled note was pinned to the jacket, but I lacked the courage to yank it off to read it.

My brother's head was missing.

I finally stood, pushed the door closed, and bolted it, although I knew the lock offered little security. They would be back. I sat down on the sofa and called the police. Someone official would show up eventually, but there was no guarantee they could be trusted.

MY NOISY ALARM jolted me awake, tearing my brain away from the grisly scene. The recurring nightmare of Roberto's murder always woke me with bone-chilling fear and disorientation, forcing me to touch things that I knew to be real. My hand on the warm plastic radio--real. My feet sliding inside fuzzy pink slippers--real. I was drenched in sweat and turned on the chrome faucet of the shower--real.

That horrific dream, revisiting the worst night of my life, continued to plague me every few weeks. It used to be almost every night, so, at least there was that improvement.

*La Linea* was part of the reason I'd remained so solitary since coming to the U.S. As the enforcement gang of the Juarez drug Cartel, *La Linea*, was also known to have branches outside of Mexico in several cities in Texas, Arizona, and New Mexico. They weren't as open and ruthless as the police allowed them to be in Mexico, but they were definitely a presence in the underbelly of some US cities, protecting their turf.

Remaining vigilant, I lived as anonymously as possible. Whenever I began to feel safe or complacent, I'd pull out the ripped paper which had hung precariously on Roberto's jacket. In a jagged scrawl in Spanish, it read: *We're coming for you next.* I kept it folded at the bottom of a little jewelry box; one of the few things I'd brought with me from Juarez.

Roberto had been both a brother and best friend. Always looking out for me and wanting to do right by our parents. That's what brought both of us to Juarez; a place where we found decent factory jobs and earned enough monthly to send extra home.

U.S. owned factories along the border, the maquiladoras, attracted a lot of the new, green graduates from the country-side. We were eager to learn a trade and bring home a steady paycheck. Speaking passable English was a plus. But the cartels weren't stupid. That's where they found their best recruits. As we left work each day, they kept their eye out for fresh-faced, bright kids ready to make serious money. They preyed upon new arrivals, recruiting the men for trafficking, sales, and enforcement, and women too, often used as drug mules.

Within a few months of arriving in Juarez someone noticed my twin, Roberto. He wanted nothing to do with *La Linea*, but they wouldn't leave him alone. When they started harassing me, making me offers, that's when he got really angry.

Now horrific dreams were all I had left. I came to Dallas hoping for escape, but also to honor his sacrifice, to show him I would do better for the both of us. Momma, a widow for the last seven months, was still back home and received an extra hundred dollars a month from me. It wasn't much, but it kept food on her table.

With documented police reports of Roberto's assassination, gruesome police photos, and the threatening note from his jacket, my immigration lawyer presented a strong case for my asylum and eventual US citizenship. But for now, I had my green card and would soon have a social security card. I couldn't wait to apply for an honest-to-God competitive job with a decent wage.

But tonight, Bright White Laundry was still my destination. I showered again, dressed, and brushed out my shoulder length brown hair, taking a little extra time to add eyeliner and lipstick, just enough to admire my own reflection for a change. At the laundry, I had a lot of regulars. Truckers, hospital employees, shift workers, who all dropped off laundry to be picked up the next day. They liked that I remembered their names, and asked about special instructions. I took an interest and they seemed to appreciate it.

"Rosario, *mi novia*."

I looked up from sweeping, knowing it was smiling Carl, one of my few Anglo customers. His Spanish accent was terrible, but then again, so was my American accent.

*"Hola* Carl. So, what kind of messes you have for me today?" He was a butcher who worked late hours at a small meat packing plant.

"Oh, the usual, blood and guts all over my whites. Give 'em your deluxe bleach treatment. Nobody gets 'em clean like you."

"Yes, it's my top-secret formula, Carl. Then I whispered, "I presoak and wash them twice."

"Well, whatever you do, it does the trick and my wife loves you for it. Hey, brought you some extras."

Carl handed me a couple small packages of frozen meat. I never knew if he bought them for me or if they just conveniently fell off a shelf, but I never asked and was very grateful.

*"Gracias*! Looks like burgers this weekend. Everything will be ready by noon tomorrow. Your wife picking up?"

"Yeah, I'll let her know. You're awesome Rosie! Catch you next time."

Although I appreciated customers like Carl, I daydreamed about being able to get up at a normal hour. Then I'd eat breakfast at home, drink a slow cup of coffee while discussing my day across a kitchen table with someone I loved. I'd be happy working my eight or nine hours, then come home and live like the real people did.

I felt like my customers and I were part of a separate underworld, the ones most people never realized were there, toiling away all night so the *normal* people's worlds were never disrupted. Maybe, once I had the magic social security card, I'd become one of them.

But where could I work? All I knew was what I *didn't* want to do. No more scrubbing port-a-potties, no more washing blood stains in the middle of the night, no more glazing donuts at six AM. I was thankful for the jobs, but currently my days consisted of hard work and little sleep, with time for almost nothing else.

Hopefully now, an opportunity was waiting around some corner. As I dropped Carl's whites into a bleach-heavy pre-soak, I began to daydream about life on the other side. What would it look like?

# CHAPTER 7
# LEARNING TO TALK
# THE WALK
VIOLET

*I*'d been acclimating for several days. In other words, doing nothing. I stretched and flexed in my deep-dish bed, swaddled in silky high-thread-count sheets. I raised my head up, looked down at a glistening pool and thought, this was all *way* too easy. Get your ass up and start preparing for whatever the hell you plan on doing. You tell yourself you don't want Mother's help, but what are you doing about it? Although…a morning swim would be invigorating about now.

I was on lap fifty-two, when I took a side breath and saw Mother's gold-heeled mules approaching pool-side. "Vi…Vi!" She clapped thinking I hadn't heard.

In mid-flip, I stopped and turned. "Yes?"

"Pulled a few strings, got you in for a one o'clock with Lexi today. I know it'll be great for the two of you to connect again." She said it as if my speech therapist and I were besties from junior-high. Although, it was almost true. I'd been seeing Lexi since fifth grade. Probably now in her mid-fifties, she had been a listener, teacher, mentor, and doctor to me for years. At one point, I considered myself done with her services; thought

I'd gleaned all I possibly could from her. But right now I honestly welcomed the sessions.

I shook the water off my face. "G-Good. Thanks for arranging."

"Well, I know how you procrastinate. I thought you'd appreciate it if I got the ball rolling. Oh, and I haven't forgotten about that email you sent the other night. Give me a week or so and we'll discuss some job options. Some of us have things to do. I'm running late, Vi. Dinner maybe?"

"Sure." Forty-eight laps to go and then perhaps a three-mile run at the lake. Plenty of time.

SHOWERED, with my damp hair pulled back in a headband, I sat in the waiting room of Lexi's new and impressive looking offices. Appointments must be booming. Perhaps speech impediments were all the rage right now? Within a few minutes, her receptionist ushered me in.

Lexi sat in a soothing-blue upholstered dome-like chair that seemed to cocoon her petite body. Her friendly brown eyes looked out through large black framed glasses as she stood up to greet me, while I quickly scoped out the soft impressionist paintings of children playing on grassy fields. I felt calm now that I was back in her safe, comfortable world.

She stood up and gave me a brief hug. Lexi knew I wasn't a hugger and kept it short. "Violet, so good to see you. Truly. When your mother called, I told Ellen to clear the decks for an hour or two. Have a seat. Let's get to it."

"Thanks, Lexi. G-G-Great to s-s-see you as well."

"So, tell me what brings you in?"

I told her about my recent job loss and explained how that job had been vital for me in so many ways. "I wanted to find something else in Austin, but M-M-Mother insisted I come back home, and now I'm incredibly anxious about g-going through a round of interviews."

"So Violet, while doing research work, were you still practicing your word re-directs, switching out the trouble consonants? How about doing your elocution drills from time to time?"

"Honestly, no. I thought it was all b-b-behind me, but maybe I got too com-pl-pl-placent. I wasn't talking to people much. Kept to my-myself mostly."

"Hmm," she said, pursing her lips together. "I see you've regressed. I can tell we've got lots of work to do. I want you strong and confident for those interviews and what lies beyond. Tell me honestly. In Austin, was it the work you loved so much or the comfort of working so often in solitude?"

I took a minute to reflect. "P-p-probably a little of b-both."

She nodded. "Hiding from people won't really solve our problems. But, let's get started, shall we?"

After a few days of Lexi sessions, and several one-on-ones between myself and a mirror, I felt a tad more confident. But I now realized it was an affliction that might never be fully cured. Instead, it was something I could make better through practice. Lexi suggested embracing it, avoiding the trouble areas, and making people aware of my stutter when the situation called for it.

At our most recent session, she explained, "While interviewing, take the elephant out of the room. Tell them about your impediment at the get-go. That way, you've put your interviewer more at ease if a stammer bubbles up. They're not caught off-guard wondering what's happening or feeling uncomfortable for you. I'm not sugar-coating it, Violet. Some people will still discriminate; it happens. Many don't even realize they're doing it. But most HR associates will appreciate your honesty."

After a thorough role-playing module, I felt ready to see

what Mother's career connections might have in store for me. I laughed, conjuring up what Mother might come up with. Possibly working as a low-budget event coordinator in charge of balloons and crepe paper? Or, maybe a science advisor for high-society women needing socially-correct green topics of conversation? It was bound to be an interesting list. I sent Mother an email letting her know I was ready for a meet and greet.

I WAS STILL in bed checking my email and dejectedly threw my phone down. Once again, I'd had zero responses from the university labs I'd sent my resume to. I'd waited eagerly for two weeks and no one was taking the bait. Then I heard a text ding. Ruffling through my sheets, I pulled out my phone. It was Magna Temple, my mother's personal assistant, up to her normal early-morning efficiency.

*Good morning, Violet. Your mother is ready to discuss a few Dallas career options with you at 10:45 this morning. Does that time slot work? Let me know. –M.T.*

Bless Magna Temple! The woman was a God-send to my mother who retained her services as secretary, financial advisor, personal assistant, and occasional lunch and bridge partner when mother fell short on friends for the day.

Anyway, about my schedule…I saw no obstacles in the way of a morning chat about jobs. There was certainly no clamor of interest through my own efforts. I texted a reply: *Morning Magna. 10:45 is fine. See you in a bit. How's the temperature in there?*

She replied: *Pleasant so far, but you never know after our Monday morning financial strategy meeting. See you later.*

When it came to Mother, Magna had always been my secret co-conspirator. Originally, Magna had served as my father's administrative assistant for years until he died ten years ago. Then Mother acquired her capable services, working together five days a week. But last year, at the age of seventy, Magna announced her semi-retirement and began coming in only three days a week. A year later, Mother was still having trouble adjusting to Magna's act of disloyalty.

I attempted a bit of makeup and nervously dressed. Viewing this as an interview rehearsal, I decided my standard suit was required. I donned my classic pin-stripe shirt and dark-navy Brooks Brothers pants and jacket. I thought it a safe choice, showing Mother I was serious about finding a good position. I walked down the steep, long drive in my flip-flops and went through the glass doors of the sunroom in the back. Approaching the office, I took a deep breath and then exhaled, saying to myself: *I am calm. I am good. I am smart.*

I walked through a set of slightly open walnut-paneled doors. "Good m-m-morning ladies!" I decided to open with enthusiasm. Both Magna and Mother, sitting at opposing double desks, looked up.

Magna smiled. "Look at you, Ms. Executive!"

Mother gave me a two-second appraisal. "Attractive suit Violet, but is it too, I don't know, too suit-y? There are so many ways to girl-up a suit now-a-days; aren't there Magna?"

"I suppose. But I like it. Simple, professional. Nothing wrong with a classic."

Then Mother stood up and peeked over her desk. "God forbid...what do you have on your feet? Those rubber things need to be outlawed."

I intervened. "Thank you b-b-both, but the flip-flops will be replaced and the suit isn't the issue here. The job's the issue."

Mother smiled and said, "So true. Have a seat darling."

I sat down in one of the two floral-print upholstered wing chairs in front of their matching desks.

"So, M-Mother, I'm ready to hear a few options."

"Aren't you the eager-beaver? OK, Magna, my files

please." Magna handed them to her. Mother opened the first manilla file folder with a flourish and seemed to be digesting the information for the first time, nodding her head at the details inside.

"Here we go. This one was an easy ask. The Perot Museum needs a coordinator and tour guide for their student tours. You recall that museum, dear… it's all about natural science, rocks, dinosaurs and such. So exciting! And I've been a big contributor for years. Think about it, Violet. This is a perfect fit for you! Answering questions from school children. You're so clever about all this science info. And, no need to be on edge regarding public speaking. By that I mean…you'd only be speaking to children."

My eyes bugged out at her remark, but I ignored it. Considering the position, I shook my head, thinking the idea sounded absurd. "Sorry, I can't think of anything I'd r-r-rather *not* do. You do know I'm a m-m-molecular b-biologist, correct? And children make me nervous." I was certainly over-qualified, and I cringed at speaking in front of large groups of children, especially ones that were certain to mimic me, like eleven-year-old assholes. To my recollection, children were like parrots, shouting out and repeating awkward phrases that I'd certainly be spewing.

Magna stood up, stepping out of the firing zone. "Who's ready for coffee? I'm getting a cup."

Mother and I ignored her hasty retreat. "Violet, so negative already? And sadly typical. You haven't even given it a chance to sink in. Keep an open mind, dear. Let's move on."

I calmed down. *One down, two to go. Hit me.* "OK M-Mother. Let's continue."

"Alright then, this next one has excellent merit. And they're willing to train, given your scientific background *and* my position on the board. It would be as Head of Food Services for North East Center Hospital. Apparently, they normally hire only registered dieticians for this, but again, I told them you were a quick study and I'm sure you learned a lot about food in your biology studies. Down side...I believe there is a hair net involved. But, it's a minor obstacle." With that mention, she flicked her hand as if swatting an imaginary fly.

I looked down at my tightly clenched hands. "That sounds like a d-damn big learning curve. I appreciate your confidence in m-my abilities but it sounds almost dangerous to put m-me in that spot." I briefly flashed on my nervous stomach disorder. Was I a wise choice in overseeing the healthy nutritional menus for sick patients? "Uh, OK. Number three?"

"Now Violet, I pulled some strings here, but I think this last one would be absolutely lovely. Just imagine...working as a head gardener at Botanicals United of Dallas, designing a new xeriscape garden featuring plants of the Southwest. I've told them about your research work at UT with that *stuff* you were conjuring up for dry soil and they had a huge interest in that. Again, you'd have to study up a bit, but maybe my new gardener could teach you a thing or two."

I had never even taken care of a house plant. Never mowed a lawn or planted a flower. I was sure Mother's lawn guy would come up woefully short on teaching me the level of garden design that Botanicals United was known for. Nodding, trying to appear positive, I asked, "So, that's it then? Thank you. I'll give those files a thorough read-through, M-M-Mother." *Thanks for not really knowing me at all.*

At that point, Magna walked in with a tray containing three cups of coffee. She stopped, leaned over with her beverage tray and said, "Everything good, Violet?"

I reached up, taking a cup and saucer. "Make mine an Irish coffee please," and gave her a smirk.

Mother stood up, clutching the strap of her nude-leather Birkin bag. "No coffee for me, thanks. Now Vi, I know it's not *exactly* what you were doing previously, but that's what makes job searches so exciting. I'm leaving now for an appointment. I want you and Magna to go over these in detail together. She knows more about the nuances of the positions than I do. We'll talk later. And keep an open mind!"

After she left, we sipped coffee in silence for a minute. "Magna…I'm serious about that whiskey in my cup. You have to know, I'm not remotely qualified for any of those po-po-posi —jobs.

Magna smiled, as gentle creases formed around her mouth and she patted the back of her heavily-sprayed perfect platinum up-do. "So, none of these three jobs sound slightly feasible to you?"

"All three are absolutely ri-ridiculous. I have no expertise in any of those areas."

Magna took another sip. "I understand you feel that way. Violet, you were lucky in Austin, being able to find a job that perfectly matched your skills. But think about it this way…A lot of people feel unsure, like a fish out of water, when they first take a job. And you're right; in some ways, you don't have detailed knowledge of these three positions."

Magna folded her hands on the desk and continued. "But one thing I *do* know is that you're at your best studying up on a subject, behind the scenes. Take cues from those around you and ask questions. I know it's scary working in new surroundings. But you are a clever woman. It wouldn't hurt to at least *apply* and find out more about the responsibilities. People are hired for their potential, their education, their intelligence, and most importantly, their ability to adapt. Be more malleable."

My eyes were directed at shoe level below her desk. Her pumps were interesting. Chunky, but not too matronly. "I don't know, Magna. I'm not a very b-b-bendy person."

"Violet, none of these jobs are a done deal. We only procured the interviews. Now, I'm sure the people conducting the interviews might be aware of your mother's influence, but you actually have to sell yourself to get hired for the position, just like anybody else applying."

I sighed loudly, sitting with my arms crossed against my chest. "M-M-Maybe you're right. Perhaps I should apply at the gardening one? At least I wouldn't be sp-speaking to a crowd of rugrats. And I'd only be killing p-plants instead of human p-patients."

Magna nodded. "Excellent points. Yes! Let's start with that and we'll do some mock interviews."

She stood up from her desk, leaned over as if to shake my hand and said, "I must say Ms. Violet Hill, you look lovely today, great suit. Have a seat. Now tell me a little about yourself."

With my eyes still glued to the floor, I responded, "Sure, but f-first tell me, where'd you get those p-pumps?"

## CHAPTER 8
## BREAK THE CHAIN
TURNER

*T*he hot shower helped tamp down the fugue and fog created by the contents of my previously full bottle of Scotch. But it would be a monumental lie to say I was feeling tip-top about addressing the biggest problem to hit the supply chain industry in decades. I was drinking way too much, feeling way too guilty, and way too uninformed on current business to offer much in the way of solutions.

I sucked it up, combing back the hair sticking up all over my head and continued to dress for the office, replacing unlaundered cargo shorts with khaki trousers and a clean white polo.

I drove the seven miles downtown to Rapid Logistics. It was a company I'd created and spun off from my father's small trucking business about twelve years ago. A little past three, I walked into the conference room. I saw Dad seated at the end of the sleek Scandinavian table surrounded by matching beech-wood chairs. I hated this room. It looked good but those chairs were so darn uncomfortable. I cursed the decorator every time I had to spend a few hours there making nice with clients. The table was surrounded by my top people. Sam in shipping, Helene, who oversaw trucking, Ed on rail, and Melissa, who headed up short-term delivery systems. All experts in their fields.

But today, they seemed to be lacking the ability to communicate with each other. I was pissed I'd been called in; so, not in the best of moods. As I entered, all went quiet. I stopped, with hands in my pockets. "So, tell me, what are the biggest problems you five clever people aren't able to solve?" Not the most positive opening line I'd ever used when greeting associates.

Dad spoke up first. "Now, son, it's a clusterfuck out there. Customers are having conniption fits, calling every few minutes wondering where their damn stuff is."

I tried to remain calm. "Yes, I understand. It's happening all over the country. Actually, all over the world. It's almost October now, folks. We started hearing rumbles about this back in July and August. And it's going to get worse. So, the question should be--how can we get ahead of this and what are we doing about it for *our* customers?"

Sam-in-shipping spoke up. "Turner, some of our containers are now in range or waiting at the LA port, but things are really backed up and neither of our contracted trucking lines are fully staffed. They can't keep up and aren't hiring drivers fast enough."

I nodded and looked at Helene who was busy tapping away on her laptop. "Helene, what 'cha got? Any breakthroughs?"

She shook her head. "Not really. A couple loads got out on trucks yesterday. But it's gonna take weeks to catch things up."

Everyone began mumbling again.

Leaning over the back of a chair at the table, I turned up the volume. "OK look, I know right now everything is a mess with delays. Who could foresee huge layoffs, hiring shortages, raw material shortages, and then every American with a laptop deciding to order shit-loads of stuff?"

Everybody's eyes were on me again. "We're one small

company with contracts to get this stuff delivered and keep our clients' flow of goods moving. Let's put our heads together and get these current delivery challenges worked out. Dad... Helene? What are we gonna do about trucking?"

Helene raised her hand timidly. "Independents? I can call around the southern Cal area. See who we can scrounge up."

"Perfect! Let's do it. And Dad?

"I still got all my old contacts. Let me make some calls." He nodded over to Helene and said, "Let's also check independents in Arizona and Nevada."

I did a thumbs up. "Exactly! Offer them twenty percent over normal rates until all this calms down. All the big boys will soon start paying extra. We need to get ahead of the curve."

I punched up the receptionist's line. "Fern? Please locate Sarah-from-sales and have her join us...and you better order some pizzas to be delivered. I explained to the team, "We need sales input. I want us to focus *only* on top clients today. They bring in sixty percent of our revenue and we can't have any of them jumping ship. Melissa, if we can't get enough trucks, do you think you can get some short-term delivery systems to haul some of the freight from the shipping containers over to the rail lines?"

She glanced up from her laptop, looking over her glasses at me. "That might work. Let me get on it. Ed, you'll have to get me up to speed on the rail connections.

Ed loosened his tie, pulled it off and nodded. "Sure thing."

Sarah-from-sales walked in looking frazzled, with her blonde hair pulled up in a bun held together with a pencil. "Sorry, boss. It's tough being on the other end of those customer calls. Nobody wants to hear *I'm not sure*, or *maybe another six weeks*."

I pulled out a seat for her. Still standing in front of the group, I said, "I know it's tough being on the receiving end. Sarah, let's take a look at our top client list. These other sharp people are going to work hard at getting you *real* delivery dates to give our clients.

And remember guys, most other supply chain companies are in the same crappy, convoluted spot we're in. But we're small and nimble. Let's cut through the red tape and get on top of things. *Now* is the time to use your charm and rapport. Pull out some favors."

I walked over to a white board behind the table and wrote up all backed-up orders from Sarah's list of top clients. "I need everyone on this list to have an accurate delivery date next to it by tomorrow morning so that Sarah can call all of them ASAP. Sarah, I'll coach you on the best way to deliver the message. Trust me, they're going to appreciate the truth, even if it's a delay. At least when you give them a definite date, they can make plans around it.

Sarah nodded. "Thanks Turner, that'll definitely help."

Laptops were clicking, everybody's cells were lighting up, a slightly more positive buzz started to fill the room instead of grumbles.

After coaching Sarah and seeing some results from each department manager, I cleared my throat and called out, "Everything gets documented. Get my dad to sign off on every discount or delivery bonus we're honoring. I have to leave now. But my cell will be open to you for any questions or problems. You may not see me for a while; need to make some decisions. But you're exceptionally smart and capable people who can be problem solvers when you work together. That's why you're here."

They were silent for a second, offered nods and small waves, and then went quickly back to their screens or phones.

I walked down the hallway, my heels echoing against the tile floor. The elevator couldn't come fast enough. I didn't want to spend another minute at the job which I had allowed to gobble up years of personal time. Precious time I could now never give back to Allie.

The ding of the elevator door startled me. The doors swished open and I was grateful it was empty. I leaned my head forward on the cold metal panel. How could I have *not ever* met a maid Allie had employed for three years? How did I *not know* that Allie always spent Wednesdays in meetings? How could I have been so oblivious to my selfishness?

Allie went through weeks of chemotherapy with her breast cancer but came back strong. *Of course* she was immunocompromised. Yet, it had still come as a shock to me. I was guilty of so many self-absorbed atrocities as a husband. I needed time away for some serious self-reflection.

I'd given *Rapid Logistics* all my time and energy. It was time for me to give something back for Allie. Maybe some type of memorial to her, something she'd been motivated by. It was too late for her, but maybe I could do something for someone else, in memory of Allie. Was I doing it to assuage my guilt? Yes. But it was something I felt driven to do.

As the doors opened to the parking garage, I told myself, *Good idea…I'll get on it tomorrow.* But right now a bottle of Dewars was calling me home.

# CHAPTER 9
# THE LAUNDRY PRINCE
ROSARIO

*T*he glass doors to Bright-White swung open with an annoying buzz, knocking me out of my blissful new-career daydream. I immediately became nervous watching hot Victor Morales walk in with his overstuffed bag of laundry. The few times he'd come in, he'd never been anything but polite to me. But was he *too* nice? And wasn't he a little *too* handsome? I reminded myself, calm down Rosario, you're just the laundry girl.

So, it was three AM and he looked as if he was going out, or possibly heading home after a night out. Either way, he looked sharp. Maybe mid-twenties, fitted black jeans, slim-cut sports jacket, flawless white shirt. Dark hair styled to perfection. Never over-the-top. Not too flashy. Just right. But what was he doing at *this* lavanderia, in *this* neighborhood?

He walked over to the counter where drop-offs were logged and weighed, looking surprised to see me. "Oh hi… you again? How do you grab all these choice work shifts?"

"*Hola.* Just lucky, I guess. You look very nice this evening."

Our conversations had never gone beyond laundry preferences, so I decided to make a stab at a friendly chat. I was thinking, *My, what perfect white teeth you have*, but instead I said, "So, you going somewhere special at three in the morning?"

"Thanks, actually yes. Have a crack-of-dawn flight at DFW, and I needed this laundry squared away for the week. It's cool I found this place; open all the time, and then there's the added bonus of an attractive uh--washer-folder-person? Sorry, what's your title? Better yet, what's your name?"

I looked down, embarrassed by the almost-complement. "Rosario, and I guess I'm the night manager."

"Night manager. Impressive."

"Oh yes, that's why they pay me the big money. So, Mr. Morales, what can I do for you this morning?"

"Impressed again... you remembered my name, Ms. Rosario.

"I try. I get a lot of regulars here but you've stood out."

He looked confused. "I just come in, drop my bag, and go."

"But you look different. So nicely dressed, stylish, clean. You should see what I see! My last customer, Carl, a very nice man. But his drop-offs—covered in blood." I stopped to laugh as Victor's mouth fell open. "Don't worry. He's only a butcher, not a criminal."

"Yeah...this crazy shift you work, I bet you see a little of everything. Hey, what do you do during normal hours? We should go for coffee sometime. Maybe find mutual interests other than laundry. When's your day off?"

"I only have Sundays off."

"Sundays are good. What's your number?"

That question immediately made me feel cautious. I rarely gave my number to anyone. But I was intrigued. "I tell you what. You give me your number and I'll call you next Sunday. I could meet you somewhere."

"Sounds good. I'm happy to pick you up though."

"No... It's best if I meet you. So, you live around here?"

"Not too far; this place is along my route. Hand me your phone and I'll put in my number."

"I have to fill out your information on the laundry form. I'll get it from that." I pulled out my pad, filled out his name and number, and asked about special instructions.

He stood there and watched me carefully, making me nervous. "You know Rosario, I've never asked anyone out that already knew whether I wore boxers or briefs."

"Or the color of your sheets," I said, pulling out a wrinkled set of navy pillowcases from the bottom of his bag. "Guess I know all your intimate secrets now," I said with a laugh.

His face actually blushed in a charming way, "I'll keep a few things under wraps. So, what do you enjoy doing? Any special requests for Sunday?"

I looked up and thought for a second. "Anything outdoors is good for me. After working all week, I love sitting outside for coffee when the weather is nice."

He snapped his fingers, and nodded. "Know the perfect place." Then he glanced at his watch. "Call me around ten, Sunday morning? But right now, I have a plane to catch. See you then, Rosario."

As the doors shut behind him, I melted in place, stuck to my office chair. Had that really happened? I had a date with an attractive, interesting man. My first date since I'd moved here, excluding hanging out with a few cousins and those weren't worth counting. Victor appeared to be friendly and successful. Then doubts immediately crept in.

If he was so successful, why was he asking *me* out? I worked at an all-night lavanderia. Wait until he heard about my other job, cleaning port-a-potties. Maybe I wouldn't mention that. Perhaps it was like the Cinderella story, and he enjoyed playing the handsome prince swooping in to put low-skilled working girls on a pedestal?

What would I wear? What did we have in common? Would

it be safe? What would Roberto tell me to do? I thought about it, picturing my twin's smirking face. He would say, *Jesus, Rosario. Just go get a free coffee, and don't worry so much. Not everyone is a reject, maniac, or gangster.*

Roberto was probably looking down and laughing at me right now. Maybe it was time to have a little fun. It was only coffee. Let's see...It was already Monday morning. Only six days to go!

I WAS STARING at my phone while holding it in my palm; it screamed out *ten-fifteen, Sunday*. My finger had been perched over Victor Morales' number since ten. What if he'd forgotten? He had asked me so casually, perhaps it was all a big joke?

I'd washed and straightened my hair, tried a new coral lipstick, and put on a pair of tight turquoise jeans and a print top. The weather outside was perfect. Just do it. Press the call button--now! It was ringing...once...twice. I'd give it four rings and then hang up. On the fourth, I heard:

"So, this is either *Scam Likely,* or this is Rosario."

Relief flooded my voice. "*Hola* Victor. Yes, it 's Rosario. *¿Qué pasa?*"

"I've been waiting for your call. I'm hungry."

"Yes, where should I meet you? The address please."

"Uh, how about the main entrance of Botanicals United of Dallas. Most people just call it BUD. Best outdoor patio in the city. You know it?"

"Sorry, never heard of that place."

"I'll tell you what. Why don't I pick you up in front of the laundry? Might be easier. Can you be there in thirty minutes?"

"Yes, I can do that. See you soon." At night I took the bus to Bright White, but today I'd walk. By ten-thirty-three, I was leaning against the window of the donut shop next door, considering grabbing a jelly donut to tide me over, but maybe I should wait. Had Victor mentioned food? I went in and got four donuts. They were always free for me; my one employee perk. When I came out there was a small black SUV waiting near the curb. I peeked inside, but it was empty.

From behind, I heard his voice and turned. "There you are; had me worried for a minute. I went inside the lavenderia to look for you. Only saw one person inside talking to his stolen shopping cart."

I glanced over at the laundry windows. "Oh, that has to be Charlie. Every morning, he goes to the donut shop, buys coffee, then goes to the lavenderia and sorts through all his stuff in the cart and pretends he's doing laundry. An hour later, he wanders out.

Victor smiled, clicked his lock and opened my door. "Hop in."

"Thanks." As he got behind the wheel, I held up my white bag. "I stopped and got donuts. Super fresh. I work there too."

"Wait, what? You worked this morning? At that donut place?"

"No, not today. Sunday is my one day off. No matter what."

"OK, so BUD's not too far from here. A few miles. It's cool...a cafe located within the gardens. If you like being outdoors, I think you'll love it."

We drove into a busy parking lot and walked to an entrance line. While walking through, Victor explained, "There's several different gardens inside. Uh... *jardins muy grandes*."

"Victor, I wondered if you spoke Spanish. You have no accent."

"I *barely* speak Spanish. Just trying out what I remember from high school. Your English seems pretty good though. Did you grow up here?"

"No. Near Jaurez, but I learned in school too. My brother

and I would practice every day together and we watched lots of American movies."

We walked into an open flag-stoned piazza and I was immediately intrigued. "Victor, this is so incredibly beautiful."

Guarding the borders of the walk-ways were thousands of orange pumpkins, surrounded by gorgeous explosions of fall colors from flowers draping over their pots in shades of gold, orange, and purple, and overhead there were broad shady trees covered with deep red leaves. Walking further within was a large sparkling fountain within a pond. I'd never seen such natural beauty layered together in my life. I breathed in all the scents, closing my eyes for a second. Fresh cool air, damp leaves, rich moist earth. Everywhere I glanced there was another unique plant, a winding path, a romantic stone bridge, and this was only near the entrance.

Victor directed me over to tables with umbrellas near the service counter. "I'll get the coffee. Let's sit here."

He pulled out a chair for me. But I wasn't really ready to sit down. I would have rather run through the place, touching the velvety petals, or try laying down on the spongy green grass. "Thank you. *Café a leche*, please."

Ten minutes later he came back with coffee, salad options, and two sandwiches. "I should have asked. Hope you're not vegetarian. These turkey paninis are the best."

"This looks wonderful. You're making my bag of jelly donuts look very sad right now."

He sat down, touching my hand on the small table. "So, Rosario, I've been waiting for a week to look into this beautiful face and those huge brown eyes of yours. Tell me about yourself."

"Well, I have some excellent news to share." I pulled out my new social security card that I'd recently received. "I'm so happy about this and you're the first person I've shown it to.

Maybe my time at Bright-White will be coming to an end. With this, I hope to start looking for better work."

"Hey, congratulations! What do you have in mind?"

I told Victor a little about my past and my vague hopes for the future, but stayed away from the dark episode of Roberto's murder. I didn't want that clouding this perfect morning. The food was delicious, the air felt cool but the sun had come out, and Victor was so handsome. It was as if our eyes had locked onto each other and we couldn't look away. As we were finishing our meal, Victor offered to walk me through the gardens. As we both stood up, his phone buzzed.

He looked down at the screen and said. "Excuse me; I need to take this." Victor walked to the patio's edge and looked concerned, talking briefly into the phone. He came back to the table shaking his head. "I'm so sorry. Bad news from work. Something has come up and I'm going to have to catch an afternoon flight to LA. I apologize for having to cut this short."

"Really? We haven't even looked around yet." *And just like that…the carriage turns back into the pumpkin.*

"Look…Rosario, you should stay… as long as you want. Just take your time and wander through. I know you'll love it." He pulled out his phone and started tapping. "I'm scheduling an Uber to take you home. Is that OK? Let's say one-thirty? That should give you plenty of time to wander. Uber will charge my account, but the driver will have your contact number. He handed me his phone. "Here, put it in for me. Have you used Uber before?"

I nodded my head, a bit upset. "Yes, I have. Thank you."

He took both of my hands. "I promise. We'll try this again. It's been a real pleasure." Before he turned for the exit, he gave me a brief hug and then quickly walked out.

I looked around. Suddenly, everything looked less vibrant as I tried to decide which garden path to take.

Of course. My first real date in Dallas would end early with him walking out. Why should I ever expect something good? He'd seen a pretty girl in a laundry, but then reality hit after we'd spent an hour talking. We were from two different worlds.

But I repeated my daily refrain to myself and thought about it. I was in a beautiful place. I had the day to myself and would make the most of it. Besides, Victor now had my number if he wanted to see me again. I hoped he would call.